ELOHIM BIBLE
COMMENTARY

William S. Holmes

ISBN 978-1-09832-888-7 eBook 978-1-09832-889-4

*Study to show thyself approved
unto God, a workman that
needeth not to be ashamed, rightly
dividing the word of truth
2 Timothy 2:*

ACKNOWLEDGEMENT

My Beloved Mom, who taught me my first Sunday school lesson. (John 3:16)

Rev. Bobby Clontz, who embodied the Good News of Jesus Christ throughout his life and ministry.

My uncle Warren – Upon my ordination into the ministry gave me the book *In His Foot Steps*. Reading the book was not the challenge ... living the Christian life is the challenge before us.

My family and friends. I like the Apostle Paul have greatly fallen short in my Christian life. (1 Tim. 1:15) Yet, my family and friends have always been there to pick me up, dust me off and set me back on the road of life.

"Certainty ... Only comes once in a life time."

– Cynthia

CONTENTS

Acknowledgement   iv

ACTS OF THE APOSTLES   182

BOOK OF JONAH   147

BOOK OF OBADIAH   146

BOOK OF RUTH   44

DEUTERONOMY   25

ECCLESIASTES   104

ESTHER   88

EXODUS   10

EZEKIEL   132

EZRA   80

FIRST LETTER OF JOHN   315

FIRST LETTER OF PETER   293

FIRST LETTER TO THE THESSALONIANS   215

FIRST LETTER TO TIMOTHY   235

GALATIANS   203

GENESIS   6

GOOD NEWS BY JOHN   175

GOOD NEWS BY LUKE   170

GOOD NEWS BY MARK   167

GOOD NEWS BY MATHEW   160

HAGGAI   154

HERORIC CHARACTER: THE PROPHET ELIJAH.   67

HOSEA   140

I CORINTHIANS   196

II CHRONICLES   77

II CORNINTHIANS   201

I & II KINGS   57

I & II SAMUEL   46

II SAMUEL   52

INTRODUCTION   1

ISAIAH   110

JEREMIAH   124

JOB   91

JOSHUA   29

JUDGES   35

LAMENTATIONS   131

LETTER OF JAMES   281

LETTER TO PHILEMON   272

LETTER TO THE COLOSSIANS   213

LETTER TO THE EPHESIANS   207

LETTER TO THE HEBREWS   276

LETTER TO THE PHILLIPPIANS   211

LETTER TO TITUS   264

LEVITICUS   16

MALACHI   158

NEHEMIAH   84

NUMBERS   19

PROVERBS   101

PSALMS   96

REFERENCE NOTES   378

ROMANS   191

SECOND LETTER OF JOHN   318

SECOND LETTER OF PETER   305

SECOND LETTER TO THE THESSALONIANS   226

THE BOOK OF AMOS   143

THE BOOK OF DANIEL   137

THE BOOK OF HABAKKUK   151

THE BOOK OF JOEL   142

THE BOOK OF MICAH   149

THE BOOK OF NAHUM   150

THE BOOK OF REVELATION   323

THE LETTER OF JUDE   322

THE SECOND LETTER TO TIMOTHY   252

THE SONG OF SOLOMON   108

THE TWO GREAT PROPHETS OF II KINGS ELIJAH AND
ELISHAI & II CHRONICLES   75

THIRD LETTER OF JOHN   320

ZECHARIAH   156

ZEPHANIAH   153

INTRODUCTION

I. SIGNIFICANT ARRANGEMENT

1.   BIBLE BEGINS WITH GOD

    a.   Gen. 1:1 – "In the beginning God."

    b.   Embodies the whole of the Bible, key to the Bible and all created things.

2.   BIBLE ENDS WITH MAN (Last of God's creations)

    a.   Rev. 22:21 – "The grace of our Lord Jesus Christ be with you all."

3.   GOD IS AT ONE EXTREME END OF THE BIBLE AND MAN IS AT THE OTHER.

4.   BIBLE IS THE MESSAGE FROM GOD TO MAN. ITS OBJECT IS TO BRING MAN TO GOD.

    a.   Middle verse of the Bible brings God and man together.

    b.   Psalms 118:8 (Middle verse) "it is better to trust in the Lord than to put confidence in man."

II. THE "LIVING WORD", COVERS ALL TIME: YESTERDAY, TODAY AND FOREVER."

1.   ITS HISTORY – GOD'S YESTERDAY.

    a.   Records lives of good and bad men.

        (1) The good to encourage us to emulation.

        (1) The bad to warn us against emulation.

2.   ITS SPIRITUAL TEACHING – GOD'S TODAY

    a.   Shows us the *Way*, the *Truth*, and the *Life*.

    b.   How to live in our todays.

    c.   Presents the Divine and Human Relationships.

3.   IT'S PROPHECY – GOD'S TOMORROW

    a.   The good amply rewarded.

b. The bad and sinful punished.

III. GOD'S METHOD OF DEALING WITH MAN

1. FROM ADAM TO THE FLOOD – CONSCIENCE

   a. No Bible for the first 2,500 years of the world.

   b. Man's guidance was Divinely Direct Conscience.

2. FROM THE FLOOD TO THE NEW TESTIMENT – LAW

   a. History not entire human race.

   b. History of the "chosen Race' Israel – through Noah, Abraham, David, etc.

3. FROM THE NEW TESTAMENT ON – GRACE

   a. Not human race, nor Chosen Race.

   God dealing with His people through Christ.

   b. Christ offers redemption to all people.

IV. GOD'S LAWS FOR MAN

1. GOD GAVE THREE SETS OF LAWS

   a. One law given to sinless man in Eden – BROKEN

   b. Ten laws given to sinful man at Sinai – BROKEN

   c. Whole law given to the Perfect Man in Palestine – KEPT.

2. TEN COMMANDMENTS CONDENSED AND REDUCED

   a. Condensed into TWO:

      (1) Matt. 22:37-40: Love to God and love to man.

   b. The two laws reduced to ONE, as in the beginning.

      (1) Gal. 5:14 - "For all the law is fulfilled in one word … 'THOU SHALT LOVE."

      (1) Rom. 13:10 – "Therefore love is the fulfilling of law."

V. PSALMS IS EXACTLY IN THE CENTER OF THE BIBLE

1. Books preceding and following Psalms tell of God's voice to man.

2. In Psalms, we hear man's voice crying out to God.

3. In the first half, God's voice thunders with Law.

4. In Psalms (center), man responds to God.

5. In the last half, God speaks through Christ, the Good news and Letters in tones of love and grace.

VI. THE OLD AND THE NEW

1. OLD TESTAMENT BEGINS WITH GOD:

   a. Gen. 1:1 – "In the beginning God."

2. NEW TESTAMENT BEGINS WITH CHRIST:

   a. Matt. 1:1 – "The book of the generations of Jesus Christ."

3. OLD TESTAMENT DEALS WITH LAW – ENDS WITH THE WORD "CURSE"

   a. Deut.27:26_– "Cursed be he that confirmeth not all the words of this law to do them."

   b. Mal.4.6 – "Lest I come and smite the earth with a curse." (End of the Old Testament)

4. NEW TESTAMENT DEALS WITH GRACE – ENDS WITH A BLESSING:

   a. Rev. 22:21 – "The grace of our Lord Jesus Christ be with you all. Amen." (End of the New Testament)

5. CONTRAST OF LAW AND GRACE:

   a. In Old Testament, the Law was given through Moses. In the New Testament, "Grace … came through Jesus Christ. (John 1:17)

6. CONTRAST OF FIRST MIRACLES OF LAW-GIVERS:

   a. First miracle of Moses was turning *water* into *blood.* (Exodus 7:19) *Type of death.*

   b. First miracle of Christ was turning *water* into *wine.* (John 2:1-11) *Type of life and joy.*

7. FIRST QUESTIONS

    a. First question in Old Testament is <u>God's call to man:</u> "Where art thou?" (Matt. 2:2)

8. OLD AND NEW INSEPARABLE

    a. They give two aspects of purpose of God.

    b. They both enshrine and present the Savior. In Old Testament, we see Christ. In New Testament, we see Jesus. In Old Testament, we see a just God. (Isa 45:21). In New Testament, we see a Savior. While the Old is the New explained. The New Is in the Old concealed, while the Old is by the New revealed. The New is enfolded in the Old, while the Old is unfolded by the New.

VII. A WORK OF GENIUS

1. GREAT RELIGIOUS LEADERS HAVE WRITTEN BOOKS

    a. Mohammed – The Koran,

    b. Buddha, Confucius, etc.

    c. They and their writings are national in scope.

    d. Bible is universal.

2. COMPARISON OF FOUR "LIVES OF CHRIST"

    a. As written by uninspired men:

Geikie's	1,200 pages
Edersheim's	1,500 pages
Hanna's	2,100 pages
Papini's	416 pages
TOTAL	5,216 pages

    b. As written by inspired men of God:

Mathew	31 pages
Mark	19 pages

Luke	31 pages
John	26 pages
TOTAL	107 pages

    c.   Uninspired writers required 5,109 pages more than the inspired writers to present the same facts about Christ.

VIII. SCIENCE

1. BIBLE AND TRUE SCIENCE NEVER DISAGREE

   a. Some theologians and some scientists do.

   b. Bible and true science prove each other.

2. SCIENTIST AND SCHOLARS OF EVERY FIELD OF THOUGHT REFERNCE THE BIBLE.

   a. A few of the long list throughout history:

   Prof. Bateson, Prof. Huxley, Mathew Arnold, Rosseau, Goethe, Michael Faraday, Charles Dickens, Thomas Carlyle, John Ruskin, J. A. Fronde, Robert Louis Stevenson, Green the Historian, Secretary Sewell, Walt Whitman, George Peabody, Lessing.

IX. SCOPE

1. OPENS WITH MANKIND RUINED – PARADISE LOST.

2. REDEEMER IS PROMISED (Gen. 3:15)

3. CLOSES WITH PROMISES REDEEMED – PARADISE REGAINED.

GENESIS

AUTHOR: MOSES

DATE: Moses lived around the 1400s BC, but the events of Genesis date to the very beginning of time.

THE BOOK OF ORIGINS: A RECORD OF THE ORIGIN OF:

1. Our universe.
2. Human race.
3. Sin.
4. Redemption.
5. Family Life.
6. Corruption of Society.
7. The nations.
8. Different languages.
9. The Hebrew Race.

GENESIS ACCOUNT OF CREATION HAS NEVER BEEN DISPROVED.

1. Does not give comprehensive account of creation.
2. Only a single chapter given to the subject.
3. Gives bare outline of fundamental facts.
4. Thirty-eight Chapters given to account the history of chosen people.

MAIN THEME: Man's sin, and the initial steps taken for his redemption by divine covenant, made with a chosen race whose early history is here portrayed.

KEY WORD: "In the beginning –"

FIRST MESSIANIC PROMISE:

1. Gen. 3:15: "And I will put enmity between thee (Serpent) and the woman, and between thy seed and her seed; it shall bruise thy head and thou shalt bruise his heel."

SYNOPSIS

I. HISTORY OF CREATION

1. Of the Universe. (Chapter 1:1-25)

2. Of Man. (Chapter 1:26-31)

3. Of Woman. (Chapter 2:18-24)

II. THE STORY OF PRIMEVAL MAN

1. Temptation and fall. (Chapter 3)

    a. Personality and character of the Tempter.

    b. Penalty of sin.

    c. Promise of the coming Redeemer. (Chapter 3:15)

2. Story of Cain and Abel. (Chapter 4)

3. Genealogy and death of patriarchs. (Chapter 5)

4. Flood. (Chapters 6, 7 & 8)

5. Rainbow covenant and Noah's son. (Chapter 9)

6. Descendants of Noah. (Chapter 10: Shem – Ham Japheth)

7. Confusion of tongues of Babel. (Chapter 11)

III. HISTORY OF THE CHOSEN FAMILY

1. Career of Abraham. "Father of the Faithful" – Wife, Sarah.

    a. His divine call. (Chapter 12)

    b. Abraham and Lot. (Chapter 13)

    c. Divine promises to Abraham. (Chapters 15, 16, 17)

        1. Promise of a son. (Name changed from Abram to Abraham)

        2. Possessions of Holy Land.

        3. Great Prosperity.

    d. Intercession for Cities of the Plain, and their destruction. (Chapters 18, 19)

e. Life at Gerard and birth of Isaac. (Chapters 20, 21)

f. Test of Obedience – sacrifice of Isaac. (Chapter 22)

g. His death. (Chapter 25:8 – 175 years old)

4. CAREER OF ISAAC. (Laughter) SON OF ABRAHAM.

a. His birth. (Chapter 21:3)

b. His marriage. (Chapter 24 – Rebekah)

c. Birth of his sons, Jacob and Esau. (Chapter 25: 20-26)

d. His later years. (Chapters 29-31)

5. CAREER OF JACOB. (Supplanter) – (Son of Rebekah)

a. Craftiness in securing birthright. (Chapter 27:1-29)

b. Vision of heavenly ladder. (Chapter 28:10-22)

c. Marriage and life in Padan-aram. (Chapters 29-31)

6. CAREER OF ESAU (Eldest son of Isaac and Rebekah)

a. A hunter. (Chapter 25:27)

b. Impulsive, dominated by appetite. (Chapter 25:32)

c. Lacked appreciation of higher things. (Chapter 25:34)

d. Married Heathen wives. (Chapter 26:34)

e. Lost his blessing. (Chapter 27:30-38)

f. Tried to repent when too late. (Hebrews 12:16-17)

7. CAREER OF JOSEPH. (Son of Jacob)

a. Youthful dreamer. (Chapter 37:5-9)

b. Dreams fulfilled. (Chapter 41:42-44)

c. Honored in Potiphar's house. (Chapter 39:1-6)

d. Resisted temptation. (Chapter 39:7-13)

e. Unspoiled by sudden prosperity. (Chapter 41:14-46)

f. Manifested brotherly love. (Chapter 43:30; 45:14)

g. Filial devotion. (Chapter 45:23; 47:7)

h. Dependence upon God. (Chapter 41:16)

ROMINENT NAMES ASSOCIATED TOGETHER

1. Adam and Eve, Adam lived 930 years.

2. Cain and Abel.

3. Abraham and Lot.

4. Isaac and Ishmael.

5. Jacob and Esau.

6. Joseph and his brethren.

FIVE GREAT SPIRITUAL CHARACTERS

1. Enoch – the man who "walked with God."

2. Noah – the Ark Builder. (Sons: Shem, Ham, Japheth)

3. Abraham – the Father of the Faithful.

4. Jacob – the man whose life was transformed by prayer.

5. Joseph – Who rose from slavery and became the *Premier of Egypt*.

EXODUS

<u>**AUTHOR AND CENTRAL CHARACTER**</u> –MOSES.

<u>**DATE:**</u> Approximately 1400s BC.

<u>**MAIN THEME:**</u> History of Israel from the death of Joseph to the erection of the Tabernacle.

<u>**KEY WORD**</u>: "DELIVERANCE"

<u>**SYNOPSIS:**</u>

Genesis closed with the Hebrews high in Egyptian favor. Exodus opens on a race of slaves. Silent centuries have elapsed between Genesis and Exodus. Not till the time for a new advance of the promised redemption is the story resumed.

I. THE PERIOD OF BONDAGE

2. THE OPPRESSION IN EGYPT (1:7-22)

a. Bondage and Exodus under Seti I. Rameses II and Menephthah.

b. Eleven sons of Israel and their families came to Egypt – Seventy people. Joseph was already there.

c. They multiplied rapidly.

d. Joseph and his generation died.

e. Hebrews were so numerous that they were considered a menace to Egypt.

f. Egyptians made slaves of Hebrews.

3. EVENTS IN EARLY LIFE OF MOSES (Forty years in Egypt)

a. His birth and adoption. (2:1-1)

b. Parents: Amram and Jachobe of tribe of Levi. Miriam and Aaron born before Seti's edict.

c. Well educated. Acts. 7:22

d. Identified himself with Israel. (Heb. 11:25)

e. Slew a taskmaster to aid his brethren. (2:11-14)

f. His flight into Midian (East of Red Sea) (2:15)

4. **40 YEARS IN MIDIAN: (East of Red Sea)**

    a.   Age 40 years. (Acts 7:23)

    b.   Married Jethro's daughter, Zipporah. (2:21)

    c.   Shepherd.

    d.   Became familiar with country thru which he was to lead Israel.

    e.   Egypt had taught him arts and sciences. His mother had taught him religion. God prepared him in Midian as Deliverer.

    f.   40 years in Midian. (Acts 7:30)

II. PERIOD OF DELIVERANCE

1. **CALL OF MOSES AT BURNING BUSH. (3:1-10)**

    a.   God heard Israelites call for help.

    b.   Called Moses to deliver them.

2. **HIS FOUR EXCUSES**

    a.   Personal unfitness. (3:11)

    b.   Feared unbelief of people. (4:1)

    c.   Lack of eloquence. (4:10)

    d.   Requests some other leader. (4:13)

3. **GOD PROMISES AID**

    a.   Divine Presence. (3:12)

    b.   Given Divine Authority. (3:13, 14)

    c.   Promised Divine Empowerment. (4:28)

    d.   Promised Human Cooperation. Aaron. (4:14-16)

4. **MOSES AND AARON RETURN TO EGYPT**

    a.   Told Elders of Israel of deliverance. (4:29-31)

    b.   Pharaoh's opposition. (5:2)

    c.   Tasks made more severe. (5: 5-23)

    d.   Divine instruction to Moses and Aaron. (Chapters 6,7)

5. **THE GREAT CONTEST: TEN PLAGUES (7:14 – 12:29)**

(Water turned to blood, frogs, lice, flies, murrain upon beasts, boils, hail, locusts, darkness, death of first born)

  1. **NATURE OF CONTEST**

    a.   Not merely struggle between slaves and oppressors.

    b.   Contest between Jehovah and gods of Egypt.

  2. **NEED OF THE CONTEST**

    a.   Israelites only race to believe in one God.

    b.   Danger of losing faith and national identity.

    c.   In Hebrews was God's only chance to preserve faith in Himself.

    d.   Egyptian Gods now gone, Jehovah lives.

  3. **END OF THE CONTEST**

    a.   Passover brings death to firstborn.

    b.   Fetters broken – Israel given freedom.

    c.   Pharaoh pursues – Israelites trapped.

    d.   Sea divides – Israelites saved – Egyptians drown.

6. **RESULTS OF SOJOURN IN EGYPT**

  1. **MADE ISRAEL A NATION**

    a.   They entered Egypt twelve nomadic families.

    b.   Jacob and his direct descendants numbered seventy.

    c.   Including servants. Entire tribe numbered two thousand or three thousand.

    d.   Had they remained in Canaan they would have been wandering tribes.

    e.   Oppression compacted them into a nation.

2. MARCH TO REPHIDIM THROUGH WILDERNESS OF SIN

 a. Could not remain on shore of triumph.

 b. Followed eastern shore of Red Sea.

 c. Sweetened Marah's bitter water. (15:23-26)

 d. Camped by Elim's twelve springs (15:27)

 e. Manna sent, when food fails. (16:14, 15)

3. CLOSING EVENTS CONFIRMED THEM IN A NATIONAL FAITH

a. Had they remained in Egypt they would have lost both national faith and national unity.

III. PERIOD OF DISCIPLINE

1. MOSES SONG OF DELIVERANCE

 a. Magnificent ode. (15:1-19)

 b. On eastern shore of Red Sea.

2. MARCH TO REPHIDIM THROUGH WILDERNESS OF SIN

 a. Could not remain on shore of triumph

 b. Followed eastern shore of Red Sea.

 c. Sweetened Marah's bitter water. (15:23-26)

 d. Camped by Elim's twelve springs. (15:27) e.Manna sent, when food fails. (16:14, 15)

3. ENCAMPMENT IN VALLEY OF REPHIDIM

 a. Entering district of Horeb.

 b. Water from rock. (17: 1-7)

 c. Amalekites attack Hebrews. (17:8)

 d. Aaron and Hur hold up Moses' hands. (17:12)

 e. Israel victorious. (17:9-13)

 f. Jethro's advice – select judges. (18:13-23)

g. Arrival at Mt. Sinai. (19: 1, 2)

IV. <u>PERIOD OF LEGISLATION AND ORGANIZATION</u> (Chapter 19-40)

1. **THE YEAR AT MT. SINAI**

    a. From Rephidim Moses led Israel to Sinai.

    b. Camped on level plain before Holy Mount.

    c. Mt. Sinai vast granite mountain fifteen hundred feet high.

2. **MOSES FIRST ASCENT (19: 3-6)**

    a. Appearance of God upon the mountain.

    b. Covenant made with God. (19:8)

3. **MOSES SECOND ASCENT (19:20) (Ten Commandments)**

    a. God manifested in fire and smoke. (19:16-18)

    b. God called Moses up to warn people (19:20-22) not to come near the Mountain.

    c. God spoke ten commandments. (20:1-17)

4. **NATIONAL FESTIVALS**

    a. Passover or Feast of Unleavened Bread. (23:15)

    b. Feast of Pentecost -- Fifty days after Passover. (23:16)

    c. Feast of Tabernacles, or Ingathering. (23:16)

5. **CONQUEST OF CANAAN PROMISED (23: 20-31)**

6. **MOSES' THIRD ASCENT (Forty days)**

    a. God called him to give tables of stone.

    b. God had written his laws on them. (24:12)

    c. Moses remained there for forty days. (24:18)

    d. God's commands to Moses. (Chapters 25-31)

7. **THE GOLDEN CALF**

a. While Moses was on the mountain the Hebrews made gold calf. (32:1-4)

b. God intended to destroy them. (32:7-10)

c. Moses' intercession. (32:11-14)

d. Moses saw Hebrew idolatry and broke tables of stone. (32:19)

8. MOSES' FOURTH ASCENT (32: 31-32)

a. Moses second intercession. (32:30)

b. God smote Israelites for idolatry. (32:35)

c. Three thousand paid penalty for crime.

9. REMOVAL OF DIVINE PRESENCE (33:1-6)

a. Sent an angel to lead them. (33:2)

b. God commanded people to remove jewelry. (33:5)

c. Never wore ornaments from Horeb on. (33:6)

10. DIVINE PRESENCE RESTORED

a. Moses' third intercession. (33:12, 13)

b. Divine leadership restored. (33:14-17)

11. A SECOND TABLE OF THE LAW GIVEN

a. Moses was to make the two stones. (34:1-10)

12. MOSES' FIFTH ASCENT (Forty days)

a. Moses took the two stones up. (34:4)

b. God told Moses to write Ten Commandments on stones. (34:27-28)

c. Was with God Mountain forty days. (34:27-28)

13. MOSES' FACE SHINES (34:30-35)

14. THE TABERNACLE SET UP (Chapters 35-40)

LEVITICUS

AUTHOR: Moses.

DATE: Approximately Mid 1400s BC.

PLACE: Before Mount Sinai.

KEW WORDS: "Access" and "Holiness"

MAIN THEME: Atonement – How can sinful man approach a holy God? (The word Holy occurs over eighty times in Leviticus.)

COMPANION BOOK: Hebrews

SYNOPSIS

I. THE WAY OF ACCESS TO GOD

1. THROUGH SACRIFICES AND OFFERINGS

a. Burnt offerings, signifying atonement and consecration. (1:2-9)

b. Meal (flour offerings, signifying thanksgiving.) (2:1-2)

c. Peace offerings, signifying fellowship. (7:11-15)

d. Sin offerings, signifying reconciliation. (Chapter 4)

e. Trespass offerings, signifying cleansing from guilt. (6:2-7)

2. THROUGH PRIESTLY MEDIATION

a. Call of human priesthood –Aaron and sons. (8:1-5)

b. Cleansing of priests. (8:6)

c. Garments of priests. (8:7-13)

d. Atonement for priests. (8:14-34)

e. Example of sinfulness of priests. (Chapter 10)

Nadab and Abihu destroyed by fire. (10:1, 2)

f. f.Scapegoat for people. (16:20-22)

II. SPECIAL ENACTMENTS GOVERNING ISRAEL

1. AS TO FOOD (Chapter 11)

    a.   All cloven-footed animals except camel-coney-hare-swine.

    b.   Of things that live in water; only those that have fins and scales.

    c.   Of fowls only; locusts, bald locust, beetle, grasshopper.

2.   AS TO CLEANLINESS, SANITATION, CUSTOMS, MORALS, MARRIAGES, ETC.

ALL EMPHASIZING PURITY OF LIFE AS A CONDITION OF DIVINE FAVOR

    a.   Leprosy – unclean (Chapters 12-20)

    b.   Unlawful marriages or lusts.

3.   PURITY OF PRIEST AND OFFERINGS (Chapters 21, 22)

    a.   Priests mourning, marriage, holiness.

    b.   Priests must be without blemish.

    c.   Unclean priests must abstain from holy things.

    d.   Sacrifices must be without blemish.

III. THE FIVE ANNUAL FEASTS

1.   FEAST OF PASSOVER, BEGINNING APRIL 14. (23:5)

    a.   Commemorating the Exodus.

2.   FEAST OF PENTECOST, JUNE 6. (23:15)

    a.   Commemorating giving of law.

3.   FEAST OF TRUMPETS. OCTOBER 1. (23:23-25)

    a.   Convocation and praise.

4.   A DAY OF ATONEMENT, OCTOBER 10. (Chapters 16 & 23: 27-32)

    a.   High priest enters Holy of Holies to make atonement for sins of people.

5.   FEAST OF TABERNACLES, OCTOBER 15. (23: 39-43)

IV. GENERAL ENACTMENT AND INSTRUCTIONS

1. THE SABBATICAL YEAR. EVERY SEVENTH YEAR

    a.   Land was given a Sabbath – rest. (25:2-7 Ex. 23:11)

2. THE YAR OF JUBILEE. FIFTIETH YEAR

    a.   Slaves were freed.

    b.   Debts were canceled.

    c.   Lands were restored. (25:8-16)

    d.   Oppression prohibited.

    e.   No land to be cultivated.

3. CONDITIONS OF BLESSINGS AND PUNISHMENT (Chapter 26)

    a.   Idolatry prohibited. (26:1)

    b.   Keep sabbeths and reverence sanctuary. (26:2)

    c.   A blessing to the obedient. (26:3-13)

    d.   A curse to the disobedient. (26: 14-39)

    e.   A promise to the penitent. (26: 40-46)

4. THE LAW OF VOWS (Chapter 27)

    a.   Sanctifying self to God. Price according to age. (27:1-8)

    b.   Sanctifying possessions. Price according to priests' estimation. (27:9-25)

    c.   First born of all animals belongs to God. (27:26)

    d.   No devoted thing may be redeemed. (27:28, 29)

    e.   Tithe of all possessions is God's. (27:30)

5. HEBREWS IS COMPANION BOOK TO LEVITICUS

    a.   Should be studied together.

NUMBERS

AUTHOR: Moses
GENERAL LESSON:
Unbelief bars entrance to abundant life (Heb. 3:7-19)
DATE: 1490 to 1451. BC Events of Numbers begin fourteen months after the Exodus from Egypt, and covers a period of forty years wandering.
PLACE: Country between Mount Sinai and Jordan.

MAIN THEME: Counting of the tribes

I. ORGANIZATION AND NUMBERS LEGISLATION

II. CHAPTER 1. THE GENISUS:

1. Men of war from twenty years up numbered. (1:1-46)

2. Levites as priests exempted tabernacle service. (1:47-54)

CHAPTER 2. ORDER OF TRIBES AROUND TABERNACLE
(Levites closely surrounded tabernacle; soldiers, far off, surrounded tabernacle.)

1. **EAST – STANDARD OF JUDAH**

   a. Junah – 74,600 soldiers

   b. Issachar – 54,400 soldiers

   c. Zebulun – 57,400 soldiers

   TOTAL – 186,400 soldiers

2. **SOUTH – STANDARD OF RUBEN**

   a. Ruben – 46,500 soldiers

   b. Simeon –59,300 soldiers

   c. Gad – 45,650 soldiers

   TOTAL – 151,450 soldiers

3. **WEST – STANDARD OF EPHRAIM**

   a. Ephraim – 40,500 soldiers

   b. Manassah – 32,500 soldiers

   c. Benjamin – 35,400 soldiers

   TOTAL – 108,100 soldiers

4. NORTH – STANDARD OF DAN

    a. Dan –   62,700 soldiers

    b. Asher –   41,500 soldiers

    c. Naphtali – 53,400 soldiers

    TOTAL – 157,600 soldiers

CHAPTER 3

1. Levites service. (3:1-39)

2. First-born freed by Levites. (3:40-43)

3. The over plus redeemed. (3:44)

CHAPTER 4

1. Levites service and office of priests. (4:1-33)

2. Number serving the tabernacle:

    a. Kohathites – 2,750

    b. Gershonites – 2,630

    c. Merarites – 3,200

    TOTAL LEVITES – 8,580

CHAPTER 5

1. Unclean removed from camp. (5:1-4)

2. Restitution commanded. (5:5-8)

3. Holy offerings belong to priests. (5:9, 10)

4. Trial of jealousy and punishment. (5:11-31)

CHAPTER 6

1. Law and vow of the Nazarite. (6:1-21)

2. Form of blessing the people. (6: 22-27)

CHAPTER 7

1. Prince's offering to Levites. (7:1-88)

2. God speaks to Moses from Mercy Seat. (7:89)

CHAPTER 8

1. Consecration of Levites. (8:5-22)

2. Age and time of service. (8:23-26)

   a.   From years old to 50 years.

CHAPTER 9

1. Observance of Passover. (9:1-14)

2. Cloud and fire guided Israelites. (9:15-23)

III. FROM SINAI TO KADESH

1. Leaving Mount Sinai. (10:11-12)

2. Fire destroys the murmurers at Tabera. (11:1-3)

3. Longing for fleshpots -- loath manna. (11:2-6)

4. Discouragement of Moses. (11:10-15)

5. Seventy elders appointed. (11:16-25)

6. Quails sent. (Israel wanted flesh) (11:31-35)

7. Jealousy of Aaron and Miriam. (12:1-15)

   a.   Miriam become leperous

   b.   Moses intercession – Miriam healed

IV. AT KADESH –THE BREAK DOWN OF FAITH (lost in sight of home)

1. Mission of the spies and their report. (13:26-33)

2. Rebellion of Israel. (14:1-10)

3. Curse pronounced upon them. (14:11-12)

4. Whole generation doomed. (14:29)

5. Moses intercedes. (14:13-20)

6. Generation doomed to die in the wilderness. (14:28-33; Heb. 3:17-19)

   a.   Only Joshua and Caleb to enter Promised Land

7. Israel defeated by Amalekites and Canaanites. (14:40-45)

V. FORTY YEARS WANDERING IN WILDERNESS

1. Wanderings of Israel predicted. (14:33)

2. Sabbath-breaker stoned. (15:32-36)

3. Rebellion of Korah, Nathan and Abiram. (16:1-40)

4.   Rebellion of people. (16:41-42)

5.   Aaron's atonement. (16:45-50)

VI. AT KADESH THE SECOND TIME

1.   Death of Miriam. (20:1)

2.   People murmur because of thirst. (20: 2-6)

3.   Moses' sin – struck the rock. (20:7-13)

4.   Moses and Aaron denied entrance to Canaan. (20:12)

VII. FROM KADESH TO THE JORDAN

1.   Detour around Edom. (20:14-22)

2.   Death of Aaron. (20:23-29)

   a.   Eleasr, his son, succeeds Aaron.

3.   Fiery serpents. (21:5-7)

4.   The Brazen Serpent. (21:8-9)

5.   Settlement of country east of Jordan. (22:1)

6.   Balaam, the prophet. (Chapters 22-25)

7.   Census of the new generation. (Chapter 26)

CONTRAST OF FIRST AND SECOND CENSUS

Only man of war numbered – Twenty years old and up

First Census	Second Census	TOTAL
TRIBE:Ruben 46,500	43,730	- 2,770
Simeon 59,300	22,200	-37,100
Gad 45,650	40,500	5,150
Judah 74,600	76,500	1,900
Issachar 54,400	64,300	9,900
Zebulum 57,400	60,500	3,100
Ephraim 40,500	32,500	- 8,000
Manasah 32,300	52,700	20,500
Benjamin 35,400	45,600	10,200
Dan 62,700	64,400	1,700
Asher 41,500	53,400	11,900
Naphtali 53,400	45,400	- 8,000
TOTAL 603,550	601,730	- 1,820

Levites exempt from census of warriors

8,580 23,000   14,420

(Only male Levites counted -- from one month old and up)

Only Joshua and Caleb of the first census of 603,550 were alive to be counted in the second census – Go's promise was fulfilled. (14:28-30)

8. Law concerning inheritance, offerings, feasts, vows, etc. (Chapters 27-30)

9. Judgment of Midian. (Chapter 31)

10. Assignment of land east of Jordan. (Chapter 32)

11. Summary of journey to Jordan. (33:1-49)

12. The cities of refuge. (Chapter 35)

13. Inheritance of daughters and their marriage. (Chapter 36)

MESSIANIC TYPES

The Smitten Rock. (20:7-11; 1 Cor. 10:4)

The Brazen Serpent. (21:6-9; Jn. 3:14)

The Cities of Refuge. (Chapter 35; Heb. 6:18)

THE SEVEN MURMURINGS

1. Concerning the way. (11:1-3)

2. Concerning the food. (11:4-6)

3. Concerning the giants. (13:33 – 14:2)

4. Concerning their leaders. (16:3)

5. Concerning divine judgments. (16:41)

6. Concerning the desert. (20:2-5)

7. Second time concerning the manna. (21:5)

DEUTERONOMY

AUTHOR: Moses, commonly accepted. With the exception of the last chapter where the account of Moses' death is given. This could not have been written by Moses, and the writing of this chapter is attributed to Joshua, who followed Moses, and is most likely true.

NAME: The name of the book is derived from two Greek words, "Deuteros," meaning second, and "Nomos," meaning law. The more correct wording in the English Version means, "A repetition of the law" or "A copy of the law."

DATE: Approximately 1400s BC.

MAIN THEME:

The former generation of Israel had died in the wilderness. Hence it was important and necessary that the law should be repeated and expounded to the new generation before they entered the Promised Land.

The scene of the books is in the plains of Moab, and the Time is the interval between the "wanderings' in the wilderness" and the "crossing of the Jordan."

It opens with the first day of the 11th month and 40th year of the Exodus. Chapters 1-3 and as the Israelites crossed the Jordan on the 10th day of the 1st month of the following year, after 30 days' morning for Moses in the Plains of Moab. (See Chapter 34:8 and Joshua 4:19) It follows that the period covered by Deuteronomy is not more than forty days.

One will notice that the main theme of the book is a rehearsal of the laws proclaimed at Sinai, with a call to obedience, interspersed with a review of the experiences of the old generation

CONTENTS

A series of discourses given by Moses just before his death, on the plains of Moab, before the crossing of the Jordan. In these discourses, Moses reviews the events and experiences of the past forty years and found on them repeated exhortations to gratitude, obedience and loyalty to Jehovah. Discourses given are as follows:

FIRST DISCOURS: (Chapter 1:4-43)

This comprises a brief survey of the history of Israel from Mt. Sinai to the Jordan. Chapters 1, 3, and concluding with an earnest appeal to the people to keep the commandments of Jehovah and remain faithful to his covenant. (Chapter 4:1-40)

SECOND DISCOURSE:

Beginning with 4:44 through the 28th, which is mainly legislative, it begins with a repetition of the Decalogue and an exhortation to cleave to Jehovah, and abstain from idolatry. Chapters 4:44 to 11 after which follows a series of laws regulating the religious and social life of the people. Chapters 12 to 26, this section forms the nucleus of the book.

THIRD DISCOURSE: (Chapters 29, 30)

In which the Covenant is renewed and enforced with promises and threatening.

FOURTH PART: (Chapters 31, 34)

These chapters are in the nature of appendices and comprises Moses' charge to Joshua and delivery of the Law to the Levitical Priests. (Chapter 31:1-13). The blessing of Moses which are both in rather poetical form. Chapter 33 and lastly the account of the death of Moses. (Chapter 34)

KEY THOUGHT: The Divine requirement of obedience. (Chapters 10, 12, 13)

SYNOPSIS AND DIVISIONS:

1. A rehearsal God's dealing with Israel in the past. (Chapters 1, 4)

2. A repetition of the Decalogue and references to the choice of Israel to be a separated people obedient to the divine commandments. (Chapter 5, 11)

3. A code of laws to be observed in Canaan. (Chapters 12-26)

4. Blessings pronounced on Obedience and curses on disobedience. Life and death set before the people. (Chapters 27-30)

5. Final words of Moses, his song, blessing, etc. (Chapters 31-33)

6. Supplemental account of the last vision of Moses and his death. (Chapter 34)

SOME PROBLEMS AND INFORMATION AS TO THE ORIGIN AND COMPOSITION OF THE BOOK OF DEUTERONOMY:

The book of Deuteronomy was most certainly in existence in the year 621 B.C. The BOOK OF THE LAW discovered by Hilkiah, the priest in the temple at Jerusalem in that year, is generally agreed to have included, if not identical with, our book of Deuteronomy.

Some commentators say there is no reason to believe that this was not the discovery of a lost work, and its identification of at least the main part of Deuteronomy.

It is inferred from the fact that the reformation as instituted by Josiah was such as the Law of Deuteronomy would require. Namely, the Prohibition of the worship of heavenly bodies. Compare II Kings 23:3, 5, 11 with Deuteronomy 17:3. This also refers to idolatrous and superstitious worship and the centralization of worship at Jerusalem. Compare II Kings 23:2, 21, 23, with Deuteronomy 12:4-28, and II Kings 23:8, 9 with Deuteronomy 18:6-8, and the language in which Josiah's reformation is spoken of in II Kings 23:2-3 with the general style of Deuteronomy 29:1-9, 25 – 30:10 and 31:24.

Like the rest of the Pentateuch, this book professes to set forth the words and laws of Moses and is ascribed by tradition to him.

It can no longer be denied that writing was practiced in the time of Moses and even before his day. Expressly asserted in several places, Ex. 17:14, 24:4-7, 34:27, Numbers 33:2, Deu. 31:9-26 where he is said to have written the law and delivered it to the custody of the priests. Yet many Bible scholars say that the book could not have been written by Moses, at least in its present form, and that the writer or compiler lived subsequently to the time of Moses and the conquest of Canaan. The phrase "beyond Jordan" suggests that the writer lived in western Palestine where Moses never lived.

It must be kept in view, however, that the book itself is given as "a repetition of the law". So, in view of the conflict of critical opinion it seems to be best to regard it as a "re-formulation" of the laws of Moses designed to meet the changing needs and circumstances of a time subsequent to its original publication.

RELIGIOUS VALUE:

Whatever may be the difference of opinion as to the date of Deu., there can be none as to its surpassing religious value.

JOSHUA

AUTHOR: JOSHUA

LEADING TOPIC: The conquest and division of the Land of Canaan.

LEADING THOUGHT: How to be successful in the battle of life? (1:8-9)

DATE: 1451-1375 BC (forty-nine years) from the crossing of the Jordan to the Death of Joshua.

MAIN THEME: **Faith, warfare, conquest, Certainty of fulfillment of Divine Purposes, as seen:**

1. In Judgments visited upon Canaanites because of their awful sins.

2. In the descendants of Abraham being given possession of the land according to Gods promise. (Gen. 12:7)

HISTORICAL SYNOPSIS

I. PASSAGE OF THE JORDAN (Chapters 1-5)

1. THE NEW LEADER (Chapters 1-2)

a. Moses left Israel camped east of Jordan.

b. Victories of Sihon and Og gave Israel land east of Jordan.

c. Canaan proper lay west of river; a mountainous country crowded with warlike people in walled cities.

d. Israel never had a second Moses.

e. God who gave Moses for deliverance and organization now gives Joshua for conquest and settlement.

2. THE JORDAN DIVIDED (Chapters 3-4)

a. Israel came to Red Sea with powerful Egyptian foes behind them.

b. Came to Jordan with powerful Canaanite foes before them.

c. In each instance miracle of divided water strengthened faith in God and leader.

d. River was flooded by melting snows of Mt. Lebanon.

e. No boats nor bridges, but waters parted as priests, carrying sacred ark, stepped into water.

f. Two stone memorials erected; one in rover bed, the other at Gilgal, where they camped that night.

3. **ENCAMPMENT AT GILGAL (Chapter 5)**

a. Circumcision, omitted during wanderings, renewed.

b. Penalty for unbelief rolled away, hence the name Gilgal.

c. Passover celebrated as on night of the Exodus.

(1) Then Egyptians awed by death angle in the land.

(1) Now Canaanites cowered in fear behind walls of Jericho.

d. Manna ceased at Gilgal.

e. Israel remained encamped here until Canaan was so far conquered as to be divided among the tribes.

4. **JOSHUA RECEIVED COMMISSION FROM GOD (5:13-15)**

a. God appeared not in burning bush as to Moses.

b. With drawn sword, symbol of conquest, to Joshua.

c. Removed shoes for ground was holy.

5. **THE CAPTURE OF JERICHORAHAB, FRIEND TO THE SPIES (Chapter 2)**

a. Before crossing Jordan, Joshua sent two spies to Jericho.

b. Rahab hid them from the officials of the King.

c. Spies promised her and relatives safety when they captured Jericho.

d. Scarlet thread in window to be the sign.

e. Rahab let spies down outside city wall.

6. **CAPTURE OF JERICHO – GATEWAY TO CANAAN**

    a.   Was to prove God's work instead of mans.

    b.   Priests, carrying ark, to precede march around the city.

    c.   Israelites to march around the city once each day for six days.

    d.   Seven circuits seventh day, and blow trumpets.

    e.   Jericho fell by power of God.

    f.   God broke yoke of Egypt, fed and led Israelites in wilderness, gave them law, parted waters of Jordan, dispossessed corrupt Canaanites and fulfilled His covenant to His people by giving them the land of promise.

II. THE CONQUEST OF CENTRAL CANAAN

1. **CAPTURE OF AI – KEY TO CENTRAL CANAAN (Chapter 7)**

    a.   Israel was beaten at first attack.

    b.   Cause was sin of Achan following capture of Jericho.

    c.   Took wedge of gold, some silver and mantle.

    d.   Achan atoned for his sin with his life.

    e.   Second attack gave Ai and central Canaan to Israel.

2. **THE ASSEMBLY OF SHECKEM (8:30-35**

    a.   Sheckem in the heart of Canaan

    b.   Hallowed by lives of Patriarchs

        (1)   Here Abraham first pitched his tent and reared his alter.

        (1)   At Bethel, close by, fugitive Jacob lived after his return from Exile, and buried relics of idolatry brought from Mesopotamia.

    c.   Moses directed a solemn assembly to be held at Sheckem. (Deut. 27)

    d.   Sheckem in valley between Mt. Ebal on north and Mt. Gerizim on south.

    e.   Joshua built an altar, wrote the law on stones and pronounced curses and blessings.

III. CONFEDERACY AND CONQUEST OF THE SOUTH (Chapters 9-10)

1. ISRAEL'S LEAGUE WITH THE GIBEONITES (Chapter 9)

    a.   Kings combined against Israel.

    b.   Gibeonites secured confederacy with Israel by deception.

    c.   Joshua made them servants of Israelites.

2. THE BATTLE OF BETH-HORON (Long Day) (Chapter 10)

    a.   Five kings of cities fought Gibeon.

    b.   Joshua rescued it – God sent hail stones.

    c.   Sun and moon stood still.

    d.   Five Kings hung.

    e.   Seven other Kings conquered.

    f.   Joshua returned to the camp at Gilgal.

IV. CONFEDERACY AND CONQUEST OF THE NORTH (Chapters 11-12)

1. JABIN, KING OF HAZOR, HEADED CONFEDERACY AGAINST JOSHUA

    a.   Joshua won battle at waters of Merom.

    b.   Utterly destroyed both cities and people.

    c.   Last combined effort of Canaanities against Joshua.

    d.   War died down to petty local battles.

2. LIST OF DEFEATED KINGS (Chapter 12)

3. MISTAKE OF ISRAEL

    a.   Failure to entirely expel Canaanites.

    b.   Peril lay in leagues of amity and intermarriages.

    c.   Only safety of Israel and pure religion was in their complete isolation.

V. <u>DIVISION OF THE LAND AND DEATH OF JOSHUA</u> (Chapters 13-24)

1.   DIVISION OF THE LAND (Chapters 13-22)

    a.   Joshua divided the land lot among the twelve tribes.

    b.   Levites not counted a tribe but given forty-eight cities.

        (1) Among these were the six cities of refuge; Golan, Ramothgilead and Bezer east of Jordan; Kedesh, Sheckem and Hebron west of Jordan.

    c.   Jacob had adopted Joseph's two sons, Ephriam and Manasseh, as his own, making twelve tribes without Levi.

        (1) They were: Reuben, Simeon, Judah, Issachar, Zebulum, Dan, Naphtali, Gad, Asher, Ephriam, Manasseh and Benjamin.

2.   FAREWELL AND DEATH OF JOSHUA (Chapter 23-24)

    a.   Calls solemn assembly of tribes at historic Sheckem.

    b.   Joshua exhorts Israel to obey God:

        (1) By former benefits. (23:1-4)

        (1) By promises. (23:5-11)

        (1) By threats. (23:12-16)

    c.   Reviewed their history. (24:1-13)

VI. <u>RENEWED NATIONAL COVENANT WITH GOD</u> (24:14-25)

    One of greatest texts in the Bible. (24:15)

    a.   Erected stone memorial of covenant. (24:26, 27)

    b.   Dismissed assembly. (24:28)

    c.   Death of Joshua at one hundred ten years of age. (24: 29)

<u>TYPES</u>: According to the common conception, the Crossing of the Jordan represents death – and Canaan, Heaven; but a better analogy is:

CANAAN: A type of the Higher Christian Life to be won by warfare. (Rom 7:23)

CANAANITES: A type of our Spiritual enemies. (Eph. 6:12) WARFARE OF ISRAEL: A type of the Fight of Faith. (I Tim. 6:12)

ISRAEL'S REST: After the conquest (Josh. 11:23) a type of the Rest of the Soul.

(Heb. 4:9)

CANAANITES PARTLY SUBDUED: A type of Besetting Sins, unconquered.

(Heb. 12:1)

<u>CHOICE SELECTIONS</u>:

    a.   God's encouragement of Joshua. (1:1-9)

    b.   Joshua's Farewell Address. (23:1-16; 24:1-27)

JUDGES

AUTHOR: Probably Samuel

DATE: 1375-1095. From the death of Joshua to the anointing of Saul – Judges, Ruth and Samuel. (1-10)

MAIN THEME:

The history of Israel during the times of the fourteen judges. The book portrays a series of relapses into idolatry on the part of God's people followed by invasions of the Promised Land and oppressions by their enemies. The narrative centers on the personalities of the heroic judges who were raised up to become deliverers of Israel, whenever they sincerely repented their sins. The dark side of the picture is especially emphasized in the records.

A study of the dates would seem to show that the people maintained an outward loyalty to Jehovah a larger part of the time than the casual reading of the book would indicate.

SYNOPSIS

I. RELIGIOUS CONDITIONS OF ISRAEL

1. A SERIES OF RELAPSES INTO IDOLATRY

   a. Their idolatrous ancestry. (Gen. 31:18; 35:2) (Josh. 24:2-14)

      (1) Abraham had abandoned idolatry.

      (2) By Jacob's marriage it had re-entered the family life.

      (3) Although Jacob buried the idols, traces of it remained.

   b. Their Egyptian Bondage. (Ex. 32:21-34) (Josh. 24:14)

      (1) Israel was deeply tingled with idolatry to have fallen so soon and so low at the very foot of Mt. Sinai.

(2) Joshua's address is conclusive evidence that the discipline of the wilderness did not wholly eradicate it.

c. The Contamination of Canaanite Tribes.

(1) Canaan was center of most debasing religion of the time.

(2) Carthage, Greece and Rome drew from Canaan the licentious features of their religions.

(3) Hence, the divine edict to either expel or exterminate the Canaanites. It was Israel's only safety.

(4) The failure to obey the edict, and the intermarriages which followed, were a perpetual menace to pure religion.

2. A SERIES OF CONSEQUENT OPPRESSIONS

a. Oppressions by neighboring tribes were a natural result.

b. The morally weak became politically weak.

c. Oppressions were disciplinary judgments.

d. Again and again, scourged into contrition by Moabites of Midianites or Philistines, Israel turned from the idolatry of their oppressors to the worship of Jehovah.

e. In the long run the purer religion won.

3. A SERIES OF DELIVERERS CALLED JUDGES

a. These were not ideal men.

b. They fall far below heroes of Christian faith.

c. Often superstitious, passionate, morally weak, they yet believed in God. In such times that was much.

d. They rose above the level of *their* age, as Paul or Luther did above *theirs*, and so deserve a place in roll of heroes of faith.

II. POLITICAL CONDITION OF ISRAEL

Politically there was no national organization, national capitol, or national head. Moses gave a religious system, but not a well-defined political policy. They were twelve tribes, sometimes wrangling almost to the point of mutual extermination. Three ties held them from breaking up into a dozen petty nations.

1. A COMMON ANCESTORY AND HISTORY

   a. Abraham was the founder of the race.

   b. They shared equally in their reverence for Isaac and Jacob.

   c. The lives of Joseph, Moses and Joshua, and the glories of the Red Sea, the Jordan and the Conquest were national heritages.

2. **COMMON LANGUAGE**

   a. Hebrew was the National language

3. **A COMMON RELIGION**

   a. The tabernacle had been set up at Shiloh.

   b. There was the one altar.

   c. There dwelt the High Priest of the Nation.

   d. There the sacrifices were offered up daily.

   e. To Shiloh went the representatives of the tribes to the three great annual feasts.

   f. Such were the centripetal forces at work.

   g. These ties held the Hebrews till they found in the Prophet Samuel and in King David the sublime faith and the genius for political organization to weld them into a nation.

III. THE CAUSE OF THE INVASIONS AND OPPRESSIONS

1. IDOLATROUS PRACTICES OF ISRAEL

   a. Idolaters had not been driven out wholly from the land.

    b. Israel dwelt among them (3:5), accepted their heathen practices and forgot God.

    c. Moses had warned in Deuteronomy that such practices would not go unpunished.

    d. Oppressions came as divine judgment for their apostasies.

I. PERIOD FROM DEATH OF JOSHUA TO THE FIRST JUDGE (1:1-3:9)

  1. CONTINUED WAR OF CONQUEST

    a. Judah succeeded Joshua as commander. (1:1, 2)

    b. Captured Jerusalem and Hebron. (1:8-10)

  2. **CANAANITES NOT DRIVEN OUT**

    a. Manasseh, Ephraim, Zebulun, Asher, and Naphtali disobeyed God by permitting them to remain. (1:27-33)

  3. **RESULT OF DISOBEDIENCE**

    a. Angel sent to rebuke Israel at Bochim. (2:1-9)

    b. Idolatry of new generation after Joshua. (2:10-19)

    c. Their punishment a testing. (2:20 3:9)

II. PERIOD OF SEVEN INVASIONS AND OPPRESSIONS (Chapters 3-16)

  1. MESOPOTOMAIN INVASION FROM EAST (Chapters 3:5-22) (Othniel, first judge, overthrows king of Mesopotamia) (3:7-11)

    a. In Abraham's time the lords of the Euphrates extended their empire to the Jordan and carried off Lot.

    b. Five hundred years later, another lord of the great valley heads another western invasion.

    c. Eight years Israel groans under the yoke.

d. Othniel, Caleb's nephew, rouses Israel to resistance and drives the invaders back to the Euphrates.

e. Land had peace for forty years.

2. **MOABITE INVASION FROM THE SOUTHEAST (3:12-20) (Ehud, second Judge, slays king of Moah.)**

a. Moabites, descendants of Lot, lived east of Dead Sea.

b. Under Eglon they subdued the southeastern tribes, crossed the Jordan and held

c. Jericho eighteen years.

d. Ehud, a Benjamite, carried the tribute of the tribes to Eglon at Jericho.

e. In private interview slew king and escaped.

f. Raised an army seized the fords of Jordan and in a battle, slew ten thousand

g. Moabites.

h. That part of Canaan had peace then for eighty years.

3. **PHILISTINE INVASION FROM THE SOUTHWEST (Shamgar, third Judge, slew six hundred Philistines)**

a. Country had peace for eighty years; then, the Philistine invasion.

b. Shamgar, one-man army, plus God's help delivered Israel.

4. **CANAANITE INVASION FROM THE NORTH (Chapters 4-5)**

(Judges, Deborah and Barak, defeat Jabin and Sisera)

a. Joshua defeated a northern confederacy, headed by Jabin.

b. Under a later Jabin, these northern Canaanites rallied and oppressed the northern tribes for twenty years.

   c. Deborah, a prophetess of faith and courage, stirred up Barak, of the tribe of Naphtali.

   d. With an army of ten thousand men Barak was victorious at Esdraelon.

   e. Sisera, Canaanite captain fled and sought refuge in the tent of Jael, wife of Heber the Kenite, a descendant of Jethro, Moses father-in-law.

   f. Jael drove a tent pin through temple of sleeping Sisera.

   g. The victory was celebrated by Deborah in an eloquent battle son. (Chapter 5)

5. MIDIANITE INVASION FROM THE EAST

(Judges, Gideon, Chapters 6-8; followed by Abimeoloch, Tola and Jair. Chapters 9-10)

   a. Midianites were Arabs, descendants of Abraham by his wife Keturah.

      (1) Invasion came after Israel had had forty years of peace.

      (2) Never settled in the land but swept over it at harvest time, loaded themselves with booty and went away.

      (3) So terrible were their raids the Israelites fled to the hills, walled cities and caves.

   b. God raised up a deliverer in Gideon of the tribe of Manasseh.

      (1) He began by destroying Baal worship in father's house and village.

      (2) Collected an army of thirty-two thousand men, reduced it to ten thousand by letting faint hearted return home; still farther reduced it by choosing those who warily drank water from their hands.

       (3) With three hundred soldiers he made a night attack and defeated them.

  c. Gideon became a hero; he was offered the crown but he declined it.

  d. His ambitious son, Abimelech slew all his brothers but one, and won a brief Kingship at Sheckem.

       (1) He lost both life and crown while quelling a revolt.

  e. <u>Tola</u>, a tribe of Issachar, judged twenty-three years.

  f. Jair, a Gileadite, judged Israel twenty-two years.

6. <u>AMMONITE INVASION FROM EAST</u> (Chapters 11-12:7)

(Jephtah, tenth Judge, son of Gilead, defeated Ammonites Ibzan, and Abdon succeeded Jephtah as judges.)

  a. Ammonites, like Moabites, descended from Lot.

       (1) At conquest of country east of Jordan they had been crowded back upon eastern desert.

       (2) Soon began to press back upon eastern tribes.

  b. Jephtah became the instrument of deliverance.

       (1) Low-born, disinherited outlaw; recalled, reinstated, and given command of army.

       (2) Before battle he vowed, if successful, to sacrifice whatever first met het him when he returned home.

       (3) Was successful, was met by his only daughter, and sacrificed her.

  c. After war Israel enjoyed peace for thirty-one years.

7. <u>PHILISTINE INVASION FROM SOUTHWEST</u> (Chapters 13-16)

(Samson, fourteenth Judge, delivered Israel after forty years of Philistine oppression- judged Israel twenty years.)

    a.   Philistines were the most inveterate foes of Israel.

        (1) Harassed Israel through the three hundred years period of Judges, and into period of monarch until effectually defeated by David.

        (2) Southern tribes, Simeon, Dan and Judah, especially exposed to their attack.

    b.   Samson, of tribe of Dan, was Hebrew Hercules.

        (1) Was born a Nazarite.

        (2) Made frequent forays against Philistines alone.

        (3) Two successive marriages with Philistine women afforded opportunity both for his success and final fall.

        (4) To Delilah he discloses secret of his strength.

        (5) Lost strength through violation of the Nazarite vow-haircut.

        (6) Blinded, imprisoned, doomed to turn corn mill.

    c.   Samson destroys both enemies and self.

        (1) Philistines gave feast to god Dagon.

        (2) Brought Samson out to amuse people.

        (3) He pulled down central pillars of temple and buried thousands of Philistines with himself under ruins.

    d.   Samson never broke power of Philistines.

        (1) His exploits rekindled Israel's courage.

        (2) Made possible more permanent work of Samuel and David.

III. <u>PERIOD JUST PRIOR TO THE JUDGES</u> (Chapters 17-21)

    1.   THE DEPTHS OF IDOLATRY

        a.   Moses' grandson officiating before an idolatrous shrine.

2. **THE DEPTHS OF IMMORALITY**

   a. Men of Benjamite town sunk to the level of Sodom

3. **CIVIL WAR**

   a. Tribes make war against tribe of Benjamin for immoral crime.

SPIRITUAL MESSAGE

1. HUMAN FAILURE, DIVINE MERCY, AND DELIVERANCE.

2. **POWER OF SINCERE PRAYER TO GOD.**

   a. Alternate sentences repeated ten times in Judges:

   "The children of Israel did evil in the sight of the Lord."

   b. God heard and answered.

3. **DISCIPLINE THROUGH WHICH IDOLATROUS ISRAEL CAME AT LAST TO BE A NATION WHOSE GOD WAS JEHOVAH.**

BOOK OF RUTH

AUTHOR: Probably Samuel.

DATE: Approximately 101-970 BC.

SUBJECT: HOW A YOUNG MOABITISH WOMAN'S LIFE WAS ENRICHED.

1. By a beautiful constancy and wise choice. (1:16)

2. **By a humble industry. (2:2,3)**

3. **By accepting counsel from an older friend. (3:1-5)**

4. **By a providential alliance. (4:10, 11)**

5. **By exaltation to a Royal Line. (4:13-17)**

MAIN THEME: To show how a gentile woman became one of the ancestors of Jesus.

SYNOPSIS

1. THE SOJOURN IN MOAB (1:1-5)

   a. Elimelech and Naomi and their two sons, Mahlon and Chilion, driven by famine from Bethlehem into Moab.

   b. Elimelech, Naomi's husband, died there.

   c. Two sons married Moabitish women, Orpha and Ruth.

   d. Two sons died.

   e. Naomi lived in Moab about ten years.

2. **THE RETURN HOME (1:6-22)**

   a. The three childless widows started back.

   b. Orpha faltered, then turned back.

   c. Ruth replied in language that has become classic. (1:16, 17)

   d. Ruth accompanied her mother-in-law.

   e. Reached Bethlehem in the beginning of barley harvest.

3. **RUTH GLEANS IN THE FIELDS OF BOAZ (Chapter 2)**

    a.   Ruth was kinswoman to Boaz by marriage.

    b.   Boaz noticed her and befriended her.

    c.   Gave orders that she was not to be molested.

4. **HER MARRIAGE TO BOAZ (3:4:1-13)**

    a.   Instructed by Naomi, Ruth claims the kinswoman's right of marriage to perpetuate her husband's name and inheritance.

    b.   United in marriage.

5. **BIRTH OF HER SON, THE GRANDFATHER OF DAVID (4:13-16)**

    a.   Obed.

6. **GENEALOGY OF DAVID (4:18-22)**

I & II SAMUEL

AUTHOR: Not stated. Samuel himself was likely involved, through some of the history of Samuel occurs after the prophet's death._

DATE: Approximately 1100 – 1000 BC.

MAIN THEME: Israel's twelve tribes united under a king. From Theocracy to Monarchy.

SYNOPSIS

I. CLOSE OF THE PERIOD OF THE JUDGES (Chapters 1-7)

1. BIRTH AND CHILDHOOD OF SAMUEL (1:1-2:21)

   a. His birth, a child of promise.

   b. Dedicated to God by his mother, Hannah.

   c. Samuel grew in favor with God and man.

2. **DOOM OF ELI'S HOUSE (2:22-36)**

   a. Eli personally was pure.

   b. Gross sins of children unrestrained.

3. **CALL OF SAMUEL TO BE A PROPHET (Chapter 3)**

   a. Samuel ministered to God before Eli.

   b. God called Samuel.

   c. Pronounced doom on Eli's house.

4. **LOSS OF ARK AND DEATH OF ELI. (Chapter 4)**

   a. Philistine invasion victorious – Ark taken.

   b. Two sons of Eli slain by Philistines.

   c. Eli, heard news, fell from seat and broke his neck.

   d. Eli was ninety-eight years old - judged Israel for forty years.

5. **THE ARK RETURNED (5:1-7: 2)**

   a. Philistines place Ark before Dagon – Dagon destroyed.

   b. Three cities stricken by presence of Ark.

    c.   Fifty thousand seventy Beth-shemite men destroyed by looking into Ark.

    d.   Philistines returned Ark to Israel.

6.   PROMOTION OF SAMUEL TO BE JUDGE OF ISRAEL (7:3-17)

    a.   Samuel called Israel to repentance of Ark.

    b.   Israel defeated Philistines.

    c.   Samuel judged Israel annually Ark to Israel.

7.   SUMMARY OF SAMUEL AND HIS WORK.

    a.   Most important between Moses and David.

    b.   His career lifts us above low levels of the period.

    c.   Reared in the Tabernacle at Shiloh.

    d.   Brought about a great national reform.

    e.   Renewed the covenant – brought Israel back to God.

    f.   Won such a victory over Philistines at Ebenezer that they never renewed the attack in his judgeship.

    g.   He organized the schools of the prophets.

    h.   He judged Israel throughout his life.

    i.   He prepared the way for and introduced the monarchy.

    j.   Anointed both Saul and David.

    k.   He was the last and greatest of the Judges.

    l.   He was the first of the great line of Hebrew prophets after Moses.

II. PERIOD OF THE MONARCHY – REIGN OF SAUL B.C. 1095-1055. (Chapters 8-31)

    1.   ISRAEL A THEOCRATIC KINGDOM FROM SINAI

        a.   Organized a Theocracy, a kingdom of God.

        b.   God was to be their real king.

    c.   Moses and judges were High Priests, God's representatives to the people.

2. ISRAEL WANTED EARTHLY KING (Chapter 8)

    a.   Demanded king for two reasons:

        1.   Unfitness of Samuels' sons to judge.

        2.   Needed king to lead them in war.

    b.   Israel rejected God as king.

3. SAUL'S ELECTION AS KING (Chapters 9-11)

    a.   His private anointing.

        1.   Saul was son of Kish of tribe of Benjamin.

        2.   Searching for stock, he called on Samuel.

        3.   Samuel anointed him secretly.

    b.   His public election.

        1.   Samuel summoned Israel to Mispah.

        2.   Saul elected by the sacred lot.

        3.   His magnificent stature arouses enthusiasm.

        4.   Some sneered at Saul.

    c.   Defeat of the Ammonites.

        1.   Ammonites besieged Jabesh-Gilead.

        2.   People appealed to Saul.

        3.   Saul gathered an army of three hundred thousand men.

    d.   The coronation at Gilgal.

        1.   Victory silenced.

        2.   Tribes assembled at Gilgal, and Saul was triumphantly crowned, king of Israel.

4. SAUL'S REIGN TILL HIS REJECTION (Chapters 12-15)

    a.   The war of independence.

1. Israel not free from Philistines.

2. Philistines disarmed Israelites.

3. Saul and his son Jonathan led victorious Israelites in battle at Michmash.

4. Broke power of Philistines.

b. Saul's other wars.

1. Different nations pressing Israel.

2. Saul waged successful wars against Moab, Ammon, Edom and Zobah.

c. Saul's rejection.

1. Forgot he was only earthly representative of God.

2. Became disloyal to God, self-willed, disobedient.

3. Sent to destroy Amalek, he saved the king Agog as a trophy.

4. From then on, he was disowned of God and abandoned by Samuel.

5. Decline of Saul and rise of David.

5. DAVID ANOINTED – WINS FAVOR (Chapters 16-20)

a. Shepherd boy anointed at his home. (Chapter 16)

b. Slew giant Goliath and was promoted to high command. (17:1-18:5)

c. Saul insanely jealous, tried to kill David. (18:6-30)

d. Jonathan effected a reconciliation but Saul tried again to kill David. (Chapters 19-20)

6. DAVID'S FLIGHT AND LIFE AS AN OUTLAW (Chapters 21-27)

a. Fled by way of Nob and Gath' was arrested, escaped to cave of Adullam and collected an army of four hundred men. (21:1-22:2)

    b.   David took his parents to Moab for safety. (22:3-5)

    c.   Saul had eighty-five priests slain because they were kind to David. (22:6-23)

    d.   Saul pursued David but fell into his power. (Chapters 23-24)

    e.   David spared Nabal's family for Abigal's sake and married two wives. (Chapter 25)

    f.   Again, David could have killed Saul but did not. (Chapter 26)

    g.   David finally went to Philistia to live. (Chapter 27)

7. SAUL'S LAST DAYS (Chapters 28-31)

    a.   Achish asked David to fight against Israel. (28:1-2)

    b.   Philistine army advancing on Israel camped at Shunen. (28:4, 5)

    c.   Saul forsaken of God, consults a witch at Endor. (28:6-25)

        1.   Wanted to know outcome of battle.

        2.   Called for Samuel – the witch brought him.

        3.   Samuel prophesied calamity and death.

    d.   David disqualified for battle by Philistines. (Chapter 29)

    e.   Amalekites had burned Ziklag and carried off David's family.

    f.   David followed and defeated them and rescued his family. (Chapter 30)

    g.   At battle of Gilboa Israel was beaten, Saul's sons slain and Saul himself, like Brutus and Cassius at Philippi, died by his own sword. So, sets in gloom on Gilboa the sun, which rose in splendor on Saul's coronation at Gilgal.

8. CHARACTERISTICS OF SAUL'S REIGN

a. Saul was not:

    1. A builder of cities.

    2. A political organizer.

    3. A patron of literature.

    4. A promoter of true religion.

b. Saul was a military genius.

    1. Gave nation military standing.

    2. He was a man after the people's heart.

c. Saul degenerated in office.

    1. Grew too self-willed and disloyal to God, to fulfill God's will Saul was removed to make way for one who would be true to the national ideal, the man after God's own heart.

SPIRITUAL MESSAGE

1. FROM LIFE OF SAMUEL – PRAYER

    a. Born in answer to prayer. (1:10-28)

    b. Name means "Asked of God." (1:20)

    c. His prayer brings deliverance at Mizpah. (7:2-13)

    d. His prayer when Israel asked for king. (8:21)

    e. His constant prayer for his people. (12:23)

2. FROM LIFE OF SAUL – RESULT OF DISOBEDIENCE

    1. Blessing and victory follow obedience.

    2. Death and disaster follow disobedience.

FIVE DEVIATIONS FROM DIVINE LAW, which results in misery.

    1. Polygamy. (1:6)

    2. Parental indulgence. (2:22-25; 8:1-5)

    3. Trust in sacred objects. (Chapters 3-4)

    4. Impatience. (13:8, 9)

    5. Partial obedience. (Chapter 15)

II SAMUEL

MAIN SUBJECT: The Reign of David. B.C. 1055-1015.
DAVID'S PLACE IN HISTORY

1. Abraham, Moses, David – the three great names in Old Testament history.

   a. Abraham the Founder.

   b. Moses the Law Giver.

   c. David preeminently the king.

2. His reign marks the climax in national power and prosperity.

3. David was more than a *king*; he was the *poet* of his people.

4. Next to Moses, David's life and writings occupy the largest place in Hebrew history.

SYNOPSIS
I. DAVID KING OVER JUDAH (Chapters 1-4)

1. **EXECUTION OF THE AMALEKITE WHO SAID HE SLEW KING SAUL** (1:2-16)

   a. Died about slaying Saul to win David's favor.

   b. David had him slain.

2. **DAVID'S ELEGY ON SAUL AND JONATHAN** (1:17-27)

   a. One of the most tender in literature.

   b. Showed the character of David.

      1. Never rejoiced over his enemy's fall.

3. **DAVID KING OVER JUDAH FOR 7 YEARS** (2:1-7)

   a. God directed David to go to Hebron.

   b. Judah anointed David as their king.

   c. Hebron, an old ancestral city.

      1. There Abraham had lived.

2. There Isaac was born.

3. There in the cave of Machpelah were buried Abraham, Sarah and Rebekah, Jacob and Leah.

4. There David made his capital.

d. Reigned over the one tribe over seven years.

4. **CIVIL WAR** (2:8-32)

a. Other tribes adhered to Saul's son, Ishbosheth.

1. He was a weakling and figure-head.

2. Abner, his general was the master-spirit.

3. Mahanaim, east of Jordan, was their capital.

b. Seven years of civil war between kingdoms.

c. King Ishbosheth quarreled with Abner.

d. Abner made overtures to David to unite kingdoms.

e. Joab, David's general, assassinated Abner.

f. Abner's death caused collapse of rival kingdom.

g. David was crowned King of all Israel.

II. <u>DAVID, KING OF ALL ISRAEL FOR THIRTY-THREE YEARS</u> **(Chapters 5-24)**

1. **PERIOD OF INCREASING PROSPERITY AND POWER** (Chapters 5-10) (Period of marked fidelity to God.)

a. Union of all the tribes under David.

b. Jerusalem taken from Jebusites by David.

1. Transfer of the Ark to Jerusalem.

2. Jerusalem became both political and religious capital.

3. From that day, Jerusalem has been chief city of all Hebrews.

c. David's great military successes.

1. Great as was Saul in war, David was far greater.

2. Conquered the Philistines, Edomites, Moabites, Ammonites and Syrians.

d. Every nation from Egypt to the Euphrates owned his authority.

1. Phoenicia retained its independence.

2. David made alliance with its king, Hiram.

e. Promise to Abraham fulfilled in its largest geographical extent in David's empire.

2. **PERIOD OF DECLINE** (Chapters 11-24)

a. Great as David was, he was not above temptation.

b. Formed a guilty attachment for Bathsheba, wife of Uriah.

c. Had Uriah exposed to death in battle, and married Bathsheba.

d. Prophet Nathan denounced David.

e. Fifty-First Psalm is expression of David's repentance.

f. No repentance could avert consequences of his crime.

g. Divine judgments for his crime:

1. Death of his child by Bathsheba.

2. One son, Absalom, perished in a revolt, which almost cost David his throne and his life.

3. His favorite son, Absalom, perished in a revolt which almost cost David his throne and his life

4. Sheba, son of Bichri, led sedition.

5. Three years' famine for Gibeonites.

6. Four successful battles against Philistines.

       7.   Plague sent upon Israel for David's sin of numbering the people. David built an alter to God – plague stayed.

   h. David's last years. (I Kings Chapters 1-2)

       1.   His trusted general, Joab, concerned in conspiracy of the oldest son, Adonijah, to be king.

       2.   To secure succession of Solomon, David had him crowned.

       3.   David died.

CHARACTERISTICS OF DAVID'S REIGN

1. IT WAS A MILITARY REIGN

   a. Egypt and Assyria had declined.

   b. David's victorious campaigns made his empire supreme between Egypt and the Euphrates

2. IT WAS A REIGN OF INTERNAL IMPROVEMENT

   a. David was a born ruler of men. A natural organizer.

   b. He organized the political administration and industrial forces of the kingdom; introduced useful and ornamental arts; built storehouses and castles; enlarged and fortified Jerusalem; built there a royal palace and made the city of David the pride of the nation.

3. A LITERARY REIGN

   a. David's Psalms are the finest poems in the Bible.

   b. David was a poet and author of unsupervised merit.

4. A RELIGIOUS REIGN

   a. Despite his one dark crime, David was deeply religious.

   b. The *current* of his life was right.

     c.   Traits of David: Faith in God, loyalty to God, and gratitude to God.

     d.   He brought religious life of Israel to the highest level it ever attained.

     e.   He furnished the highest type of the Messiah.

CHOICE SELECTIONS

1. David's generosity to Mephibosheth. (Chapter 9)

2. Nathan's parable. (12:1-6)

3. David's Psalm of Thanksgiving. (Chapter 22)

I & II KINGS

AUTHOR: Ascribed to Jeremiah by Jewish Tradition.

TITLE: I and II Kings were originally one book.

DATE: 970 – 850 BC. 1 Kings was probably written sometime after the Babylonian destruction of Jerusalem in 586 BC.

MAIN THEME: The death of King David, his charge to his son King Solomon, and drifting of the Kingdom of Israel and Judah from God ending in a nation divided.

SYNOPSIS:

The Book may be divided into three divisions

PART ONE: CLOSING DAYS OF DAVID'S REIGN (Chapters 1-2:10)

I. FOUR MAJOR THINGS RECORDED

1. **ADONIJAH'S ATTEMPT TO USURP THE THRONE**

   a. Joab, David's general, concerned in the conspiracy to secure throne for Adjonijah, David's oldest son.

2. **SOLOMON CROWNED KING**

   a. Chosen because of his qualifications and because of David's affection for his mother, Bathsheba.

3. **DAVID'S CHARGE TO SOLOMON**

   a. To keep statutes of God.

   b. Concerning Joab and Shimei.

4. **DAVID'S DEATH.**

   a. This closed record of one of the greatest men of history.

   b. His Psalms more widely read than any other part of Scripture.

PART TWO: REIGN OF SOLOMON (Chapters 2-11)

I. EARLY YEARS. THE GOLDEN AGE OF ISRAEL. MADE FAMOUS BY:

1. **THE KING'S WISE CHOICE** (3:5-14)

   a. Offered a thousand offerings at Gibeon.

    b.   There he chose wisdom.

2. HIS DISCRIMINATING JUDGMENT (3:16-28)

    a.   Discovered mother of baby.

3. HIS SURPASSING WISDOM (4:29-34)

    a.   Wiser than all men.

4. GROWTH OF HIS SOMINIONS (4:21)

    a.   Reigned over all kingdoms from Euphrates to Philistia and Egypt.

5. SPLENDOR OF HIS COURT AND PALACES
(Chapters 4:22-28; 7:1-12)

    a.   Required thirteen years to build his house.

    b.   Built a palace for Pharaoh's daughter, his true queen.

6. THE BUILDING OF THE TEMPLE (Chapters 5-6)

    a.   Hiram, King of Tyre, furnished cedars from Lebanon.

    b.   Number of workmen:

1.   Thirty thousand helped servants of Hiram.

  2.   Seventy thousand burden bearers.

  3.   Eighty thousand stone masons.

  4.   Three thousand three hundred foremen.

    c.   Seven years required to build the temple.

    d.   Main building only thirty by ninety feet.

    e.   Small but its richness was unrivaled.

    f.   Line with gold at a cost of six hundred million dollars.

    g.   No image of God in it – stood for sublime spirituality.

    h.   Temple stood over four hundred years, until destroyed by Nebuchadnezzar.

7. **OTHER BUILDING ENTERPRISES AND GREAT WEALTH.** (9:17-23; 10: 14-29)

    a. Numerous fortresses and cities in his empire.

    b. Ivory throne covered with gold-vessels of gold.

    c. "So, King Solomon exceeded all the kings of the earth for riches and for wisdom."

8. **SOLOMON'S COMMERCE**

    a. Through Tyrian alliance carried on trade along the Mediterranean as far as Tarhish in Spain.

    b. Through ports on Red Sea had extensive trade with India.

    c. Exchanged products with Phoenicians, Egyptians and Arabians.

9. **VISIT OF THE QUEEN OF SHEBA** (10:1-13)

    a. Of Solomon's wisdom and wealth, Sheba said, "The half was not told me."

II. LATER YEARS OF HIS REIGN. DECLINE OF KINGDOM BROUGHT ABOUT BY:

1. **VIOLATION OF THE LAW OF THE KING**

    a. Moses laid down the law of the king in Deut. (17:4-20)

    b. In three ways Solomon violated it:

    1. By multiplying horses. (I Kings 10:26) Symbol of militarism.

    2. My multiplying wives until his harem contained thousand women.

    3. By multiplying gold and silver, which could only be done by impoverishing his people.

2. **VIOLATION OF THE LAW OF GOD**

    a. "Thou shalt have no other gods before me."

    b.   Mission of Israel was to displace polytheism with a pure spiritual worship.

    c.   Israel had no other reason for existence.

    d.   "When Solomon was old his wives turned away his heart after other gods."

3. HIS EXTRAVAGANT LUXURY (10:14-29)

    a.   Used wealth for selfish indulgences

4. HIS NOTORIOUS SENSUALITY (11:1-3)

    a.   Loved many women forbidden to Israelites.

5. ENEMIES, WHICH GOD STIRRED UP AGAINST SOLOMON (11:14-40)

    a.   Hadad, the Edomite.

    b.   Rezon, of Zobah.

    c.   Jeroboam, son of Nebab.

        1.   Ahijah prophesied Jeroboam would be king over ten tribes.

        2.   Solomon tried to kill Jeroboam but he fled to Egypt.

6. SOLOMON'S DEATH (11:42-43)

Reigned over all Israel forty years.
Died and was buried at Jerusalem.

III. RISE OF PROPHETS.

1. BEGINNING WITH MOSES

    a.   In his age, Moses stood out in solitary grandeur.

    b.   No prophet mentioned between Joshua and Samuel.

    c.   With Samuel and the monarchy, era of great prophets began.

2. IMPORTANCE OF THE PROPHET

    a.   The necessary counterpart of the King.

b. Samuel more important than Saul.

c. David, the Prophet-King was advised and warned by prophets.

d. Throughout the Old Testament Prophets played an important part.

3. PROPHETS OF THE PERIOD

a. Nathan. (II Sam. 7:2-17; 12:1-12; I Kings 1:8-24)

b. Iddo. (II Chron. 9:29; 12:15; 13:22)

c. Ahijah. (I Kings 11:29-39; II Chron. 9:29)

PART THREE: HISTORY OF THE KINGDOMS OF ISRAEL AND JUDAH

(Chapters 12-22)

I. DIVISION OF SOLOMON'S KINGDOM

1. ACCESSION AND POLICY OF REHOBOAM

a. "Solomon had a thousand wives and only one son, and he was a fool."

b. People petitioned Rehoboam to lighten their taxes.

c. Rehoboam rejected advice of his older counsellors and followed that of young men.

1. Told people he would increase their burden.

2. JEROBOAM AND THE REVOLT

a. At Solomon's death Jeroboam returned from Egypt.

b. People petitioned Rehoboam to lighten their taxes.

c. Rehoboam rejected advice of his older counsellors and followed that of young men.

1. Told people he would increase their burden.

3. THE TWO KINGDOMS COMPARED

a. The Northern Kingdom more national than the southern.

1. Included ten of the twelve tribes.

2. It retained the name, Israel.

3. Territory far larger and vastly richer.

4. Retained majority of foreign alliances.

b. Religion of the Norther Kingdom

1. All the kings of Israel were idolatrous.

2. People grew more and more so themselves.

3. Nearly all great early prophets, by birth or mission, belong to Israel: Abijah, Shemaiah, Elijah, Elisha, Micaiah, Jonah, Hosea, Amos, Zechariah and Jehu.

4. Though often idolatrous, Judah was far more loyal to God.

c. Reasons for Judah's greater stability.

1. Never had but one capital, Jerusalem, city of David and Solomon and of the Temple.

2. Israel had several capitals in succession: Schechem, Tirza, Samaria.

3. Israel continued only two hundred fifty years, yet in that time dynasties with nineteen kings sat on the throne. Every new dynasty began and ended in bloody revolution.

4. Judah endured for nearly four hundred years with only twenty kings, and all except the usurper, Athaliah, belonged to the line of David.

II. <u>HISTORY OF THE NORHTERN KINGDOM</u> (Chapters 12:20-22:53)

1. IDOLATRY TAKING ROOT: FIFTY YEARS. THREE DYNATIES: FIVE REIGNS

a. Leading character was Jeroboam, founder of the kingdom.

1. Selected Dan in the north and Bethel in the south as places of worship.

    2.   Instituted idolatrous calf worship.

    3.   Policy half worldly, half religious, blasted Israel forever.

    4.   "Jeroboam the son of Nebat who did sin and who made Israel to sin."

b. Remaining kings of the period

    1.   Nabad, Boasha, Elah, and Zimri.

    2.   Israel and Judah hostile. Broke out at times into open war.

2. IDOLATRY TRIUMPHANT: FIFTY YEARS. ONE DYNASTY: FOUR REIGNS

a. Omri, army officer, founder of dynasty.

    1.   Defeated usurper Zimri who burned palace at Tirzah over his own head.

    2.   Omri abandoned Tirzah, bought and built Samaria, which continued to be the capital till the fall of the kingdom, and gave its name to a district and a people.

b. Ahab and Jezebel – the Baal worship

    1.   Ahab, Omri's son, married Jezebel, daughter of Ethball, the priest-king of Sidon.

    2.   Jezebel introduced the licentious Baal worship.

    3.   Fiercely persecuted worship of God.

    4.   Ahab dominated by Jezebel.

3. ERA OF THE PROPHET ELIJAH

    a.   The one sublime character of the period.

    b.   Boldly confronted Ahab with his sins, prophesied a three-year famine for national apstacy; was fed by ravens at brook Cherith and later by widow of

    c.   Zarephath in Jezebel's own land.

d. Finally faced Ahab again and summoned a national assembly on Mt. Carmel, and there prophesied to the hundreds of priest-prophets of Baal and Ashtarte a test - The God who answered by fire should be the nation's God.

e. Elijah's God triumphed and four hundred fifty false prophets were slain.

f. Elijah ran in triumph before Ahab's chariot to Jezebel.

g. Jezebel sent threatening message to Elijah, who fled to Horeb.

h. There God met him and told him there were seven thousand loyal souls.

i. God commissioned Elijah to return and anoint Hazael king of Syria, Jehu king of Israel, and Elisha to be prophet.

j. Elijah pronounced doom upon Ahab and Jezebel for murdering Naboth for his vineyard.

4. AHAB SLAIN – AHAZIAH, HIS SON, WAS KING

a. Ahaziah followed example of his parents.

b. Worshipped Baal - caused Israel to sin.

III. HISTORY OF THE SOUTHERN KINGDOM (Chapters 12;1-22:50)

1. DECLINE UNDER REHOBOAM AND ABIJAM

a. Religion

1. Paganism began under Solomon increased for next twenty years.

2. Despite protests of prophets, worship of God fell off.

3. Heathen altars sprang up all over the land.

4. Gross immoralities spread among the people.

b. **Relations to Israel.**

    1. At the revolt of ten tribes Rehoboam raised an army to quell the revolt.

    2. Prophet Shemaiah advised Rehoboam against it and war was avoided.

    3. During Abijam's reign of three years, he defeated Israel in battle of Zemaraim.

c. **Invasion of Shishak**

    1. Shishak, a king of Egypt, invaded Palestine, captured Jerusalem, and stripped the temple of its golden splendors.

2. **REVIVAL UNDER ASA AND JEHOSHAPHAT. PERFORMS:**

a. **Asa's reign of forty-one years was a marked contrast with the two proceeding ones both in purity and vigor.**

    1. For several years he enjoyed profound peace.

    2. Removed heathen altars and images.

    3. Reorganized worship of God.

b. **Jehoshaphat reigned righteously for twenty-five years.**

    1. Carried further his father's reforms.

    2. Provided for religious instructions.

    3. Reorganized and improved the judicial system.

c. **Invasion of Zerah the Etheopian**

    1. Asa's peace was broken by an invasion of one million Etheopians under Zerah.

    2. Asa went into battle with an earnest prayer to God and won such a decisive victory that

Judah never suffered another invasion from that quarter for three hundred years.

HERORIC CHARACTER: THE PROPHET ELIJAH.

<u>CHOICE SELECTIONS:</u>

1. Solomon's wise choice. (3:5-14)

2. Solomon's prayer at the dedication of the temple. (8:22-53)

3. The ministry of Elijah. (Chapters 17, 18, 19, 21)

4. The call of Elisha. (9:19-21)

<u>SYNOPSIS:</u>
<u>PART 1 - HISTORY OF NORTHERN KINGDOM CONTINUED FROM I KINGS.</u>

I. IDOLATRY CHECKED: ONE HUNDRED YEARS. ONE DYNASTY. FIVE REIGNS.

1. PERIOD OF ISRAEL'S GREATES PROSPERITY

a. Last flicker of the flame – "Indian Sumer."

2. ELISHA'S REFORMS

a. More successful than reforms of Elijah.

3. WORK OF JEHU, FOUNDER OF THE DYNASTY

a. Exterminated the house of Ahab.

b. Destroyed Baal worship.

c. Resumed calf worship of Jeroboam.

4. SUCCESSORS TO JEHU

a. Jehoahaz, Jehoash, Jeroboam II and Zachariah.

b. Jeroboam II reigned forty-one years.

1. Raised the kingdom to its greatest power.

2. He was aided by Prophet Jonah.

3. Prophet Hosea denounced idolatry.

II. IDOLATRY ENDING IN RUIN: FIFTY YEARS. FOUR DYNASTIES. FIVE REIGNS.

1. KINGS WHO WERE MERE PUPPETS OF ASSYRIA

a. Shallum, Menahem, Pekahia, Pekah and Hosea.

b. Assyrians begin deporting in reign of Menahem.

c. Pekah, a king of some vigor, forms an alliance with Syria against Assyria and Judah, which had become tributary to Assyria.

d. Tiglath - pileser II, of Assyria, puts an end to Syria and puts Israel to heavy tribute.

e. The end comes when Hosea revolts against Assyria.

1. Shalmanezer IV invades the land and besieges Samaria.

2. The city holds out for three years, during which time Sargon succeeds Shalamanezer IV to Assyrian throne.

3. Sargon completes the siege and captures Samaria, and carries away the Ten Tribes into captivity, from which they never return.

4. Untrue to God and their national mission, they lose their national identity forever.

5. Imported Assyrians mingled with the remnants of the Ten tribes.

6. This mixed race, with a mongrel religion, continued for centuries and constituted the Samaritans of the time of Christ.

PART II - HISTORY OF SOUTHERN KINGDOM CONTINUED FROM I KINGS

I. SECOND DECLINE AND REVIVAL: NINE REIGNS. TWO HUNDRED YEARS.

1. THE DECLINE.

a. <u>Jehoram and Athaliah.</u>

    1. Jehoram, Jehoshaphat's son, succeeded to the throne.

    2. Jehoram had married Athaliah, daughter of Ahab.

    3. Athaliah carried Judah into the gross Baal worship of her mother, Jezebel.

    4. After eight years, Jehoram was succeeded by his son, Ahaziah.

    5. In a year Ahaziah perished in the doom, which Jehu of Israel visited upon the house of Ahab.

    6. Athaliah escaped, seized the throne, murdered all the royal family but the infant Jehoash, and for six years was the Jezebel of Judah.

    7. Line of David was reduced to a single babe, while a heathen queen sat on the throne.

b. Joash and the reaction.

    1. Athaliah was slain in an uprising under the aged High Priest, Jehoiada,

    2. who placed young Joash on the throne. After Jehoiada's death, Prophet Zachariah was martyred under Joash.

c. Uzziah

    1. Of the three reigns which followed, Amaziah, Uzziah and Jotham, that of Uzziah was best.

    2. Vigorous and prosperous reign for fifty-two years.

    3. His successes were his ruin. Presuming to offer incense, which was a priestly, not a royal,

duty, he was smitten with leprosy from which he died.

    d.   Ahaz and Apostasy.

          1.   Idolatry under Ahaz became general apostasy.

          2.   He had images and altars of Baal everywhere.

          3.   Sacrificed his children to the god Moloch.

          4.   Moral decay was followed by political decline.

          5.   Ahaz was harassed by Edomites.

2. THE REVIVAL UNDER HEZEKIAH

    a.   Isaiah and the reform.

          1.   Most prominent character in Hezekiah's reign.

          2.   First prophet of Judah to overshadow both priest and king.

          3.   Destroyed Baal worship and horrible Moloch rites.

          4.   Destroyed brazen serpent made by Moses, which had become an object of idolatrous worship.

          5.   Restored the worship of Jehovah and the Passover festival at Jerusalem.

    b.   Invasion of Sennacherib, the Assyrian.

          1.   Hezekiah, against Isaiah's advice, exchanged the Asssyrian for an Egyptian alliance.

          2.   Sennacherib invaded Judea, captured many cities, carried off two hundred thousand captives and besieged Jerusalem.

II. <u>THIRD DECLINE AND REVIVAL. THREE REIGNS. NINETY YEARS</u>.

1. JUDAH PLUNGED DOWNWARD UNDER MANASSEH. HEZEKIAH'S SON.

a. All known idolatries seem to have been adopted; Baal worship, Moloch worship, Chaldean star worship, witchcraft, fierce persecution, which filled Jerusalem with blood—such were the crimes of Manasseh's reign of fifty-five years.

b. Isaiah was martyred.

c. Manasseh's son, Amon, succeeded him, imitated his father's worst practices and perished in a revolt.

2. **THE REVIVAL UNDER JOSIAH. (Jeremiah and the Reforms.)**

a. Death of Amon brought Josiah, a child of eight year, to the throne.

b. He reigned thirty-one years. Last rally of a dying empire.

c. Jeremiah was to Josiah what Isaiah had been to Hezekiah.

d. The reforms:

1. At sixteen years of age Josiah took affairs into his own hands.

2. He turned personally to God.

3. At twenty, he began to purge Jerusalem of idolatry.

4. At twenty-six, he undertook to repair the temple.

5. Found a copy of the Law in the temple, which during the long, Dark reign of Manasseh, had been lost.

6. Inspired by its teaching, he kept the most famous Passover since the days of Samuel.

7. Abolished calf worshiping at Bethel and other cities of Samaria.

e. The battle of Megiddo.

    1.   Josiah's prosperous reign had a disastrous ending.

    2.   Assyrian and Egyptian empires were at war.

    3.   Josiah unwisely interfered and at the battle of Meggido lost his life.

    4.   Death of Josiah proved the doom of Judah.

    5.   He was the last king who "walked in the ways of David."

III. FINAL DECLINE AND CAPTIVITY

1. MORAL DECAY

    a.   Josiah's reforms not rooted in the hearts of people.

    b.   Enforced by royal authority and fell as soon as that authority was withdrawn.

    c.   Jeremiah, Daniel and his friends remained true.

    d.   Mass of the nation were hopelessly corrupt.

    e.   Jeremiah's writings show a deepening darkness.

    f.   Idolatry, drunkenness, greed, lust and violence are characteristic

vices.

    g.   Moral decay was forerunner to political dissolution.

2. A SUCCESSION OF CAPTIVITIES.

    a.   Four kings followed Josiah.

        1.   Johoahaz, Jehoiakim, Jehoiachin and Zedekiah.

        2.   The third was a grandson, the others were sons of Josiah.

        3.   All were puppets either of Egypt or Babylon.

    b.   First Captivity

        1.   Nebuchadnezzar captured Jerusalem, B.C. 606.

    2.   Spared King Jehoiakim, but carried certai people into captivity, among whom were Daniel, Shadrach, Meshach andAbed-nego, all princes of royal blood.

    3.   Jehoiakim came to a violent death after a reign of eleven years.

c. Second Captivity

    1.   Nebuchadnezzar made his second invasion in B.C. 597.

    2.   Carried away King Jehoiachin, who was kept a captive for thirty-five years.

    3.   Prophet Ezekiel, with ten thousand of the upper classes, went into captivity at the same time.

    4.   Zedekiah was placed on the throne, and for eleven years reigned as the poppet of the monarch of the Euphrates.

d. Third Captivity

    1.   Jeremiah announced the judgment of God upon the nation to be seventy years captivity in Babylon, and counselled submission to that power.

    2.   For this he was imprisoned in a dungeon.

    3.   Rebellion brought Nebuchadnezzar's armies once more against Jerusalem.

    4.   He captured Jerusalem in B.C. 586, slew Zedekiah's sons before his face, put out his eyes, and carried him in chains to Babylon.

    5.   Walls of the city were broken down, the temple and palaces burned, and the upper classes carried away into captivity.

6. Jerusalem, the City of David, was no more, save in the hearts of a few faithful ones who, through seventy years of exile, longed for the Holy City, and looked forward to the promised return.

THE TWO GREAT PROPHETS OF II KINGS
ELIJAH AND ELISHA
I & II CHRONICLES

AUTHOR: Probably Ezra. First and Second Chronicles are one book in the Jewish bible.

DATE: Probably written during, or shortly after, the captivity. 1010 BC to about 970BC.

A SUPPLEMENT: I Chronicles supplements the books of I and II Samuel, and I and II Kings. Some of the historical descriptions are almost identical with those of the preceding books.

DISTINCTIVE FEATURES: The books of Samuel and Kings refer to events in both Kingdoms, whereas Chronicles deals almost exclusively with the history of Judah.

MAIN THEME: The Sovereignty of God, the Temple and Public Worship. (4:4-10; 5:20; 11:14; 12:18; 14:2, 10, 14, 15; Chapter 22)

CENTRAL CHARACTER: David.

SYNOPSIS:

PART ONE: GENEALOGIES OF THE TRIBES OF ISRAEL (Chapters 1-9)

1. Adam's line to Noah; Sons of Japheth, Ham and Shem; Shem's line to Abraham; sons Of Ishmael and Keturah; the Kings of Edom. (Chapter 1)

2. Sons of Israel; posterity of Jodah; children of Jesse; posterity of Caleb, of Hezron, of Jeraheel, and Sheshan. (Chapter 2)

3. Sons of David; David's line to Zedekiah; successors of Jeconiah. (Chapter 3)

4. Posterity of Judah by Caleb, the son of Hur; of Ashur, the son Hezron; of Jabez. (Chapter 4)

5. The line of Reuben, and their country. (Chapter 5)

6. Sons of Levi, the line of the priests; office of Aaron and his sons. (Chapter 6)

7. Sons of Issachar; of Benjamin; of Naphtali; of Manasseh; of Ephriam and of Asher. (Chapter 7)

8. Sons and chief persons of Benjamin; stock of Saul and Jonathan. (Chapter 8)

9. Original registers of Israel and Judah's genealogies; the charge of certain Levites; line of Saul and Jonathan. (Chapter 9)

PART TWO: THE REIGN OF DAVID (Chapters 10-29)

1. His accession to the throne, the capture of Jerusalem, and his mighty men and armies. (Chapters 11-12)

2. His mistake in attempting to transport the Ark on a "new cart." (Chapter 13)

3. His victory over the Philistines. (Chapter 14)

4. The Ark brought to Jerusalem. (Chapter 15)

5. The great festival of rejoicing. (Chapter 16)

6. The King's desire to build a temple for Jehovah denied. (Chapter 22)

7. Great military victories. (Chapters 18-20)

8. The sinful census. (Chapter 21)

9. The Preparation of materials for the building of the temple, and a charge to Solomon. (Chapter 22)

10. The further organization of the affairs of the temple. (Chapters 23-27)

11. David's last charge to the people and to his son, Solomon; Solomon made King; the death of David. (Chapters 28-29

CHOICE SELECTION:

1. Prayer of Jabes. (4:10)

2. David's Psalm. (16:7-36)

3. Description of David's Chorus Choir and Orchestra.

4. David's last blessing and prayer. (29:10-19)

II CHRONICLES

<u>AUTHOR</u>: Probably Ezra

<u>A SUPPLEMENT</u>: II Chronicles is a sequel to I Chronicles, and also is a supplement to the book of Kings.

The history of Judah as related here is on the whole a dark picture of instability and apostasy, interspersed with periods of religious reformation.

<u>DISTICTIVE FEATURES</u>:

1. **The spiritual element in the history is more emphasized in Chronicles than in Kings.**

2. **References found only in II Chronicles**:

   a. Abijah's devout address. (13:5-12)

   b. Asa's neglect of God. (16:12)

   c. Jehoshaphat's foolish alliances. (20:35)

   d. Cause of Uzziah's leprosy. (26:16-21)

   e. Manasseh's captivity and restoration. (33:11-13)

<u>FIVE PERIODS OF REFORMATION DESCRIBED</u>:

1. Under King Asa. (Chapter 15)

2. Under King Jehoshaphat. (17:6-10)

3. Under the priest Jehoiada and King Joash. (23:16-19)

4. Under King Hezekiah. (Chapters 29-31)

5. Under King Josiah. (Chapters 34-35)

<u>SYNOPSIS</u>:

PART ONE: THE REIGN OF SOLOMON

1. Solomon's sacrifices at Gibeon and his wise choice. (Chapter 1)

2. The building of the temple. (Chapters 2-4)

3. The glory of the Lord fills the house. (Chapter 5)

4. Solomon's prayer at the dedication of the temple. (Chapter 6)

5. Jehovah appears to Solomon again at night. (Chapter 7)

6. The prosperity and fame of Solomon. (Chapter 8)

7. The visit of the Queen of Sheba and the death of Solomon. (Chapter 9)

P ART TWO: THE FOLLY OF REHOBOAM

1. Division of the Kingdom. (Chapter 10)

PART THREE; HISTORY OF THE REIGNS FROM REHOBOAM TO ZEDEKIAH

1. Abijah (Chapter 13)

2. Asa. (Chapters 14-16)

3. Jehoshaphat (Chapters 17-20)

4. Jehoram (Chapter 21)

5. Ahaziah (22:1-9)

6. Athaliah (Queen) (22:10-23:15)

7. Joash (Chapter 24)

8. Amaziah (Chapter 25)

9. Uzziah (Chapter 26)

10. Jotham (Chapter 27)

11. Ahaz (Chapter 28)

12. Hezekiah. Chapters 29-32

13. Manasseh (33:1-20)

14. Amon (33: 21-25)

15. Josiah (Chapters 34, 35)

16. Jehoahaz (36:1-3)

17. Jehoiakim (36:4-8)

18. Jehoiachin (36:9-10)

19. Zedekiah (36:11-13)

SPIRITUAL MESSAGE: The power of prayer to give success and victory. (11:16; 13:13-18; 14:11; 15:12; 17:4; 20:3; 26:5; 27:6; 30:18-20; 31:21; 32:20; 34:3.)

SPIRITUAL LESSONS:

1. The preeminence of wisdom. (1:7-12)

2. The glory of the Lord fills the prepared temple. (5:13-14)

3. The Spirit of Praise renders God's people invincible.
    (20:20-25)

EZRA

INTRODUCTORY – REVIEW AND SUMMARY

We have traced the history of man, of sin, and of the earlier stages of redemption. We have followed the fortunes of the Chosen People for fifteen hundred years, from Creation, through the call of Abraham and through successive periods: Patriarchal, Bondage, Wanderings, Conquest, Judges, United Kingdom, Double Kingdom, and Judah alone. We have seen, in the day of David and Solomon, a glorious outburst of national life, succeeded by division and decline.

The Northern Kingdom has gone down in political and spiritual night. Judah, after one hundred and forty years more of fitful life, broken up, Jerusalem in ruins, and king a people borne to Babylon, seven hundred miles distant, into helpless captivity. Everywhere brutality, gross superstition and idolatry are triumphant. To all human appearances, the experiment of human redemption is a failure; the knowledge of God is forever lost. But it is no experiment. Out of the darkest night there arose the highest star of hope. It was after the fall of the Northern Kingdom, and during the decline and exile of Judah, that such prophets as Micah, Isaiah, Jeremiah, and Daniel and Zechariah wrote their sublime prophecies of the coming Christ and his worldwide spiritual reign. Hebrew Theocracy is only the thorny stalk of which a purely spiritual kingdom is to be the consummate flower and fruit. Till the flower blooms, the thorny stalk must stand. Therefore, though exiled and scattered, there must be, for Judah, a return and renewal of national life. The captivity, which dated B.C. 586- 536, had been repeatedly foretold by such prophets as Isaiah, Micah, Huldah, and Jeremiah (2 Kings 20:17; 21:10-15; 22:14-17; Jer. 25:9011; 34:2-3; Micah 3:8-12).

These prophecies were unconsciously fulfilled by Nebuchadnezzar in his successive captures of Jerusalem and deportation of the Jewish people. The seventy years have been spent in exile in Babylon, which has fallen under Persia and the Jews are now permitted to return to their own land. This was in B.C. 536. Judah is now under Persia, the second world empire. The Sacred Narrative of the return of the Jews and the work of rehabilitation is recorded in the Book Ezra.

AUTHOR: EZRA, who was both scribe and priest, being a lineal descendent from Phinehas, the son of Aaron, and a Jewish exile in Babylon. (7:1-6)

DATE: Approximately 530 BC to the mid 400s BC.

MAIN THEME: The return of the Jews from their captivity in Babylon, the rebuilding of the temple, and the inauguration of social and religious reforms. The power of the word of God in human life. Referred to as the "Word of the Lord" (1:1; 9:4, "Law of Moses" 3:2; 6:18; 7:6; "Commandments" 6:14; 10:3-5; "Law of the Lord" 7:10-14.)

SYNOPSIS:

PART ONE: THE RETURN EXPEDITION UNDER ZERUBBABEL (Chapters 1-6)

1. **EDICT OF KING CYRUS TO RETURN TO JERUSALEM AND REBUILD THE TEMPLE** (1:1-4)

    a. This was predicted by Isaiah one hundred seventy-five years before, in which Cyrus is named. (Isaiah 44:28).

    b. Babylon, the first universal empire, destroyed the temple and carried Judah into exile; Persia the second world empire, sent them back home to rebuild their temple and become re-established in their land.

    c. Cyrus restored the sacred vessels which Nebuchadnezzar had looted from the temple. (1:7-11)

2. THE NUMBER OF PEOPLE THAT RETURNED UNDER THE LEADERSHIP OF ZERUBBABEL. (Chapter 2)

    a. Forty-two thousand three hundred sixty Jews returned

    b. Seven thousand three hundred thirty-seven servants.

    c. Returning remnant composed of people, priests, Levites, descendants Solomon's servants, and their substance and gifts.

3. THEIR BUILDING ENERPRISES

   a. The alter rebuilt and worship established. (3:1-6)

   b. The foundation of the temple laid. (3:8-13)

   c. Samaritans offered to help work. (4:1-2)

   d. Their offer rejected, wrote to Artaxerxes who stopped their work. (4:7-24)

   e. Building resumed by an edict of King Darius. (Chapter 5)

      1. Haggai and Zechariah prophesy.

   d. The temple completed and dedicated. (Chapter 6)

      1. Decree of Darius to advance work.

      2. The temple finished.

      3. Feasts of dedication and of the Passover B.C. 515.

PART TWO: THE SECOND RETURN EXPEDITION UNDER EZRA.
(Chapters 7-10)

(This was eighty years after the first expedition and in the 7th-year of Artaxeres. B.C. 457).

   1. EZRA'S REQUEST AND THE KING'S COMMISSION (Chapter 7)

   2. LIST OF EZRA'S COMPANY AND RETURN TO JERUSALEM (Chapter 8)

   a. One thousand six hundred fifty-four males.

   b. Fast proclaimed, entreating protection on journey.

   c. Safe arrival in Jerusalem.

   3. EZRA'S REFORMS (Chapters 9-10)

   a. Jews had intermarried with heathen.

   b. Separation of such alliances.

   c. Better establishment of Masaic institutions.

LITERARY AND RELIGIOUS WORK OF EZRA:

1. Probably the author of First and Second Chronicles.

2. Associated with Nehemiah in starting a revival of the study of the Scriptures. (Neh. Chapter 8.)

3. Reputed to be the organizer of the Jewish synagogue.

4. Reputed to have assembled most of the books of the Old Testament.

CHOICE SELECTIONS:

1. Ezra's sublime trust in divine protection when called upon to carry great treasures through dangerous places. (8:21-32)

2. Ezra's prayer and confession for the people. (9:5-15)

NEHEMIAH

<u>AUTHOR AND COMPILER</u>:Nehemiah, who was neither prophet nor priest, but a layman.

<u>DATE:</u> Approximately 445 BC.

<u>MAIN THEME:</u> Rebuilding the walls of Jerusalem, implementing certain Divine Laws and restoration of Ancient Ordinances.

<u>SYNOPSIS:</u>

<u>PART ONE: NEHEMIAH'S COMMISSION</u> (Chapters 1-2:10)

    1.   HIS FEELINGS REGARDING THE STATE OF THINGS IN JERUSALEM

        a.   Hanani brought Nehemiah the news. (1:1-3)

        b.   Mourns, fasts, and prayers. (1:4-11)

    2.   NEHEMIAH'S REQUEST AND THE KING'S COMMISSION

        a.   Requested permission to rebuild the walls. (2:1-5)

        b.   Artaxerxes Longimanus commissioned him to do the work. (2:6-10)

            1.   King sent letters, captains and horseman with Nehemiah.

<u>PART TWO: FIRST VISIT TO JERUSALEM</u> (2:11 – Chapter 7)
<u>(Twentieth year of the reign of Artaxerxes, B.C. 445, and twelve years after Ezra had led his expedition to Jerusalem)</u>.

    1.   INSPECTION OF THE CITY AND PEOPLE'S RESPONSE

        a.   Nehemiah inspected Jerusalem at night. (2:11-16)

        b.   Determination of people to rebuild the wall. (2:18-19)

        c.   Scorn and ridicule of Sanballat and Tobiah. (2:19-20)

    2.   BUILDING OF THE WALL AND OPPOSITION OF SANBALLAT AND TOBIAH.

    a.   Names and order of those who built the wall. (Chapter 3)

    b.   Enemies scoffed. Nehemiah prayed and set guards for protection. (Chapter 4)

3.   USURY PROHIBTED – NEHEMIAH APPOINTED GOVERNOR.

    a.   People complained of debts, mortgages and bondage. (5:1-5)

    b.   The usurers rebuked. (5:6-10)

    c.   Debts abolished and possessions restored. (5:11-13)

    d.   Nehemiah appointed governor; served twelve years. (5:14-19)

4.   WALL COMPLETED INSPITE OF ENEMIES. Ch. 6

    a.   Sanballat repeatedly tried to hinder the work.

    b.   The wall finished.

5.   THE REGISTER OF THOSE WHO CAME FROM BABYLON. (Chapter 7)

    a.   Repetition of genealogies, in Ezra. (Chapter 2)

PART THREE: NEHEMIAH'S SECOND VISIT TO JERUSALEM (Chapter 8-13)
(Thirteen years after his first visit or B.C. 432).

   1.   **INSTRUCTION IN THE LAW**. (Chapter 8)

    a.   Manner of reading and hearing the Law. (8:1-8)

    b.   Nehemiah comforted the people. (8:9-15)

    c.   People kept the feast of tabernacles. (8:16-19)

   2.   THE ATTITUDE OF THE PEOPLE. (Chapters 9-10)

    a.   Confession of God's goodness and their wickedness.

    b.   Prayer.

    c.   People covenanted to obey God's commandments.

3.   SELECTION OF DWELLING PLACES. (Chapter 11)

    a.   Ruler, voluntary man, and every tenth man chosen by lot, lived at Jerusalem.

    b.   The others lived in other cities of Judah.

4.   DEDICATION OF THE TEMPLE. (Chapter 12)

    a.   Priests appointed to different places in city.

    b.   Great rejoicing at the dedication.

5.   NEHEMIAH'S SOCIAL AND RELIGIOUS REFORMS. (Chapter 13)

    a.   Mixed multitude separated from Jews.

    b.   Tithe restored to Levites.

    c.   Desecration of the Sabbath abolished.

A STUDY IN TYPES:

I. REBUILDING THE WALLS OF JERUSALEM AS A TYPE OF THE UPBUILDING OF THE KINGDOM OF GOD.

1.   The walls broken down (1:3) typify the defenses of God's kingdom weakened.

2.   The preliminary season of fasting and prayer (1:4-11) typifies the state of mind, which should precede all great spiritual enterprises.

3.   Nehemiah's sacrifices of a fine position for the good of the cause (2:5) typifies the sacrificial service always needed when a great work is to be accomplished.

4.   The night inspection of the city (2:15-16) typifies the necessity of facing the facts before beginning constructive work.

5.   The seeking of cooperation (2:17-18) typifies an essential element in all successful work.

6.   The enlistment of all classes (Chapter 3) typifies the importance of thorough organization.

II. THE SAME METHODS MAY BE USED IN OVERCOMING HINDRANCES TO SPIRITUAL WORK.

1. *Ridicule* (2:19) overcome by *confidence* in God. (2:20)

2. *Wrath and contempt* (4:3) overcome by *prayer and hard work.* (4:4-6)

3. *Conspiracy* (4:7-8) overcome by *watchfulness and prayer.* (4:9)

4. *Discouragement* of friends (4:10-12) overcome by *steadfast courage.* (4:13-14)

5. *Selfish greed* (5:1-5) overcome by *rebuke* and *self-sacrificing example.* (5:6-17)

6. Work will be completed, and enemies will be defeated by persistent endeavor. (6:1-15)

ESTHER

AUTHOR: Unknown. Ascribed to EZRA by Augustine. Clemens ascribes it to Mordecai.

DATE: Approximately 486 – 485 BC. During the reign of King Ahasuerus of Persia. Esther became queen around 479 BC.

NAME AND CHARACTERISTICS OF ESTHER: Esther is a Persian word. Her Hebrew name was Hadassah. The Bible represents her as Jewess of pronounced piety, faith, courage and patriotism.

CANONICITY: The right of this book to place in the Scripture Canon has been greatly disputed. The name of God does not appear in it, while a heathen king is referred to over one hundred and fifty times. There is no allusion to prayer or spiritual service of any kind with the possible exception of fasting.

The truth is, that in the days in which the book was written God's people were in such a godless condition that the Almighty would not allow his name to be publicly associated with them, in the book inspired by His Holy Spirit to form a permanent part of the Sacred records; thus, solemnly confirming the awful words: "If ye forsake him, he will forsake you." (2 Chron. 15:2) But, and here is the wonderful part of it, it is not correct to say the name of God is not to be found in the book of Esther. It *is* there (as Dr. Bullinger has shown) four times over – not easily dis-concerned, it is true, but in an acrostic form in the Hebrew.

The Hebrew word Jehovah originally consisted of the four consonants – JHVH (that is, no vowels were used at all in Hebrew) and it is this name, JeHoVaH, which lies hidden in this book.

First, in the initial letters of four Hebrew words in Chapter 1:20 read forwards - that is, from right to left (Hebrew is read from right to left) **H-V-H-J.**

Second, in the initial letters of four Hebrew words in Chapter 5:4 read backwards – that is, from left to right: **J-H-V-H.**

Third, in the final letters of four Hebrew words in Chapter 5:13, read forwards – that is, from right to left: **H-V-H-J.**

Fourth, in the **final** letters of four Hebrew words in Chapter 7:7 read backwards – that is, from left to right: **J-H-V-H.**

In each of these cases **JHVH** may be spelled. How wonderfully this is in keeping with the whole teaching of the Bible; that while God does seem to withdraw himself from his people who forsake him (2 Chron. 24:20), never the less, he never absolutely and finally leaves his redeemed (Rom. 11:2). Although because of their unfaithfulness, he may so hide his face that outwardly he cannot be traced. This is illustrated in David's pathetic cry: "Hide thy face *from my sins*," but, "Cast me not away from thy presence."

MAIN THEME: Without doubt it occupies its place in God's word because of its hidden teaching of an overshadowing Providence in connection with God's people and the certainty of retribution overtaking their enemies.

SYNOPSIS:

Main events of the history center around three feasts:

I. THE FEAST OF AHASURERUS, KING OF PERSIA.

1. On the seventh day of the feast, when the king was merry with wine, he ordered Queen Vashti to appear before the assembled princes and she refused to do so. (1:1-12)

2. The angry king decided to accept the advice of his wise men, and dethroned the queen. (1:13-22)

3. After a kingdom-wide search for a new queen, Esther, the Jewess, was chosen. (2:1-17)

II. THE FEAST OF ESTHER, QUEEN OF PERSIA. (Preliminary events and the final outcome)

1. Mordecai, the Jew, the queen's foster father, saved the king's life. (Chapter 2:7 and 2:21-23)

2. The promotion of Haman to Prime Minister and the failure of Mordecai to bow and reverence him enraged Haman and he decided to destroy all the Jews. (Chapter 3:1-15)

3. The mourning among the Jews on the discovery of Haman's plot. (4:1-4)

4. The heroic determination of Esther to appear before the king with a plan in her mind to counteract the plot. (4:5-7)

5. Esther's gracious reception by the king, and her invitation to himself and Haman to attend her feast. (5:1-8)

6. Haman's erected a gallows on which to hang Mordecai. (5:9-14)

7. During a sleepless night the king examined the court records and discovered that Mordecai had received no reward for saving his life. (6:1-3)

8. Haman's selfish vanity resulted in his own humiliation, and great honor for Mordecai. (6:4-11)

9. Esther's feast and Haman's plot revealed. He was hung upon the gallows he had built for Mordecai. (Chapter 7)

III. THE FEAST OF PURIM, A MEMORIAL OF DELIVERANCE.

1. Preliminary events:

   a. The vengeance of the Jews against their enemies authorized by the king.(Chapter 8)

   b. Vengeance executed: Haman's sons hung. (Chapter 9)

2. The Feast instituted. (9:20-31)

3. The exaltation of Mordecai. (Chapter 10)

JOB

AUTHOR: Unknown

DATE: Unclear, however, many Bible scholars believe the story of Job is one of the oldest stories in the Bible, perhaps 200BC.

MAIN THEME: THE PROBLEM OF SUFFERING, ESPECIALLY THAT OF JOB.

This book attempts to solve the problem of how the afflictions of the righteous and the prosperity of the wicked can be consistent with the moral government of God. Fearlessly, the author grappled with the dark problem of the apparent injustice of the Divine rule among men.

A DRAMATIC POEM:

Job is the first of the five poetical books. By Hebrew poetry is meant the books from Job to the Song of Solomon. As a dramatic poem, Job ranks among the highest, if not the highest, of all literature. Beginning with 3:3 the reader is in the field of poetry. The prologue (Chapters 1, 2) and the epilogue (42:7-17) are in prose: All else is poetry except the brief words introducing each speaker in the dialogue.

As a dramatic poem, the analysis may be divided into scenes.

SYNOPSIS:

I. THE PROLOGUE (Chapters 1, 2)

1. **SCENE I. JOB AND HIS FAMILY BEFORE HIS TROUBLE.**

    a. Job was a godly father, unspoiled by prosperity.

    b. He ministered as a priest to his family.

2. **SCENE II.**

    a. Satan told God there was no such thing as disinterest goodness, that even Job served him because of special favors. (1:9-11)

    b. Satan was permitted to test Job by inflicting the loss of property and children. (1:12-22)

    c. Job retained his integrity. (1:21-22)

3. **SCENE III.**

a. Satan told God that if Job's body was afflicted, he would curse him. (2:1-5)

b. Satan was permitted to afflict Job with a horrible disease. (2:7-8)

c. The blasphemous advice of his wife, and the triumphant submission of Job. (2:9-10)

4. **SCENE IV.**

a. The arrival of Job's three friends, and the seven days of silent sympathy. (2:11-13)

b. Eliphaz the Temanite, Bildad the Shuhite and Zophar the Naamathite.

II. <u>ACT I</u>. <u>THE FIRST SERIES OF SPEECHES</u> (Chapters 3-14)

1. **SCENE I.** (Chapter 3)

a. Job cursed the day he was born.

b. He complained of life because of his anguish.

2. **SCENE 2. DISCUSSIONS BETWEEN JOB AND HIS THREE FRIENDS CONCERNING HIS AFFLICTIONS.** (Chapters 4-14)

(Of his three friends who came to comfort Job, but ended by tormenting him, Eliphaz was something of a prophet, Bildad was a traditionalist, and Zophar was an impatient debater who attack Job without mercy.)

III. <u>ACT II</u>. <u>SECOND SERIES OF SPEECHES.</u> (Chapters 15-21)

1. **SCENE I.**

a. The position of the friends was that repentance will restore to God's favor, while rebellion only adds to sin and suffering.

b. Job insisted that the justice of God cannot always be discerned in his government of the world.

c. Job claimed that he had a right to justify himself before God.

IV. ACT III. THIRD SERIES OF SPEECHES. (Chapters 22-31)

1. **SCENE I.**

    a. The position of the friends was that repentance will restore to God's favor, while rebellion only adds to sin and suffering.

1. **SCENE II.**

    a. Job modified his positive attitudes to the government of God, and treated the problem in a calmer frame of mind.

    b. Job at one time seemed on the point of renouncing his faith in God, as Satan said that he would do when the test became sever enough, but the honest servant of God fought his hard way to a higher faith; boldly affirmed that he would be vindicated after death by his kinsman Redeemer.

V. ACT IV.

1. **SCENE I. THE SPEECH OF ELIHU.** (Chapters 32-37)

    a. Elihu acted as a judge of the debate.

    b. He condemned the friends who failed to establish their case.

    c. He reproved Job for laying such stress upon his self-justification.

    d. Elihu presents affliction as meant to be corrective and disciplinary.

2. **SCENE II. GOD SPEAKS TO JOB.** (Chapters 38-39)

    a. God speaks to Job out of the whirlwind, and teaches him the folly of sitting in judgment of the deep problems of the moral rule of the world, when even the simpler tasks are beyond his powers.

3. **SCENE III. JOB'S CONFESSION** (40:3-5)

    a. Job humbled himself, and confessed his sins.

4. **SCENE IV. GOD SPEAKS TO JOB AGAIN.** (40:7 Chapter 41)

    a. Showed Job his righteousness, power and wisdom.

5. **SCENE V. JOB'S SECOND CONFESSION.** (42:1-6)

    a. Job confessed his mistakes in challenging God, and gets a vision of his sinfulness that overwhelms him.

6. **SCENE VI.SOLUTION OF THE PROBLEM.**

    a. God did not solve for Job the intellectual problem. The solution consisted in God revealing himself to Job, and this vision of God satisfied Job as no intellectual solution could have done.

VI. <u>THE EPILOGUE.</u> (42:7-17)

1. **SCENE I. GOD'S REBUKE OF THE THREE FRIENDS.** (42:7-9)

    a. Rebuked Eliphaz, Bildad, and Zophar for their foolish words.

    b. Commanded them to offer sacrifices.

2. **SCENE II. RESTORATION OF JOB'S PROPERTY.** (42:10-15)

    a. Job prayed for his friends.

    b. God gave him twice as much as he had before.

    c. God blessed the last part of his life more than the first part of it.

3. **SCENE III. JOB'S DEATH** (42:16-17)

    a. After this Job lived one hundred forty years, covering four generations of his family.

    b. "So Job died, being old and full of days."

<u>**MESSAGE OF JOB:**</u>

From the book as a whole, we learn that suffering may be sent as a test of one's faith, rather than a punishment for one's sins.

It is also made plain that the problem of the inequalities of rewards and penalties in this life is too hard for the mind of man, and that there must be a future life in which all will be set right.

PSALMS

DEVOTIONAL BOOK

One hundred and fifty spiritual songs and poems were used by the Church in all ages in worship and devotional exercises.

The Psalms were collected for use in the temple service. In the later history of the Jews, they were used also in the synagogues and in the family circle.

AUTHOR: According to the titles, seventy-three Psalms are ascribed to David; twelve to Asaph; eleven to the sons of Korah; two to Solomon; one each to Moses; Heman and Ethan, Haggai, Ezra, and Zechariah, a doubtful number to Hezekiah, and the remainder anonymous.

David, however, was the founder of Hebrew psalmody and one of the most brilliant psalmists Israel ever had.

DATE: Approximately 1400 BC (Moses' time) through the 500 BC. The time during the Jews Babylonian exile.

MAIN THEME: The Psalms cover a great variety of religious experiences. They are more frequently quoted in the New Testament than any other book, except *Isaiah*.

The Christian Scriptures have no book corresponding to the *Psalms*, but Christians in all ages have made large use of the *Psalms* in public worship and in private devotion. The prayer-life of the Christians has been largely shaped by the prayers of the ancient Hebrew psalmists. At the heart of the book – Prayer and Praise.

DIVISIONS OF THE PSALSM:

The Hebrew divides the Psalms into five books:

1.   Psalms 1-41

2.   Psalms 42-72

3.   Psalms 73-89

4.   Psalms 90-106

5.   Psalms 107-150

Each of the books end with the word "Amen" except the last, which closes with the grandest "Hallelujah Chorus" ever put onto human lips.

PLAN OF THE BIBLE:

The beautiful and harmonious plan of the Bible is seen in the fact that these five books of Psalms correspond in a very wonderful way with five books of the Pentateuch:

The first book answers to Gene is – the *Book of Beginning.*
(See Psalms 8)
Second book answers to Exodus – the *Book of Redemption and Passover.*
(See Psalms 51)
Third book answers to Leviticus – the *Book of the Sanctuary or Atonement.*
(See Psalms 84)
Fourth book answers to Numbers – the *Book of Wilderness or Sojourn.*
(See Psalms 90)
Fifth book answers to Deuteronomy – the *Book of the Work of Obedience.*
(See Psalms 119)

TWENTY-ONE HISTORICAL PSALMS RELATE TO THE FOLLOWING PERIODS:

1. Mosaic (106, 114)

2. Judges (106, 34-46)

3. Davidic:

   a. During the reign of Saul (3, 7, 11, 18, 54.)

   b. During David's reign (24, 30, 32, 51, 55, 60.)

4. Solomonic (72)

5. Exilic and post-exilic (64, 79, 80, 85, 127, 137.)

MESSIANIC PSALMS:

The Psalms are replete with Messianic announcement. Christ declared that all things must be fulfilled, which were written in the Psalms concerning him. (Luke 24:44)

1. Messiah's advent and mission. (40. Heb 10:5-10)

2. Messiah's sufferings:

   a. His betrayal (41:9) (John 13:8)(Ps.109. Acts 1:20)

      b.   Crucifixion (Ps. 22) (John 19:24) (Ps. 69)

3.   Messiah's resurrection and ascension. (Ps. 16:8-11) (Acts 2:25-27; 13:34-37) (Ps. 68:18) (Eph. 4:8-10)

4.   Messiah's Kingship. (Ps. 2, 72, 110) (Every part of Ps. 110 applies to Christ). (Ps. 118:19-23) (Matt. 21:41-46) (Acts 2:30)

TOPICAL ARRANGEMENT:

(Each Psalm is arranged under some topic which appears prominently in it.)

1. MAN

    1.   Exaltation of man. (Ps 8)

    2.   Sinfulness of man. (Ps. 10, 14, 36, 55, 59)

2. WORLDLY AND WICKED

    1.   Contrasted with the godly. (Ps. 1, 4, 5)

    2.   The delay of the punishment of worldly and wicked. (Ps. 10)

    3.   Prosperity of worldly and wicked. (Ps 37, 73)

    4.   Fate of worldly and wicked. (Ps. 9, 11)

    5.   Trust in riches. (Ps. 49)

3. RELIGIOUS EXPERIENCES

    1.   Penitence. (Ps. 25, 38, 51, 130)

    2.   Pardon. (Ps. 32)

    3.   Conversion. (Ps. 40)

    4.   Consecration. (Ps. 116)

    5.   Trust. (Ps. 3, 13, 20, 23, 27, 31, 34, 42, 61, 62, 91, 121)

    6.   Teachableness. (Ps. 25)

    7.   Aspiration. (Ps. 42, 62, 143)

    8.   Prayer. (Ps. 55, 70, 77, 85, 86, 142, 143)

    9.   Praise. (Ps. 96, 98, 100, 103, 107, 136, 145, 148, 149, 150)

10. Worship. (Ps. 43. 84, 100, 122, 132)

11. Affliction. (Ps. 6, 13, 22, 69, 88, 102)

12. Old age. (Ps. 71)

13. Vanity of life. (Ps. 39, 49, 90)

14. Home. (Ps. 127)

15. Homesickness, typical. (Ps. 137)

4. **THE CHURCH (typical)**

   1. Safety of the Church. (Ps. 46)

   2. Glory of the Church. (Ps. 48, 87)

   3. Love for the Church. (Ps. 84, 122)

   4. Unity in the Church. (Ps. 133)

5. **THE WORD OF GOD.** (Ps. 19, 119)

6. **MISSIONARY.** (Ps. 67, 72, 96, 98)

7. **DUTY OF RULERS.** (Ps. 82, 101)

8. **DIVINE ATTRIBUTES:**

   1. Wisdom, Majesty and Power. (Ps. 18, 19, 29, 62, 66, 89, 93, 97, 99, 118, 147)

   2. Mercy. (Ps. 32, 85, 136)

   3. Infinite knowledge. (Ps. 139)

   4. Creative power. (Ps. 33, 89, 139)

9. **ISRAEL'S EXPERIENCES:**

   1. Unbelief. (Ps 78)

   2. Desolation and misery. (Ps. 79, 80)

   3. Backsliding of Israel. (Ps. 81)

   4. Divine Providence. (Ps. 105, 106, 114)

CHARACTERISTICS OF THE BOOK OF PSALMS:

   1. More chapters than any book in the Bible.

   2. Longest chapter in the Bible. Psalm 119.

3. Shortest chapter in the Bible. Psalm 117.

4. Psalms is exactly in the center of the Bible.

   a. Books preceding and following Psalms tell of God's voice to man.

   b. In Psalms, we have man's voice crying out to God.

   c. First half of the Bible, God's voice thunders with Law.

   d. In Psalms (center) man responds to God.

   e. Last half of the Bible, God's voice is softened with love and grace through the gospels and epistles.

5. Middle verse of the Bible brings God and man together.

   a. Psalms 118:8 (middle verse): "It is better to trust in the Lord than to put confidence in man."

6. Psalms is the greatest book of devotions in all literature.

7. Psalms deals with a greater number of human problems than any other book in all literature.

   a. It presents no argument for their solution.

   b. It lifts them up to God in prayer and praise and trusts God for their solution.

8. There is no other book in all literature like Psalms. It stands alone, supreme and eternal as interpreting man's heart to the living God.

PROVERBS

AUTHORS: Primarily Solomon with sections attributed to Agur and King lemuel. Little is known of the latter two. Credited with

DATE: Solomon reigned approximately 970 – 930 BC.

MAIN THEME: Instructions concerning living right, wisdom, justice, temperance, industry, and purity. The sharp contrast between Wisdom and folly. "Prudence to the simple, and to the young man knowledge and discretion." Key thought throughout the book is "The fear of the Lord." (Occurs fourteen times)

SYNOPSIS:

1. Fatherly counsels and warnings, with exhortations concerning the attainment of wisdom. (Chapters 1-7)

2. Wisdom's call. (Chapters 8, 9)

3. Proverbs of Solomon: Contrasts between good and evil, wisdom and folly.
   (Chapters 10-20)

4. Proverbial maxims and counsels. (Chapters 21-24)

5. Proverbs of Solomon copied by men of King Hezekiah. (Chapters 25-29)

6. The words of Agur, the oracle. (Chapter 30)

7. The words of King Lemuel - a Mother's advice. (Chapter 31:1-9)

The description of an ideal wife. (Chapter 31:10-31)

I. CHOICE SELECTIONS

1. The call of wisdom. (Chapter 1:20-23; Chapter 8)

2. The source of wisdom. (Chapter 2:6)

3. The preciousness of wisdom. (Chapter 3:13-26)

4. The principle thing. (4:5-13)

5. The richest treasure. (8:11-36)

6. The feast of wisdom. (9:1-6)

II. SUBJECTS SPECIALLY DISCUSSED

1. **ANGER.** (14:17, 29 ... 15:18 ... 16:32 ... 19:11)

2. **BENEVOLENCE.** (3:9, 10 ... 11:24-26 ... 14:21 ... 19:17 ... 22:9)

3. **CORRECTION OF CHILDREN.** (13:24 ... 19:18 ... 22:6, 15 ... 23:13-14)

4. **ENTICERS.** (4:14 ... 9:13 ... 16:29)

5. **FEAR OF GOD.** (1:7 ... 3:7 ... 9:10 ... 10:27 ... 14:26,27 ... 15:16, 33; 16:6 ... 19:23 ... 23:17 ... 24:21)

6. **FOOLS**

   a. Slanderous. (10:18)

   b. Short-lived. (10:21)

   c. Mischief-makers. (10:23)

   d. Self-righteous. (12:15)

   e. Irritable. (12:16)

   f. Mock at sin. (14:9)

   g. Talk nonsense. (15:2)

   h. Insensible. (17:10)

   i. Dangerous. (17:12)

   j. Visionary. (17:24)

   k. Meddlesome. (20:3)

   l. Despise Wisdom. (23:9)

   m. Stupid. (27:22)

   n. Self-confident. (14:16 ... 28:26)

   o. Garrulous. (29:11)

7. **FRIENDSHIP.** (17:17 ... 18:24 ... 19:4 ... 27:10, 17)

8. **INDOLENCE.** (6:6-11; 10:4, 5 ... 12:27 ... 13:4 ... 15:19 ... 18:9 ... 19:15, 24 ... 20:4, 13; 22:13 ... 24:30-34 ... 26:13-16)

9. **DIVINE KNOWLEDGE.** (15:11 ... 21:2 ... 24:12)

10. OPPRESSION. (14:31 … 22:22 … 28:16)

11. PRIDE. (6:17 … 11:2 … 13:10 … 15:25 … 16:18, 19 … 18:12 … 21:4, 24 … 29:23 … 30:13)

12. PRUDENCE. (12:23 … 13:16 … 14:8, 15, 18 … 15:5 … 16:21 … 18:15 … 27:12)

13. SCORNERS. (3:34 … 9:7 … 14:6 … 19:25 … 24:9)

14. STRIFE. (3:30 … 1012 … 1518 … 16:28 … 17:1, 14, 19 … 18:6, 19 … 20:3 … 22:10 … 25:8 … 30:33)

15. THE TONGUE. (4:24 … 10:11-32 … 12:6, 18, 22 … 13:3 … 14:3 … 15:1-7, 23 … 16:13, 23, 27 … 17:4 … 18:7, 21 … 19:1 … 20:19 … 21:23 … 26:28 … 30:32)

16. TEMPERANCE. (20:1 … 21:17 … 23:1-3, 20 … 23:29-35 … 25:16 … 31:4-7)

17. UNJUST GAIN. (10:2 … 13:11 … 21:6 … 28:8)

18. WEALTH. (10:2, 15 … 11:4, 28 … 13:7, 11 … 15:6 … 16:8 … 18:11 … 19:4 … 27:24 … 28:6, 22)

19. EVIL WOMEN. (2:16-19 … 5:3-14, 20, 23 … 6:24-35 … 7:5-27 … 9:13-18)

20. GOOD WOMEN. (5:18, 19 … 31:10-31)

III. <u>SPIRITUAL LESSON:</u>

Solomon was a *guide-post,* rather than an *example.* He pointed the way to Wisdom, but in the latter part of his life he did not walk in it; therefore, his son Rehoboam, followed his *example,* rather than his *counsels,* and become a foolish and evil rule.

ECCLESIASTES

NAME: Borrowed from the Septuagint. In the Hebrew Bible, it is called "Koheleth," which means "Preacher," or one who addresses an assembly.

AUTHORSHIP: Ascribed to Solomon, Chapter 1:1, 2.

DATE: Approximately 900 BC.

MAIN THEME: The reflections and experiences of a Philosopher whose mind was in conflict over the problems of life. After speaking of the disillusionments that had come to him, he presents the view of the Epicurean materialist, that there is nothing better than the carnal enjoyment of the pleasures of life. As this reappears all through the book, it is quite evident that the writer was struggling with it while at the same time he was uttering profound truths concerning man's duty and obligations to God. At last he seems to emerge from his speculations and doubts, and reaches the noble conclusion in Chapter 12:13, "Fear God and keep his commandments; for this is the whole duty of man."

KEY WORDS: "Vanity" and "under the sun" – each expression more than twenty-five times.

SYNOPSIS:

CHAPTERS I and II

1. **INTRODUCTION:**

    a. Reflections on the monotonous round of life. (Chapter 1:1-11)

2. **THE SEARCH OF THE NATURAL MAN FOR SATISFACTION AND HAPPINESS.**

    a. Not to be found in the acquisition of wisdom. (Chapter 1:12-18)

    b. Not to be found in worldly pleasure. (Chapter 2:1-3)

    c. Not to be found in art or agriculture. (Chapter 2:406)

    d. Not to be found in great possessions. (Chapter 2:7-11)

3. **CONCLUSIONS**

a. The wise man is superior to the fool. (Chapter 2:12-21)

b. Of the Epicurean – there is nothing better than to eat and drink and enjoy life. (Chapter 2:24-26)

CHAPTER 3

1. **THE NATURAL MAN'S VIEW OF THE WEARY ROUND OF LIFE**

   a. There is a time for everything. (Verse 1-8)

   b. The conclusion of the Materialist. (Verse 13-22)

CHAPTER 4

1. **STUDY OF SOCIAL EVILS APART FROM FAITH**

   a. Vanity is increased by oppression, envy, idleness, covetousness and willfulness. (Verse 1-15)

   b. Conclusion: All is vanity and vexation of spirit. (Verse 16)

2. **THE SEARCH OF THE NATURAL MAN FOR SATISFACTION AND HAPPINESS**

   a. Not to be found in the acquisition of wisdom. (Chapter 1:12-18)

   b. Not to be found in worldly pleasure. (Chapter 2:1-3)

   c. Not to be found in art or agriculture. (Chapter 2:406)

   d. Not to be found in great possessions. (Chapter 2:7-11)

   e. The wise man is superior to the fool. (Chapter 2:12-21)

   f. Of the Epicurean – there is nothing better than to eat and drink and enjoy life. (Chapter 2:24-26)

CHAPTER 5

a. Advices concerning religious duties. (Verse 1-7)

b. The vanity of riches. (Verse 9-17)

    c. Conclusion – Eat and drink and enjoy life. (Verse 18-20)

CHAPTER 6

    a. The vanity of a long life. (Verse 3-12)

CHAPTER 7

    a. A series of wise sayings. (Verse 1-24)

    b. Conclusions concerning the evil woman. (Verse 25-28)

CHAPTER 8

    a. Civil duties. (Verse 1-5)

    b. The uncertainty of life. (Verse 6-8)

    c. The certainty of Divine judgment, and the injustices of life. (Verse 10-14)

    d. Epicurean conclusion. (Verse 15)

    e. The work of God and man. (Verse 16-17)

CHAPTER 9

    a. The same things happen to the righteous and the wicked; the grave is the goal of life, man is the creature of circumstances. Epicurean conclusion: "Let us eat and drink, for tomorrow we die." (Verse 1-9)

    b. Wisdom is preeminent, though often unappreciated. (Verse 13-18)

CHAPTER 10

    a. Various wise sayings, the contrast between wisdom and folly, etc.

CHAPTER 11

    a. Advices concerning benevolences. (Verse 106)

    b. Advice to the young. (Verse 9-10)

CHAPTER 12

    a. A poetical description of old age. (Verse 1-7)

b. The closing words of the Preacher, and the final
    conclusion concerning the highest duty of man.
    (Verse 8-14)

THE SONG OF SOLOMON

AUTHOR: Solomon

This book has been criticized because of its descriptive language. Its right to a place in the Bible has been defended by many saintly souls in all ages. They have regarded it as a Spiritual Allegory, representing the holy affections existing between God and His Chosen People, or between Christ and His Church.

DATE: Approximately 970 – 930 BC.

MAIN THEME: The ardent expressions of this book are in no sense offensive when it is understood that they represent the cultured descriptive of the Orientals of Solomon's day. Translated into the English language, and in the light of Western civilization, this book loses much of its oriental poetic beauty. Mature spiritual minds can best interpret it properly.

1. Spiritual communion between the Bride and the heavenly Bridegroom. (1:1-2:7)

2. The Bride misses her Companion and seeks him. (2:8-3:5)

3. The ardent discourses of the Bride and Bridegroom on their mutual love and the graces of each other. (3:6-8:14)

KEY THOUGHT: "My Beloved," the believer's title for Christ. (2:16)

SYNOPSIS:

COMPANION PASSAGE: The forty-fifth Psalm.

SIDE LIGHTS

1. THE HEAVENLY BRIDGROOM

   a. His love covers all defects of the Bride. (Son of Solomon 4:7)

   b. He rejoices over her. (Isa. 62:5)

   c. He gave his life for her. (Eph. 5:25)

   d. He will come to claim her as his own. (Matt. 25:6)

2. THE BRIDE

   a. Loves the Bridegroom. (Song of Solomon 2:16)

   b. Feels her unworthiness. (Song of Solomon 1:5)

   c.   Has been purified and dressed in spotless robes. (Rev. 19:8)

   d.   Wears the jewels of Divine grace. (Isa. 61:10)

   e.   Issues the invitations to the wedding. (Rev. 22:17)

3. THE MARRIAGE SUPPER

   a.   Prepared by the Father for the Son. (Matt. 22:2)

   b.   Costly preparations made. (Matt. 22:4)

   c.   Invitations to, a great honor. (Rev. 19:9)

   d.   Invitations scorned by many. (Matt. 22:5)

   e.   Invitation include all classes. (Matt. 22:10)

   f.   Neglect of wedding garment leads to exclusion from the Supper. (Matt. 22:11-14)

The Song of Solomon is the last of the five books of Hebrew Poetry – Job, Psalms, Proverbs, Ecclesiastes and the Song of Solomon.

A FINAL WORD:

Solomon began his reign gloriously with perfect trust in God, then apostatized by serving other gods; after a devious route, which led into materialistic experiences and problems of life, he summed up life as "Vanity and vexations of spirit," and came back to his first and correct conception of right living, "Fear God and keep His commandments; for this is the whole duty of man."

ISAIAH

AUTHOR: Isaiah

Isaiah's name is attached to the entire work, while throughout the New Testament Isaiah is quoted by name as the author of all portions of the book, including these parts declared by some to be the work of another author.

DATE: Approximately 740 – 700 BC, starting "in the year that King Uzziah died." (6:1)

THE PROPHET:

1. **The Son of Amos.**

   Prophesied during the reigns of Uzziah, Jothan, Ahaz, and Hezekiah. (Chapter 1:1)
   Isaiah exercised his ministry as a prophet for over forty years; from about 750 to 701 B.C.
   Isaiah prophesied during the reigns of the Assyrian monarchs, Tiglath-pileser III, Shalmaneser IV, Srgon, and Sennacherib.
   He was a contemporary of Hosea and Amos, prophets of Israel, and was the co- worker of Micah of Judah.

2. **Isaiah's Call and Anointing.**

   (Chapter 6)
   His lips cleansed with a coal of fire.
   His spirit of obedience: "Here I am: Send me."

3. **His Family.**

   (Chapters 7:3, 8:3-4)
   Two sons mentioned.

ISAIAH, THE GREATEST PROPHET OF ALL TIME:

The first of the Major Prophets, and the greatest prophet of all.

Isaiah was preeminently the Prophet of Redemption, and of the coming Messiah. Many of the passages in his book are among the finest in all literature.

Tradition represents him as suffering martyrdom under the cruel and reactionary King Manasseh.

MAIN THEME:

Isaiah prophesied about 750 BC, and therefore stands just midway between Moses, who gave the Law about 1500 BC, and Christ, who gave us the New Law.

Isaiah's prophecy divides itself naturally into three parts, each part beginning with a solemn call and ending with a solemn warning:

First part, Chapter 1:1 to Chapter 48:22, commencing, "Hear, O heavens, and give ear, O earth" (1:2); ending "There is no peace, saith Jehovah, to the wicked."

Second part, Chapter 49:1 to Chapter 57:21, commencing, "Listen, O isles, unto me; and harken, ye people, from afar;" ending, "There is no peace, saith my God, unto the wicked."

Third part, Chapter 58:1 to Chapter 66:24, commending, "Cry aloud, spare not, lift up thy voice like a trumpet"; ending, "Their worm shall not die," neither of which calls being regarded. The third part begins with instruction to the prophet to cry louder still in the hope of awakening a sleeping world before its doom was sealed.

In this connection, the closing words of each part are full of interest and instruction. In Parts 1 and 2, those who will neither "hear" nor "listen" are warned that for them "There is no peace." While at the close of the third part the final doom of all who resist the threefold call is revealed with awful faithfulness.

But this is not all. If we take the middle (or second) section of this prophecy, which stands, as we have seen midway between Moses and Christ, we shall find the middle chapter of that middle section is fifty-third, and in the very center of the fifty-third chapter stand the words which constitute the central truth of the whole Bible – "He is brought as a lamb to the slaughter." (Verse 7)

How beautiful is such a plan which brings into prominence the substitutionary work of Christ on behalf of those who so long refused to listen to God's repeated calls, and thereby incurred for themselves the doom recorded at the close of each section of the prophecy.

How true it is that "all we like sheep have gone astray; we have turned everyone to his way; and Jehovah hath laid on him the iniquity of us all." (Isa. 53:6)

While the Hebrew divides the book into *three* parts, scholarship divides the English translation into but *two* parts: Part one, composed of the first thirty-nine chapters; part two, composed of the last twenty-seven chapters.

This division is significant and symbolic. The book of Isaiah is a miniature Bible. The Bible has sixty-six books; Isaiah has sixty-six chapters. The Bible has two divisions; Isaiah has two divisions also. The Old Testament (1st division) of the Bible has thirty-nine books; the first division of Isaiah has thirty-nine chapters. The New Testament (2nd division) of the Bible has twenty-seven books; the second division of Isaiah has twenty-seven chapters. The first division, or Old Testament deals with the history of Israelites with interspersed prophetic gleams of the coming Messiah; the first division of Isaiah also a history of the Israelites with prophetic statements of the coming Messiah. The second division of Isaiah deals principally with Christ and his salvation. The main theme of the entire Bible is "Salvation," and the very word "Isaiah" means "Salvation of Jehovah."

SYNOPSIS:

SECTION ONE – Chapters 1-39
Refer chiefly to the events leading up to the Captivity.

1. **Chapter 1** arraigns the nation for its ingratitude; declares ritual no satisfactory substitute for right-living; predicts a thorough purging of Jerusalem.

2. **Chapter 2-4** show that Zion must suffer terrible judgments before it can be exalted.

    a. Isaiah pictured the ideal Zion of the future. (2:2-4)

    b. Present sinful people must suffer much before it can be the people of God. (2:5- 4:1)

    c. Names sins that needed punishment. (2:6-9)

    d. Announced all things proud would be brought low:

        1. Inanimate things that minister to pride. (2:10-21)

2. Rulers (2:22-3:15).

3. Proud and wanton women. (3:16-4:1)

e. God's blessing would rest upon the purified Zion. (4:2-6)

3. Chapter 5

a. Parable of the disappointing vineyard. (Verse 1-7)

b. Series of woes against six classes of sinners. (Verse 8-24)

c. Description of a fierce invading army. (Verse 25-30)

4. Chapter 6

Inaugural vision of the prophet.

a. Isaiah in the Temple, witnessing worship of the heavenly host. (Verse1-4)

b. In response to his cry and confession, his guilt is removed. (Verse 5-7)

c. Offered to go as messenger for God. (Verse 8)

d. His difficult task is then described. (Verse 9-13)

e. From the heavenly vision, Isaiah received an impression of the holiness of God from which he could never escape. Throughout the Book of Isaiah, God is always "The Holy One of Israel." Moral and spiritual perfection is found in God, and in him alone.

5. Chapters 7-12

Chiefly about the person of Immanuel.

a. **Chapter 7** recounts two interviews with Ahaz about 735 BC, when Syria and Israel invaded Judah with a view of deposing Ahaz and putting a tool of their own on the throne of Judah.

1. In the first interview, Isaiah tries to encourage Ahaz, but warns him that he must have faith. (Verse 3-9)

2. In the second interview, the prophet offers a sign to Ahaz, and when the king tries to evade the issue by a pretense to piety, Isaiah announces the birth of Immanuel as a sign from God. (Verse 10-17) (Compare 9:1-7 and 11:1-10. All these prophecies are fulfilled in Jesus' birth and Messianic reign.)

3. The chapter closes with four pictures of the desolation to be wrought by the Assyrian armies. (Verse 18-25)

b. Chapters 8-12

1. Again, Isaiah announces the desolating judgments will be followed by great salvation. (8:1-9:7)

2. The Son who is to rule on the throne of David has four names pointing to his Divine nature. (9:6)

3. Next follows a fourfold judgment on wicked Samaria. (9:8-10:4) (This prediction was delivered prior to 724 BC)

4. The last prophecy in this collection describes the pride of the Assyrian, and the defeat that awaits him, in contrast to the happy future of the people of God through the reign of the Prince of Peace. (10:5- 12:6) The most beautiful passage in this brilliant prophecy is the description of the Messianic King and the effect of his reign. (11:1-10).

6. **Chapter 13-23**

Prophecies of Isaiah against foreign nations, and a few brief passages dealing with Jerusalem and Judah.

a. Babylon shall fall before the attack of the army which God assembles against her, and shall be forever desolate. (13:1 –14:23)

b. God will surely break the Assyrian in Palestine. (14:24-27)

c. Philistia will suffer terribly while Zion escapes. (14:28-32)

d. **Chapter 15 and 16** describes the overthrow of Moab for its pride. The prophet sympathizes with Moab, but predicts its overthrow within three years.

e. **Chapter 17**

1. Predicts the destruction of Damascus. (Verse 1-3)

2. Severe Chastisement of Israel for its idolatry. (Verse 4-11)

3. Sudden destruction of the nation's invading Judah. (Verse 12-14) (The prophecy against Damascus was fulfilled in 732 BC when Tiglath-pileser sacked the city. The prophecy against Israel was fulfilled in 722 BC, when Sargon captured Samaria. The prophecy against the heathen invaders was fulfilled in 701 BC, when Sennacherib lost one hundred eighty-five thousand men by a supernatural stroke in Palestine.)

f. **Chapter 18-20** deal with Ethiopia and Egypt, announcing that the alliance of Judah with these powers will not avail, but that the people of those lands shall be led into captivity by the king of Assyria. (Isaiah was required to walk in captive garb for three years as a sign to his people.) The prediction of the union of the world in the worship of God (19:23-25) is one of the most daring utterances in all the realm of prophecy. Already, Israel's God is worshipped by a third of the human race, and his rule is rapidly spreading among the backward nations.

g. **Chapter 21**

1. A second prediction of the overthrow of Babylon is made. (21:1-10)

2. Dumah (Edom) is to have mingled experiences of light and darkness. (Verse 11-12)

3. Arabia shall suffer from invasion. (Verse 13-17)

h. Chapter 22

1. Most hopeless deliverance of Isaiah. (Verse 1-14)

2. Judah has suffered defeat through cowardice and fugitives in Jerusalem give themselves up to reckless feasting. Such conduct must spell ruin. Isaiah boldly confronts the Prime Minister Shebna, and tells him that Eliakim will supplant him. (Verse 15-25)

3. Later, Eliakim appears as Prime Minister, but Shebna's attitude must have changed toward God and his prophet, for he is second to Eliakim in authority. (37:2)

i. Chapter 23 predicts the fall of Tyre, the rich merchant city; but it will revive and be of service to God's people.

7. Chapters 24-27

A world judgment.

a. God will bring down the most severe judgments upon the earth. (Chapter 24)

b. He is praised for his overthrow of a proud city. (25:1-5)

c. Next comes one of the most remarkable pictures in all the Bible, God spreading a feast in Zion for all the people of earth and wiping tears from off all faces. (Verse 6-8)

d. The proud Moab shall be brought low. (Verse 9-12)

    e.   A song of praise over the downfall of the proud city, and prayers to god for help, (Chapter 26)

    f.   The promise that Israel's dead shall rise from their graves. (26:19)

    g.   Oppressors shall perish while Israel revives, the scattered exiles returning to worship God in his holy mountain. (Chapter 27)

8. Chapters 28-33

Another small collection of Isaiah's messages, many of them belonging to the latter part of Hezekiah's reign, while some of the politicians advocated an alliance with Egypt against Assyria.

    a. Chapter 28

        1.   A woe pronounced upon the drunkards of Ephraim. (Verse 1-6)

        2.   Drunken scoffers of Judah denounced. (Verse 7-23)

        3.   Illustrations from farming. (Verse 23-29)

    b. Chapter 29

        1.   Jerusalem is to be besieged, but her foes shall fail to capture her. (Verse 1-8)

        2.   Chastisements lead her people from blindness to clear vision. (Verse 9-24)

    c. Chapter 30

        1.   Egypt helps in vain. (Verse 1-8)

        2.   Judah shall suffer because she turns from God to boastful Egypt for help. (Verse 9-17)

        3.   God shall be gracious to his people. (Verse 18-26)

        4.   Will deliver Judah from the Assyrian by supernatural stroke. (Verse 27-33)

    d. Chapter 31

1. Isaiah shows the folly of leaning on Egypt; predicts that Jerusalem shall be helpless before the attack of Jehovah, but by a sudden change on the part of both the people and God, the heathen invaders are destroyed by the sword of the mighty God.

e. **Chapter 32**

1. A glimpse of the Messianic King. (Verse 1-8)

2. Contrast between the distress of the careless women and the quietness that shall return when justice again prevails in the land. (Verse 9-20)

f. **Chapter 33**

1. Isaiah announces that the cruel invader who has broken the covenant shall be overthrown. (Verse 1-12)

2. The righteous man and the righteous city abides and prospers under God's protection. (Verse 13-24)

9. **Chapter 34 and 35**

a. A contrast is drawn between the enemies of Israel, especially Edom, and the returning exiles, for whom God prepares a highway to Zion.

10. **Chapter 36 and 37**

a. a. Description of the invasion of Sennacherib in 701 B.C.

11. **Chapters 38 and 39**

a. An account given of the sickness of Hezekiah, and the visit of the ambassadors from Babylon after his recovery.

SECTION TWO
CHAPTERS 40-66

The second part of the book contains Predictions, warnings and promises which refer to events beyond the Captivity, and reach down the centuries through the Christian dispensation.

This portion of the prophecy is especially rich in Messianic references.

I. PREPARATION OF GOD FOR THE DELIVERANCE OF HIS PEOPLE FROM BABYLON. (Chapters 40-48)

1. Good news from Zion: The all-wise and all-powerful God will not fail his people. (Chapter 40)

2. God controls history and predicts the future. (Chapter 41)

3. The office of Christ and his work. (Chapter 42)

4. The grace of God promises redemption. (Chapters 43:1-44:5)

5. Contrast between powerless idols and the living God. (Chapter 44:6-23)

6. The mission of Cyrus. (Chapters 44:24-45:25)

7. Overthrow of the gods of Babylon. (Chapter 46)

8. Fall of Babylon, the mistress of nations. (Chapter 47)

9. Exhortations to take advantage of the work of Cyrus and flee from Babylon. (Chapter 48)

II. SALVATION COMES THROUGH THE CHRIST OF GOD (Chapters 49-55)

1. Exaltation of Christ and Zion. (Chapter 49)

2. Contrast between Israel's sinfulness and the steadfast devotion of Christ to his work. (Chapter 50)

3. Exhortation to trust in Christ for salvation and deliverance. (Chapters 51:1-16)

4. Let Zion arise and adorn herself for deliverance is at hand. (Chapters 51:17-52:12)

5. Christ should pass through deepest humiliation to supreme exaltation. (Chapters 52:13- 5312)

     a.   Christ to be a sin offering for mankind. (53:4-6)

     b.   Greatest work picture of Christ. (Chapter 53)

6.   Vast growth and blessedness of Zion predicted. (Chapter 54)

7.   Everyone invited to partake of the great salvation. (Chapter 55)

III. PROMISES AND WARNINGS (Chapters 56-66)

1.   Salvation to be without respect of persons. (56:1-8)

2.   Sharp arraignment of the godless rulers and idolaters in Israel. (56:9- 5:21)

3.   Contrast between false and true worship. (Chapter 58)

4.   The prophet arraigns his people for their sins, confesses their blackness, but announces the coming of a Redeemer. (Chapter 59)

5.   Transcendent glory of Church – to include Gentiles. (Chapter 60)

6.   Gracious mission of Christ, the anointed of God. (Chapter 61)

7.   New picture of the glory of the church. (Chapter 62)

     a.   A new name prophesied – given by God. (Chapter 62:2)

     b.   This prophecy fulfilled. (Acts 11:26; I Peter 4:16)

8.   Christ described, and his victory over his enemies. (Chapter 66:1-6)

9.   Prayer of penitent Israel. (Chapters 62:7-64:12)

10. Because of their sins and idolatry, the Jews are rejected and the Gentiles are called. Sharp contrast between the fate of the wicked and the blessedness of the righteous. (Chapter 65)

11. The glorious God will be served in humility and sincerity – gracious benefits of the church – judgments against the

wicked – the Gentiles shall have a holy church. (Chapter 66)

MESSIANIC PROPHECIES BY CHAPTERS:

1. Christ's birth and kingdom. (Chapters 2, 9)

2. Christ's ancestry. (Chapters 11, 12)

3. Kingship of Christ. (Chapters 32-35)

4. Forerunner of Christ. (Chapter 40)

5. Christ the servant of God and his work of redemption. (Chapters 49-59)

6. Call of the Gentiles. (Chapter 65)

ISAIAH'S PORTRAYAL OF CHRIST:

1. **HISTORY OF CHRIST**

   a. Birth. (7:14)

   b. Family. (11:1)

   c. Anointing. (11:2)

2. **MISSION OF CHRIST** (Nine Phases)

   a. Illuminator. (9:2)

   b. Judge. (11:3)

   c. Re-prover. (11:4)

   d. Law-giver. (42:4)

   e. Liberator. (42:7)

   f. Burden-bearer. (53:4)

   g. Sin-bearer. (53:6)

   h. Intercessor. (53:12)

   i. Only Savior. (53:5)

3. **TITLES OF CHRIST** (Nine Titles)

   a. Immanuel. (7:14)

   b. Mighty God. (9:6)

   c. Everlasting Father. (9:6)

    d.   Prince of Peace. (9:6)

    e.   Righteous King. (32:1)

    f.   Divine Servant. (42:1)

    g.   Arm of the Lord. (53:1)

    h.   Anointed Preacher. (61:1)

    i.   Mighty Traveler. (63:1)

4. CHARACTERISTICS OF CHRIST

    a.   Wisdom. (11:2)

    b.   Spiritual discernment. (11:3)

    c.   Justice. (11:4)

    d.   Righteousness (11:5)

    e.   Silence. (42:2; 57:3)

    f.   Gentleness. (42:3)

    g.   Perseverance. (42:4)

    h.   Radiance. (9:2; 42:6)

    i.   Compassion. (53:4)

    j.   Meekness. (53:7)

    k.   Vicarious suffering. (52:14; 53:10)

    l.   Sinlessness. (53:9)

    m. Greatness. (53:12)

    n.   Saving Power. (53:11)

KEY WORD: "SALVATION"

"Isaiah" means "Salvation of Jehovah."

1. SALVATION

    a.   Wells of salvation. (12:3)

    b.   Joy of salvation. (25:9)

    c.   Walls of salvation. (26:1)

    d.   Everlasting salvation. (45:17)

    e.   Day of salvation. (49:8)

    f.   Feet of the heralds of salvation. (52:7)

    g.   Spread of salvation. (52:10)

    h.   Arm of salvation. (59:16)

    i.   Helmet of salvation. (59:17)

    j.   Garments of salvation. (62:10)

    k.   Light of Salvation. (62:1)

SEVEN EVERLASTINGS

1. Strength. (26:4)

2. Judgments. (33:14)

3. Joy. (35:10)

4. Salvation. (45:17)

5. Kindness. (54:8)

6. Covenant. (55:3)

7. Light. (60:19)

JEREMIAH

<u>**AUTHOR:**</u> The book of Jeremiah contains the Biography and Message of "The weeping Prophet."

Jeremiah was born of a priestly family in Anathoth, a village about three miles northeast of Jerusalem, and was called to be a prophet in the thirteenth year of Josiah's reign (628 BC). He began to prophesy when he was about twenty-two years without committing to writings his messages.

In the fourth year of Jehoiakim (605 BC), he was directed by Jehovah to write down all the messages of his ministry. Jeremiah even then preferred to use a secretary, and so dictated his messages to Baruch, the son of Neriah. We do not know the exact limits of the roll as it was composed by Baruch; but it probably forms the greater part of Chapters 1-20 of our present Book of Jeremiah.

Under good King Josiah the young prophet had a comparatively easy time, though he never hesitated to rebuke and reprove, like the great prophets before him; but dangers thickened about Jeremiah from the accession of the reactionary Jehoiakim until the aged prophet died in exile in Egypt.

Jeremiah read the events of his time with clearer vision than all the politicians in Judah, and proclaimed it as the will of God that Nebuchadnezzar of Babylon should rule the world; that rebellion against the God who had called him as his servant. King Jehoiakim was so angered when the roll of Jeremiah's prophecies was read in his hearing that he cut it to pieces with his knife and burned it.

Zedekiah, the last king of Judah, recognized Jeremiah as a true prophet, and treated him with respect; but he was too weak to defend the prophet against the men who accused him of treason, so Jeremiah was persecuted terribly during the final siege of Jerusalem. His trials never ended with the fall of Jerusalem, for he was carried by force into Egypt by a band of Jews under Johanan, and his last days were spent in a vain effort to wean his people from Idolatry.

Tradition represents him as having finally suffered martyrdom at the hands of his ungrateful countrymen.

<u>**DATE**</u>: Approximately 585 BC.

THE HEART OF THE PROPHET:

More than any other prophet, Jeremiah gives us information concerning himself and the struggles through which he passed. He not only tells the story of his outer life, but lets us look into his heart and see what is going on within him. He records the cries of his soul, and lets us see his tears. When a beautiful vision of a brighter day comes to him by night, he tells us that his sleep was sweet to him. We hear his imprecations on his implacable foes, and the curse on the day of his birth. He hides nothing from us.

THE PERIOD:

Dark days in the Kingdom of Judah – from the thirteenth year of Josiah (the last good King) until some years beyond the captivity.

MAIN THEMES: The backsliding, Bondage and the Restoration of the Jews.

LIFE OF JEREMIAH:

Family. (Chapter 1:1)

Birth, and Divine choice as Prophet. (Chapter 1:5)

Youthful call – in the days of King Josiah. (Chapter 1:2-6)

Divine Endowment. (Chapter 1:9)

Commission. (Chapter 1:10)

Promise of Divine Presence. (Chapter 1:19)

Pressure of Duty. (Chapter 20:9)

Sustained by the Word of God. (Chapter 15:16)

Persecution of Jeremiah Predicted. (Chapter 1:19)

Put in Stocks. (Chapter 20:2)

Put into a Dungeon of Mire, without water. (Chapter 38:6)

Carried into Egypt. (Chapter 43:5-7)

SYNOPSIS:

1. **CALL OF THE PROPHET**. (Chapter 1)

2. **REBUKES, WARNINGS, AND PROMISES TO THE JEWS** (Chapters 2-20)

   a. Throughout Chapters 2-6, Israel and Judah are arraigned sharply for their many and grievous sins; warnings of the coming of fierce invading armies recur, and the prophet pleads with his people to repent. The sins, which receive chief emphasis in these early prophecies, are idolatry, which is spiritual adultery; brazen self- righteousness, oppression, covetousness and deceit. False prophets were misleading the people, and the priests were in leagues with them. These prophesies were made during Josiah's reign.

b. Chapters 7-20 probably come from the reign of Jehoiakim. The sermon recorded in 7:1-15 led to the arrest of Jeremiah by the priests and prophets, as recorded in Chapter 26. One of Jeremiah's heaviest trials was the command not to pray for his people (7:16; 11:14; 14:11). One of the most striking paragraphs is 7:21-26, where he taught that obedience is far more important than burn offerings. In Chapter 8:1 to 9:22, we learn that obstinate Judah must be punished by captivity, and Jeremiah is in great distress and sorrow for his people. Wisdom of knowing God is contrasted with the folly of idolatry (9:23-10:25). Judah is treacherous as Jeremiah's people seek his life (Chapters 11, 12). Two symbols – linen girdle and bottles filled with wine – show the fate of Judah (Chapter 13). A drought, Jeremiah confesses people's sins and earnestly intercedes for them, only to learn that not even Moses could save them from exile (Chapters 14, 15). Jeremiah is forbidden to marry because of the evils about to come upon the land; but there will be a better day for Judah (Chapter 16). Judah's sin demands exile (17: 1-11). The prophet prays for relief and safety (17:12-27). The meaning of the potter's handiwork (18:1-12) Jeremiah predicts exile, they threaten him, and he prays that they may be punished (18:13-23). He broke an earthen bottle as a symbol of the destruction of Jerusalem, and is arrested and put in stocks. He tries to quit preaching, but the internal fires compel him to speak, and he laments he was ever born (Chapters 19, 20).

3. **A DENUNCIATION OF RULERS, FALSE SHEPHERDS AND PROPHETS** (Chapters 21-23)

    a. These chapters possibly belong to the brief reign of Jehoiachin (598 BC), and contain Jeremiah's denunciation of false shepherds and his prophecy of the coming of a righteous ruler for Jehovah's people. He also attacks vigorously the prophets who speak pleasant messages.

4. **PREDICTIONS OF DIVINE JUDGMENTS, THE OVERTHROW OF JERUSALEM, AND THE SEVENTY YEARS OF CAPTIVITY.**

(Chapters 24-29)

    a. These chapters belong to the reign of Zedekiah (597-587 BC). Chapter 24 likens the captives in Babylon to good figs, and the folks in Jerusalem to bad figs. Chapters 27-29 insist that God means that Babylon shall rule the nations for a long time.

5. **PROMISES OF THE RESTORATION OF THE JEWS.** (Chapters 30-33)

    a. Of the reign of Zedekiah, they are full of consolation for Jeremiah and his people. Prophecy of the Jews' deliverance, and their ancient privileges restored in Chapter 30. Christ is promised, and His care for the church (Chapter 31:22-30). One of the most sublime prophecies of the Old Testament is that concerning the New Covenant (Chapter 31:31-34). In Chapter 32 Jeremiah is imprisoned, the captivity is confirmed, and the prophecy is made that the Jews shall be gathered back into Jerusalem. In Chapter 33 Christ is presented as the Branch of Righteousness.

6. **PROPHECIES OCCASIONED BY THE SINS OF JEHOIAKIM AND ZEKEKIAH.** (Chapters 34- 39)

   a.   Jerusalem is actually besieged (34:1-7), and the Hebrew slaves in the city are set free. But when the Chaldeans raise the siege to meet the Egyptians in battle, the slaves are put back to their tasks (37:1-10; 34: 8-22). Jeremiah's trials multiply (37:11-38:13; 39:15-18). Jerusalem is finally captured and destroyed (38:14-39:14). Zedekiah's sons slain before him; his eyes blinded, and Judah's nobles put to death; the people carried away captives to Babylon, including Jeremiah (Chapter 39).

7.   **THE WRETCHED CONDITION OF THE REMNANT LEFT IN JUDAH, AND PROPHECIES UTTERED TO THEM.** (Chapters 40-44)

   a.   In Chapter 40 Jeremiah is set free and returns to Judah. The Jews come to him. Ishmael kills Gedaliah, the appointed governor of Judah, and others. Jeremiah supported Gedeliah until he was assassinated; then, Johanan carries him into Egypt. There Jeremiah prophesies the conquest of Egypt by the Babylonians (Chapter 40). The desolation of Judah for Idolatry; their continued ignoring of God; Jeremiah's statement against them in Chapter 44.

8.   **CONSOLATION TO BARUCH.** (Chapter 45)

   a.   Jeremiah comforts him.

9.   **PROPHECIES CONERNING THE HOSTILE NATIONS.** (Chapters 46-51)

   a.   Overthrow of Pharaoh's army, and the conquest of Egypt by Nebuchadnezzar in Chapter 46. The destruction of the Philistines in Chapter 47. Judgment of Moab for sins, and their restoration in Chapter 48. Judgment of Ammon, Edom, Damascus, Kedar, Hazor, and Elam, and the restoration of Elam in Chapter 49. Certain destruction of Babylon, and the redemption of Israel in Chapter

50. Sever judgments of God against Babylon because of their treatment of Israel in Chapter 51.

10. A BRIEF HISTORICAL SUMMARY AND CONCLUSION. (Chapter 52)

THE MESSAGE OF JEREMIAH:

1. Some High Spots:

a.   The fountain and cistern. (Chapter 2:13)

b.   The indelible stain of sin. (Chapter 2:22)

c.   The search for a man. (Chapter 5:1)

d.   The old ways are best. (Chapter 6:16)

e.   The lost opportunity. (Chapter 8:20)

f.   The tearful call to repentance. (Chapter 9:1)

g.   The depravity of the human heart. (Chapter 17:9)

h.   The clay and the potter. (Chapter 18)

i.   The false shepherds. (Chapter 23)

j.   How to find God. (Chapter 29:13)

k.   The New Covenant. (Chapter 31:31-34)

l.   The mutilation of God's Word. (Chapter 36:21-24)

2. His Message Rejected:

a.   By his neighbors. (Chapter 11:19-21)

b.   By his own family. (Chapter 12:6)

c.   By the priests and prophets. (Chapter 20:1, 2)

d.   By his friends. (Chapter 20:10)

e.   By all the people. (Chapter 26:8)

f.   By the King. (Chapter 36:23)

THE VALUE OF JEREMIAH'S MESSAGE FOR OUR DAY:

Jeremiah helped men to see that the religion of Jehovah was not discredited by the destruction of the Jewish State in 587 BC; for it was Jehovah who gave victory to Nebuchadnezzar, his servant, and individual believers would worship Jehovah wherever they might go.

Jeremiah is the prophet of a spiritual religion that can dispense with sacred ark and temple. Jehovah will write his law in the hearts of his people.

Jeremiah also stresses the doctrine of individualism, and shows that Jehovah deals with each individual as a separate moral entity.

Jeremiah stresses that the kingdom of God is not destroyed so long as individual souls love and obey Him; that sin and disobedience result in individual and national bondage and disaster.

ALPHABETICAL ARRANGEMENT

All the chapters except the third contain each twenty-two verses, the number of letters in the Hebrew alphabet; the third chapter contains sixty-six verses, or exactly three times the number of any other chapters.

In the Hebrew, all these five poems, except the last are alphabetical; that is, the first letter in the opening word of each successive verse follows the order of the Hebrew alphabet of twenty-two letters. In the third chapter, *Aleph* is the first letter in the opening word of each of the first three verses, *Beth* is formed at the beginning of the second group of three verses, and so on to the end of the alphabet. Hence, there are three times twenty-two verses in this chapter.

LAMENTATIONS

AUTHOR: Not stated but traditionally attributed to Jeremiah.

DATE: The book was doubtless written soon after the destruction of Jerusalem by the Babylonians in 587 BC while the recollection of the horrors of the siege was fresh in the mind of the author

MAIN THEME: The book of Lamentations consists of five poems on the sorrows of captive Zion. Her grievous sins are confessed, and her miseries pathetically described, "and yet he presents this to us in so many lights, alludes to it by so many figures, that not only are his mournful strains not felt to be tedious reiterations, but the reader is captivated by the plaintive melancholy which pervades the whole."

SYNOPSIS:

Chapter 1:

The Departure of Judah. Zion's great sins. Judah has gone into exile. Zion rejected by God. O God, I am despised. Is any sorrow like mine? There is no one to comfort me.

Chapter 2:

The Devastation of Jehovah. Jehovah's anger against Jerusalem. The God has not pitied Jacob. The Prophet Describes Jerusalem's Destruction. The Lord has left his sanctuary. Young and old both got slaughtered in the streets. Zion Speaks Out: The Lord Destroyed Me.

Chapter 3:

Jeremiah expresses his feelings and hope. The Discernment of Jeremiah. He has driven me into darkness. But the steadfast love of the God never ceases. Let us return to the God! You will repay my enemies. The Prophet, A Man of Hope.

Chapter 4:

Zion Is Punished. The Discipline of Jehovah. The holy stones lie scattered. The children beg for food. Women boil their own children. The God has poured out his fierce anger. O Zion, your punishment will end.

Chapter 5:

The Deterrent for Judah. Look, O God, and see our disgrace! People's prayer for restoration. A Request for Mercy. We have become orphans. Slaves rule over us. But you, O God, reign forever. Restore us as of old!

EZEKIEL

AUTHOR: *Ezekiel,* which means "God Strengthens." Ezekiel was carried captive to Babylon with Jehoiachin in 598 BC. Five years later he was called to be a prophet.

According to the dates given by the prophet, his ministry extended from 593 BC, twenty-two years, or to the twenty-seventh year of the captivity, to 571 BC. Born of a priestly family, he never lost interest in public worship. In the restoration, as pictured it, the Temple was to have central place.

DATE: Approximately 590s – 570s BC.

COMPARISON:

This prophecy, like Daniel and Revelation might be termed a mystery book. It contains much imagery, which is difficult of interpretation. Nevertheless, many of its teachings are clear and of the highest order.

Ezekiel paints his pictures with much attention as to details, more indeed than any other Old Testament prophet. There is danger that the reader will become so interested in the details of the picture that he will fail to get the prophet's central message. For instance, the account of the living creatures and the wheels, in the opening chapter, must not keep one from seeing the likeness of a man on the throne above the platform; for this was the glory of Jehovah.

MAIN THEME: Though Israel is in exile, the Nation will be restored as God promised.

SYNOPSIS

SECTION I. The Preparation and Call of the Prophet. (Chapters 1-3)

1. Son of the priest. (Buzi, 1:3)

2. Carried away captive to Babylon. (1:1, 2 Kings 24:11-16)

3. His vision of God. (Chapter 1)

4. His call to be a prophet. (1:3)

5. His commission: Sent to rebellious Israel. (2:3)

6. Spiritual food. (3:1-3) (See Rev. 10:10)

7. His task, a Spiritual Watchman. (3:4-11, 17-21)

8. Ezekiel claims the highest degree of Inspiration. The words, "Thus saith Jahovah" are reiterated over and over throughout the book.

SECTION II. A Portrayal of the Apostate Condition of Judah before the Captivity.

1. Depicts destruction of Jerusalem by four symbols. (4:1-5:4)

2. Announces she is to be delivered to famine, sword and captivity because of her unparalleled wickedness. (5:5-17)

3. Announces impending disaster. (Chapter 6)

4. People are warned to expect the chain of the captor. (Chapter 7)

5. Jerusalem's guilt and punishment are described in a group of prophecies of the year 592 BC. (Chapters 8-19)

   a. In a trance, the prophet is swept through the air from Babylon to Jerusalem, where he sees all the abominations done in the city and the punishment about to fall upon it. (Chapters 8-11)

   b. He describes four abominations in the Temple. (Chapter 8)

   c. When the wicked are falling under the stroke of the destroyers, the prophet pleads for his people. (Chapter 9)

   d. Coals of fire are scattered over the wicked city. (Chapter 10)

   e. In the midst of denunciations of sin and sinners, Ezekiel again intercedes for the remnant of Judah. (11:1-13)

   f. The exiles may be despised by the wicked men in Jerusalem: but the time is coming when the faithful among the exiles will be brought back to possess the land of Israel. (11:14-21)

g. The prophet is brought back, in vision, to Chaldea, and tells his vision to his fellow exiles. (11:22-24)

h. Ezekiel continues his preaching against the sins of Jerusalem predicting its capture and overthrow (Chapter 12-19)

i. The prophet gives two signs of the approaching capture of Jerusalem. (12:1- 20)

j. He thunders against the prophets and prophetesses who daub with untampered mortar and hunt for souls. (12:21; 13:23)

k. Idolatrous Jerusalem is so wicked that its destruction is inevitable. The city is like a half-consumed vine – branch and a wanton harlot. (Chapters 14-16)

l. In connection with the riddle of the vine and the two eagles, judgment is pronounced on the covenant breaking Zedekiah. (Chapter 17)

m. The people are suffering for their own sins, and not for the sins of their fathers. (Chapter 18)

n. Next follows a lamentation for the princes of Israel. (Chapter 19)

6. **A group of prophecies from the year 591 BC** (Chapters 20-23)

a. For his name's sake, Jehovah has led Israel and will yet bless them. (20:1-44)

b. Fire and sword against Jerusalem, Ezekiel is commanded to sigh and wail because of the drawn sword in the hand of the King of Babylon. (20:45-21:32)

c. The prophet enumerates Jerusalem's sins that have brought judgment upon her. (Chapter 22)

d. Samaria and Jerusalem are vile harlots. (Chapter 23)

7. **In 589 BC the prophet announces the siege of Jerusalem has commenced**. His wife's sudden death, and the lesson of his strange conduct. (Chapter 24)

8. **Divine judgments upon the seven surrounding nations**. (Chapters 25-32)

   a. Anmon, Moab, Edom and Philistia. (Chapter 25)

   b. Tyre, the mart of nations. (Chapters 26-28)

   c. Egypt, the mighty. (Chapters 29-30)

   d. Assyria, the glorious. (Chapter 31)

SECTION III. Chiefly the Predictions and Promises concerning the means by which the glory of *the nation is to be restored* (Chapters 33-48). (After the fall of Jerusalem in 587 BC, when the Temple was burned to the ground, and most of the inhabitants of Judah were carried away to Babylon, Ezekiel's message became one of hope and consolation.)

1. By Heeding the Warnings of the Spiritual Watchman, and repenting of Sin. (Chapter 33)

2. By displacing the False Shepherds, and the coming of the Good Shepherd, who will feed the flock. (Chapter 34)

3. By a National Revival, and a Spiritual Resurrection in the Valley of dry Bones. (Chapters 36-37)

4. By the Overthrow of the Enemies of the Nation. (Chapters 38-39)

5. By the Building of a New Sanctuary. (Chapters 40-42)

6. By the returning of the Glory of the Lord. (Chapters 43:4, 5:44:4)

7. By the Ministry of a Loyal Priesthood. (44:9-31)

8. By Life-giving Waters issuing from the Sanctuary. (Chapter 47) (See Rev. 22:1-2) (The portions of the twelve tribes, Chapter 48).

OUTSTANDING EVENTS IN THE BOOK

1. The Departure of the Glory of the Lord from the Temple (10:16-18; 11:23)

2.   The fall of Jerusalem. (33:21)

3.   The return of the Shekinah Prophesied. (44:4)

KEY NOTE OF THE BOOK:

"I am Jehovah".

THE BOOK OF DANIEL

(Companion Book to Revelations)

AUTHOR: DANIEL. Captive in Babylon.

1. Brought before Nebuchadnezzar while young.

2. Trained in Chaldean language and sciences.

3. Career resembled that of Joseph.

4. Promoted to highest rank.

5. Maintained his spiritual life in midst of heathen court.

DATE: The period of the Babylonian captivity, approximately 605 – 539 BC.

MAIN THEME: THE SOVEREIGNTY OF GOD

1. Over affairs of men of all ages.

2. Pagan king's confessions of this fact constitute the Key Verses of the book. (Chapter 2:47; 4:37; 6:26)

SECTION I

LARGELY A NARRATIVE OF PERSONAL BRIOGRAPHY AND LOCAL HISTORY.

Refers to six Moral conflicts in which Daniel and his companions participated.

1. **First Conflict**

   a. Between pagan self-indulgence, and conscientious abstinence, in promoting health.

   b. Abstinence wins. (Chapter 1:8-15)

2. **Second Conflict**

   a. Between pagan Magic and heavenly Wisdom in interpretation of dreams.

   b. Divine Wisdom wins. (Chapter 2:1-47)

3. **Third Conflict**

   a. Heathen Idolatry arrayed against Loyalty to God.

    b.   Loyalty to God wins. (Chapter 3:1-30)

  4. Fourth Conflict

    a.   Pagan King's pride arrayed against Divine Sovereignty.

    b.   God wins. (King turned out to eat grass.) (Chapter 4:4-37)

  5. Fifth Conflict

    a.   Impious Sacrilege against Reverence for sacred Objects.

    b.   Reverence wins. (Belshazzar dethroned and Handwriting on the wall.) (Chapter 5:1-30)

  6. Sixth Conflict

    a.   Between Malicious Plotting and the Providence of God over his Saints.

    b.   Providence wins. (The lion's mouth stopped.) (Chapter 6:1-28)

SECTION II
VISIONS AND PROHECIES RELATING TO THE CONTROLLING HAND OF GOD. (Chapters 7-12)

  I. INTERPRETATION (Companion book to Revelation).

    1.   Both contain much Imagery, which is mysterious. Conflict of opinions in fitting prophecies of Daniel and Revelation into facts and events of human history.

    2.   True Interpretation not always clear.

    3.   TWO FACTS GENERALLY ACKNOWLEDGED:

      a.   That the Prophecies represent a partly veiled Revelation of Future Events in Secular and Sacred History.

      b.   That visions point to the ultimate triumph of God's Kingdom over all Satanic and World Powers.

  II. SOME FIGURES AND PROPHECIES

1. In Chapter Seven the four Beasts represent the Four Great Empires. Babylon, Medo-Persia, Greece, and Rome, followed by a vision of the coming Messiah.

2. In Chapter Eight another period of Medo-Perisian and Grecian history appears under the figure of a Beast.

3. In Chapter Nine is Daniel's prayer and a veiled prophecy of the time of the coming of the Messiah.

4. Chapters Ten to Twelve contain additional far-reaching predictions and revelations of future events.

    a. These three chapters have been the battleground of theological controversy with many varied interpretations.

HOSEA

AUTHOR: Hosea, the son of Beeri. (Chapter 1:1)
A contemporary of Isaiah and Micah. His message was addressed to the Northern Kingdom.
DATE: Approximately 750 – 722 BC.
SPECIAL FITNESS FOR HIS TASK

1. He is supposed to have been a native of the North, and was familiar with the evil conditions existing in Israel. This gave a special weight to his message.

2. It would appear from the narrative that he married a wife who proved to be unchaste. This statement is doubted by some scholars, but if true would have enabled him to vividly portray God's attitude toward Israel, his adulterous spouse. (Chapter 1:2-3; 2:1-5). But the style of the book is highly figurative, and it may be that this account of his experience with his wife was allegorical.

MAIN THEME:

1. Apostasy from God is Spiritual Adultery.

    a. God, the Husband. (Chapter 2:20; Isa. 54:5)

    b. Israel, the unfaithful wife. (Chapter 2:2)

SYNOPSIS:
SECTION I

1. ISRAEL'S APOSTASY

    a. Symbolized by the experience of the prophet in his marriage. (Chapters 1-3)

SECTION II

1. PROPHETIC DISCOURSES

    a. Chiefly descriptions of the backsliding and idolatry of the people mingled with threatening and exhortations. (Chapters 4-13)

    b. The formal call to repentance, and promises of future blessings. (Chapter 14)

ILLUSTRATION OF THE HIGHLY FIGURATIVE LANGUAGE USED TO EXPRESS THE EVIL CONDITIONS IN ISRAEL

1. The Valley of Achor for a door of Hope. (Chapter 2:15)

2. "Joined to idols." (Chapter 4:17)

3. "Mixed among the people." (No longer a separated and holy nation). (Chapter 7:8)

4. "A cake not turned." (Dough on one side expressing half-heartedness). (Chapter 7:8)

5. "Strangers have devoured his strength." (Weaken by evil associations). (Chapter 7:9)

6. "Grey hairs are here and there upon him." (Premature old age, and unconscious deterioration). (Chapter 7:9)

7. "Israel swallowed up." (National identity lost). (Chapter 8:8)

8. "A vessel wherein there is no pleasure." (A marred and useless vessel unto the Lord). (Chapter 8:8)

9. "The balances of deceit." (Commercial trickery in business). (Chapter 12:7)

THE BOOK OF JOEL

AUTHOR: Joel, a prophet of Judah, the Southern Kingdom. Besides the fact that he was the son of Pethuel, very little is known concerning him. (Chapter 1:1)

DATE: Not really clear on the date of writing. Possibly sometime before the Babylonian invasion of Judah 586 BC.

NAME: "Joel" means "Jehovah is God."

STYLE: The style is lofty; the book is forcefully and elegantly written.

MAIN THEME: National repentance and its blessings.

THE DAY OF THE LORD

1. **A TIME OF JUDGMENTS ON THE PEOPLE FOR THEIR SINS**

   a. The plague of locusts. (Chapter 1:4-9)

   b. The severe drought. (Chapter 1:10-20)

   c. The invasion of enemies. (Chapter 2:1-10)

2. **CALLS TO PENITENCE AND PRAYER.** (Chapter 2:12-17)

3. **PROMISES FUTURE DELIVERANCE.** (Chapter 2:18-20)

4. **WIL BE A SEASON OF GREAT REFRESHING**

   a. In nature, plenty of rain will insure abundant harvests. (Chapter 2:23-24)

   b. The outpouring of the Holy Spirit will usher in a great revival. (Chapter 2:28-32) (Refers to Pentecost. See Act 2)

5. **IN THE VALLEY OF DECISION**

   a. The Gentile nations will be judged. (Chapter 3:1-16)

   b. Zion shall receive a glorious blessing. (Chapter 3:17-21)

THE BOOK OF AMOS

AUTHOR: Amos, whose name means "burden" or "burden-bearer."

A citizen of Tekoa, in the tribe of Judah.

> A herdsman and dresser of sycamore trees. (R.V. Chapter 7:14)
>
> His call. (Chapter 7:15)
>
> The attempt to silence him (Chapter 7:10-13)

DATE: Prophesied during the reigns of Jeroboam II in Israel, and Uzziah in Judah.

Approximately 760s BC.

STYLE: Simple but picturesque.

The book abounds in striking metaphors.

Illustrations:

1. The straining of God's mercy by sinners compared to the overloading of a wagon. (2:13)

2. The pressure of duty upon the prophet compared to the roaring of a lion in his ears. (3:8)

3. The narrow escape of a remnant of Israel compared to a shepherd removing two legs or the piece of an ear from a lion. (3:12)

4. The scarcity of God's Word compared to a famine in the natural world. (8:11, 12)

AMOS, AS A PROPHET, WAS IN MANY RESPECTS LIKE CHRIST

1. In his occupation, a working man. (7:14)

2. In his humility, acknowledged his lowly origin. (7:15)

3. In his method of teaching by illustrations.

4. In his claim of Divine Inspiration, "Thus saith the Lord," occurs forty times in his prophecy.

5. In being charged with treason. (7:10; John 19:22)

6. In the pressure of duty, which was upon him. (3:8; John 9:4)

7. In denouncing the selfishness of the rich. (6:4-6; Luke 12:15-21)

MAIN THEME: Real religion isn't just ritual, but treating people with justice.

SYNOPSIS:

1. Impending judgments upon surrounding nations. (1:3-15; 2:1-3)

2. Threatening discourses:

   a. Against Judah. (2:4, 5)

   b. Against Israel. (2:6-16)

3. The call to Israel to seek God in sincerity. (Chapter 5)

4. Luxurious living condemned. (6:4-14)

5. A series of five visions:

   a. A Vision of the Locusts. (7:1-3)

   b. A Vision of the Fire. (7:4, 5)

   c. A Vision of the Plumbline. (7:7-9)

   d. A Vision of a Basket of Summer Fruit. (8:1-3)

   e. A Vision of a Smitten Sanctuary. (9:1-10)

6. The visions interrupted by an attempt to intimidate the prophet. (7:10-13)

7. The prediction of the dispersion and the restoration of Israel.

THE MESSAGE OF AMOS FOR OUR TIME

I. THE PROPHET'S WARNING (Amos 6:1-14)

1. v. 3. "Ye that put far away the evil day;" that is, you who fail to realize that what a man or a nation soweth, that shall he reap.

2 v. 4. You are idle and lazy.

3 v. 5. You are pampered and luxurious gluttons.

4. v. 5 Even your music is debauched.

5. v. 6. (See 4:1) You are drunken fops.

II. PROPHESIED RESULT OF THAT KIND OF LIFE

1. v. 7. The nation shall go into captivity.

2. v. 9. Death ("Wages of sin is death").

3. 7:7-9. Parable of the plumbline, teaching that the nation was out of plumb and would fall like a tottering wall.

4. 8:1-3 Parable of the basket of summer fruit, teaching that the nation was rotten to the core like over-ripe fruit.

5. 9:8-9. The nation to be sifted as grain in a sieve, the chaff to be blown away, but the wheat to be saved.

AMOS CURE FOR A SICK WORLD (5:4-9, 14, 15, 21-24)

1. vs. 4-6 "Seek Jehovah, and ye shall live."

2. v. 14. "Seek good and not evil, that ye may live."

3. v.15. "Hate the evil and love the good."

4. v.15. "Establish justice."

5 v .24. "Let justice roll down as waters, and righteousness as a mighty stream."

CONCLUSION:

1. Amos is rightly called, "The Prophet of Righteousness."

2. The world is sorely in need of such courageous prophets for our time.

BOOK OF OBADIAH

AUTHOR: This little book of one chapter was written by and called, "The vision of Obadiah."

DATE: Many believe possibly written thirty years after Babylon's invasion of Judah sometime in 586 BC.

THE PROPHECY: Centers around an ancient feud between Edom and Israel. The Edomites were descendants of Esau, and had a grudge against Israel a passage through their country during their "Wandering" following deliverance from Egyptian bondage. (Numbers 20:14-21)

The Edomites rejoiced over the capture of Israel. (Psalms 137:7)

MAIN THEME: Edom will suffer for participating in the destruction of Jerusalem.

SYNOPSIS:

1. The doom of Edom for their pride and wrong unto Jacob. (vs. 1-16)

2. The deliverance of the Chosen People, and the inclusion of Edom in the future kingdom. (vs. 17-21; Numbers 24:18)

SPIRITUAL LESSON:

God's special providential care over the Jews, and the certainty of punishment upon those who persecute them.

BOOK OF JONAH

AUTHOR: Jonah, a native of Galilee, and one of the earlier prophets. (2 Kings 14:25) Called to go as missionary to Nineveh, and warn the enemies of his country. He went with great reluctance.

DATE: Approximately 760 BC. Jonah prophesied during the reign of King Jeroboam II. 795 – 753 BC.

PROOF OF THE PERSON AND WORK OF JONAH

This narrative has been ridiculed as a myth by unbelievers, and regarded as a legend or a parable by some.

1. **Jonah is an historical character.**

   a. Was a native of Galilee, and one of the earlier prophets.

      1. 2 Kings 14:25: "He restored the border of Israel from the entrance of Hamath unto the sea of the Arabah, according by his servant JONAH the son of Amittai, the prophet, who was of Gathhepher."

      2. Jonah 1:1-2: "Now the word of Jehovah came unto Jonah the son of Amittai, saying, Arise, go to Ninevah, that great city, and cry against it; for me."

      3. Jonah was a prophet who lived during the reign of Jeroboam II in Israel, just before Amos and Hosea, or between 780 and 750 BC (2 Kings 14:25). Unlike those two prophets, however, he prophesied victory and prosperity for Israel. He was a supporter of the King.

2. **The person and book of Jonah**

   a. The Jews accepted as historical. (Antiquity, Book IX, 10:2)

   b. Jesus Christ vouched for their truth. (Matt. 12:39-41; Luke 11:29-30)

3. **Parables are never dated, nor proper names used.**

a. Christ gave forty-eight parables none of which were dated and named, and is as truly history as the life of Christ.

b. Jonah is both dated and named, and is as truly history as the life of Christ.

THE CHARACTER OF JONAH

1. "Sanctified in spots," a strange mixture of strength and weakness.

2. Self-willed. (1:1-3)

3. Godly. (1:9)

4. Courageous. (1:12)

5. Prayerful. (2:1-9)

6. Obedient after chastisement. (3:3-4)

7. Bigoted and selfish, and disappointed after the Ninevites repented. (3:4-10; 4:1)

8. Had too much concern for his own reputation. (4:2-3)

MAIN THEME: When God calls you to serve Him, don't try to run away.

SYNOPSIS:

Chapter 1 The Divine command evaded; the flight and punishment of the prophet.

Chapter 2 The Prayer and the Deliverance.

Chapter 3 The Second Commission Obeyed.

Chapter 4 The Childish Complaint of the prophet; the great exhibition of Divine Mercy, coupled with the rebuke to the prophet.

SPIRITUAL LESSONS:

1. The peril of running away from duty.

2. The temptation to selfish patriotism and religious bigotry.

3. The Divine employment of imperfect men as channels of Truth.

4. The wideness of God's Mercy.

THE BOOK OF MICAH

AUTHOR: Micah, a native of Moresheth, in Judah. He prophesied during the reigns of Jotham Ahaz. He was a contemporary of the Prophet Isaiah.

DATE: Approximately 700 BC.

MAIN THEME: Words of judgment and hope for Judah and Israel for their idolatry and injustice.

SYNOPSIS:

Chapter 1 The time when Micah prophesied. Samaria Doomed. Lord said, "I will make Samaria a ruin." The Enemy Approaches Jerusalem.

Chapter 2 Brutality of the Rulers. Woe to The Oppressors of God's People. A promise of restoring Jacob.

Chapter 3 Brutality of the Rulers. Israel's Leaders Denounced. The falsehood of the prophets. Zion's Destruction.

Chapter 4 Prophecy of the Millennial Kingdom. The Lord Will Deliver Zion. Lord said, "I will give you horns of iron."

Chapter 5 Prophecy of Christ's Birth. A Ruler from Bethlehem. The land to be cleansed. The Lord said, "I will punish the nations that did not obey."

Chapter 6 Jehovah's Controversy with His People. Brings A Charge Against Israel. Lord requires justice, loyalty, modesty. Lord said, "I will make you desolate for your sins."

Chapter 7 Desolation, But God Will Triumph. The church, complaining of her small number. God's Steadfast Love and Compassion. Micah's prayer and praise to God. God comforts by promises of confusion to enemies.

THE BOOK OF NAHUM

AUTHOR: Nahum. "The book of the vision of Nahum the Elkoshite." (1:1). Little else is known of him. His name means "Compassionate," or "full of comfort."

DATE: Sometime before the fall of Nineveh.

MAIN THEME: The Destruction of Nineveh.

HISTORICAL SETTING:

This book is regarded by some scholars as a sequel to Jonah. It would appear that the Assyrians, after their repentance at the preaching of Jonah, soon relapsed into gross idolatry. They plundered other nations; Nineveh, became like a lions' den full of prey. (2:11-12)

PURPOSE OF THE BOOK:

To pronounce Divine Vengeance upon the bloody city, and to console Judah with promises of future deliverance. (3:1; 1:13-15)

SYNOPSIS

Chapter 1 A vision of the majesty and invincible power of Jehovah, who will break the yoke of the Assyrians and deliver Judah.

Chapter 2 A dramatic description of the Siege of Nineveh.

Chapter 3 A woe pronounced upon the bloody city, and her complete ruin foretold.

PROPHECY OF MODERN AUTOMOBILE:

2:4. "The chariots rage in the streets; they rush to and fro in the broad ways; the appearance of them is like torches, they run like the lightning."

THE BOOK OF HABAKKUK

AUTHOR: Habakkuk. Nothing is known of the personal history of the prophet. Some have inferred from him Psalm Chapter 3, and the direction to chief musician, that he was a chorister in the Temple, but this is purely conjectural.

From a careful reading of his prophecies, we can get a distinct and definite impression of his great moral energy. He hated oppression and injustice, and longed for a more perfect understanding of Jehovah and His ways in human history.

DATE: The exact date is uncertain, but he certainly lived and labored in connection with the Chaldean invasion of 605 BC. Many scholars fix the time of the prophecy during the reign of Jehoiakim.

MAIN THEME: The Mysteries of Providence.

KEY VERSE: 1:3 "Why dost thou show me iniquity, and look upon perverseness? For destruction and Violence are before me; and there is strife, and contention riseth up."

SYNOPSIS:

The book opens with the prophet in perplexity over the mystery of unpunished evil in the world. The first two chapters are mainly composed of a dialogue between Habakkuk and Jehovah.

1. The Prophet complains to God that he sees sinful violence on every hand, yet no punishment is visited upon the evil-doers. (1:1-4)

2. He receives a reply revealing the divine plan of using the Chaldeans as a swift and terrible instrument of judgment upon the wicked nations. (1:5-11)

3. Still the moral problem is unanswered in the mind of the prophet.

    a. How can a holy God use these wicked heathen to waste and destroy people more righteous than they? Are wrong and violence to continue forever? (1:12-17)

4. The prophet ascends the watch-tower to look over the world.

a. He receives the reply of Jehovah, and is told the Purpose of God is soon to be fulfilled, and is encouraged to wait for it. (2:1-3)

b. Then follows the sentence that has been a watchword in the church. (2:4) "Behold, his soul is puffed up, it is not upright in him; but the righteous shall live by faith." (Quoted in Rom. 1:17 and Heb. 10:38)

5. Content with the new light received, the prophet utters a series of five woes against the awful sins of the great world power:

a. Woe against dishonesty. (2:6-8)

b. Woe against covetousness. (2:9-11)

c. Woe against building cities with blood and iniquity. (2:12-14)

d. Woe against the individual or nation that makes drunkards. (2:15-17)

e. Woe against idolatry. (2:18-20)

6. Finally, the prophet utters a sublime prayer (or psalm of praise) speaking of the majesty and glory of Jehovah and declaring his unwavering trust in the divine plans. (3:1-19)

NOTABLE PASSAGES:

Chapter 2:4_The Morning Star of the Reformation. (See Rom. 1:17; Heb. 10:38)

Chapter 2:14 The Triumph of Missions.

Chapter 2:15_The Woe to those who make drunkards, or even give their neighbor a drink.

Chapter 3:17-18 An All-Conquering Faith in spite of every adversity.

ZEPHANIAH

AUTHOR: Zephaniah. Evidently a direct descendant of King Hezekiah. (Chapter 1:1) Tradition says that Zephaniah was associated with Huldah, the Prophetess, and Jerimiah in the initiation of the reformation of the kingdom.

DATE: It is thought he uttered his prophecy near the beginning of Josiah's reign, before the religious revival, which swept over the kingdom of that period. (See 2 Kings, Chapters 22, 23)

MAIN THEME: The Searching Judgments of God.

KEY VERSE:

1:12 "And it shall come to pass at that time that I will search Jerusalem with lamps; and I will punish the men that are settled on their lees, that say in their heart, Jehovah will not do well, neither will he do evil."

CONTENTS: The book is exceedingly somber in its tone, and it is filled with threats and denunciations; but the sun breaks through the clouds in the last chapter, and the prophet foretells the coming of a glad day, when the Hebrews shall become a praise among all the people of the earth.

SYNOPSIS:

1. The announcement of coming judgments upon Judah. (Chapter 1)

2. The Call to Repentance. (Chapter 2:1-3)

3. Judgments threatened upon surrounding nations. (Chapter 2:4-15)

4. A woe pronounced upon the sinners of Jerusalem because of their corruption and spiritual blindness in continuing in wickedness, in spite of all the judgments meted out to the heathen nations (Chapter 3:1-8)

5. A universal judgment foretold, which only a godly remnant should escape. (Chapter 3:8- 13)

6. The future glory of Israel, when Jehovah shall deliver his people, and cause them to become famous throughout the earth. (Chapter 3:14-20)

HAGGAI

"The Prophet of the Temple" was reputed to have been born during the seventy years' captivity in Babylon, and to have returned to Jerusalem with Zerubbabel. He was a colleague of Zechariah. (Ezr. 5:1; 6:14)

MAIN THEME: Sharp rebukes for the neglect to rebuild the Temple, coupled with cheering exhortations and promises to those undertaking the work.

DATE: Sometime during the second year of King Darius (1:1) approximately 520 BC.

KEY VERSE: Chapter 2:4 "Yet now be strong, O Zerubbabel, saith Jehovah; and be strong, O Joshua, son of Jehozadak, the high priest, and be strong, all ye people of the land, saith Jehovah, and work: for I am with you, saith Jehovah of hosts."

HISTORICAL OCCASION:

The remnant that had returned from captivity were selfishly preoccupied with their own affairs, and were more concerned in beautifying their own dwellings than in rebuilding the Lord's house.

The work had ceased for years. (Chapter 1:4)

SYNOPSIS:

THE MESSAGE:

1. A cutting reproof, showing that God has withheld his natural blessings, because his temple was left in ruins. (Chapter 1:3-11)

2. Words of encouragement as the work of rebuilding the temple was resumed. (Chapter 1:12-15)

3. Inspiring promises to the older people who had seen Solomon's Temple, and were discouraged at the inferiority of the structure they were able to build. (Chapter 2:3)

4. A reminder of their unworthiness to erect a house for the Lord of Hosts. (Chapter 2:10-14)

5. Predictions of the doom of the heathen nations, and the words of commendation for Zerubbabel, as God's chosen instrument. (Chapter 2:20-23)

CHOICE SELECTIONS:

Divine Presence, strengthening. (v. 4)

Divine Power, moving. (v. 6)

Divine Glory, filling. (v. 7)

Divine Peace, coming. (v. 9)

MESSIANIC ELEMENT:

The Kingly Messiah:

    a.   First Coming in lowliness. (Chapter 9:9)

    b.   The Prince of Peace. (Chapter 9:10)

    c.   Crucified. (Chapter 12:10)

    d.   A Shepherd forsaken by his sheep. (Chapter 13)

CHOICE SELECTIONS:

1. *The secret of Success* in spiritual enterprises. (Chapter 4:6-10)

2. *The Coming of the Prince* of Peace. (Chapter 9:9, 10)

3. *The Fountain of Cleansing.* (Chapter 13:1)

ZECHARIAH

AUTHOR: Zechariah, son of Berechiah. (Chapter 1:1)
Little is definitely known concerning this prophet. He was a contemporary of Haggai, and joined him in arousing the Jews to rebuild the Temple of Jerusalem. (Ezr. 6:14) Evidently, he was a young man at the time of his prophecy. (Chapter 2:4) In the Septuagint version, several psalms are accredited to Zechariah and Haggai.

DATE: Two months after Haggai's prophecy (Compare Hag. 1:1 and Zech 1:1.) 520 – 475 BC.

THE PROPHET OF THE LONG VISION

Like Haggai, he saw the sinful condition and religious indifference of his people, and uttered stirring exhortations, which aided in the rebuilding of the Temple.

But his prophecy had a broader scope – he looked down the ages and beheld the coming of the Messiah king and the dawning of a brighter day for Zion.

KEY VERSES:

(1) Chapter 1:3 "Therefore say thou unto them, thus saith Jehovah of hosts: Return unto me, saith Jehovah of hosts, and I will return unto you, saith Jehovah of hosts."

(2) Chapter 4:6 "Then he answered and spoke unto me, saying, This is the word of Jehovah unto Zerubbabel, saying, Not by might, nor by power, but by my Spirit, saith Jehovah of hosts."

FUTURE HOPE: "At evening time it shall be light." (Chapter 14:7)

SYNOPSIS:

Opening Exhortation. (Chapter 1:1-6)

1. A Series of Eight Visions

   a. The Man among the Myrtle Trees, and the Drove of Horses. (Chapter 1:7-17)

   b. The Four Horns and the Four Carpenters. (Chapter 1:18-21)

    c. The Man with the Measuring Line. (Chapter 2)

    d. The cleansing of the High Priest. (Chapter 3)

    e. The Golden Candlestick, and the Two Olive Trees. (Chapter 4)

    f. The Flying Roll. (Chapter 5:1-4)

    g. The Woman in the Epha. (Chapter 5:5-11)

    h. The Four Chariots. (Chapter 6:1-8); the Crowning of the High Priest. (Chapter 6:10-15)

2. The answer to the deputation from Bethel concerning the fasts. In the end the fasts shall become festivals. (Chapters 7, 8)

3. Predictions concerning a period of the History of the Jews, and a vision of the Ultimate Triumph of God's Kingdom. (Chapters 9-14)

MALACHI

AUTHOR: Nothing is known of the prophet's life except what is found in his book. He was probably a contemporary of Nehemiah; the conditions described in the prophecy best answer to that time.

DATE: Approximately 450 BC.

MAIN THEME: A graphic picture of the closing period of Old Testament history, showing that great reforms were needed to prepare the way for the coming Messiah.

KEY TEXT: Chapter 3:8 "Will a man rob God? Yet ye rob me. But ye say, wherein have we robbed thee? In tithes and offerings."

SYNOPSIS:

1. **Dark side of the picture**

    The sins of a dishonest, ungrateful people, and an unfaithful priesthood.

    a. Robbing God.

        1. By failure to respond to Divine Love. (Chapter 1:2)

        2. By dishonoring God's name. (Chapter 1:6)

        3. By presenting blemished offerings. (Chapter 1:7, 8, 13, 14)

        4. The priests, by evil example, becoming stumbling-blocks, instead of Leaders, (Chapter 2:1-8)

        5. By honoring sinners. (Chapters 2:17; 3:15)

        6. By selfishly withholding tithes. (Chapter 3:8)

        7. By justifying impiety. (Chapter 3:14)

2. **Social Sins**

    a. Treacherous dealing with brethren. (Chapter 2:10)

    b. Inter-marriage with the heathen. (Chapter 2:11)

    c. Divorcing wives. (Chapter 2:14-16)

    d. Sorcery, impurity, oppression.

3. The Light side of the picture.

Glorious Promises

    a.   Of the coming of the Messenger of the Covenant. (Chapter 3:1-4)

    b.   Of the outpouring of a Great Blessing. (Chapter 3:10,12)

    c.   Of the saints becoming Jehovah's peculiar Treasure. (Chapter 3:16-18)

    d.   Of the dawning of a New Day in which righteousness shall triumph. (Chapter 4:2, 3)

    e.   Of the appearance of a Spiritual Reformer before the Day of the Lord is ushered in. (Chapter 4:5, 6)

GOOD NEWS BY MATHEW

AUTHOR: Mathew (also called Levi), one of the twelve apostles (Mark 2:14). Undoubtedly a Jew who was a publican, or Roman tax collector (Chapter 10:3). He made a great feast for Christ, who attended it despite the fact that publicans belonged to a despised class (Luke 5:29).

DATE: The Greek Letter of Mathew was written about AD 70, when Rome destroyed the temple in Jerusalem.

TO WHOM ADDRESSED: Primarily to the Jews. This view is confirmed by the fact that there are sixty-five references to the Jewish prophecies and about forty quotations from the Old Testament. Christ's mission to the Jews is especially emphasized. (Chapter 10:5, 6; 15:24)

KEY WORDS: "Fulfilled," which is frequently repeated to indicate that the Old Testament prophecies were fulfilled in Christ. The word "Kingdom" appears fifty times, and "The kingdom of Heaven" thirty times. Jesus as the "King" is stressed in Chapters 2:2; 21:5; 22:11; 25:34; 27:11; and 37:42.

PURPOSE: To show that Jesus of Nazareth was the Kingly Messiah of Jewish prophecy. Mathew is the most important letters ever written because it has exerted the greatest influence on the human race. The deity of Jesus is clearly shown, as well as his humanity. Frequently, quotations from the Old Testament show that the Life of Jesus is the prophetic picture of the Messiah.

In the writing for the Jews with a view of establishing the Messianic claims of Jesus we can understand why Matthew should give the royal and covenant descent of our Lord by tracing his genealogy to David, and Abraham. While Luke, whose design was entirely different, traced it to Seth and Adam.

PLAN OF THE LETTER: The plan of the Letter is largely topical, especially in the earlier portions. We have a group of miracles in Chapters 8 and 9, and a group of parables in Chapter 13.

There are extended discourses in Matthew; as, the Sermon on the Mount (Chapters 5-7), the controversy in the temple (Chapters 20-23), and the discourse on the Mount of Olives (Chapters 24-25).

The Letter opens with the legal genealogy of Jesus through Joseph, and the birth story is given from the standpoint of Joseph.

The ministry of John, the Baptizer, is given, with the baptism and temptation of Jesus.

Jesus' work in Galilee is given the chief place, next to the account of the events in Jerusalem at the close of the book.

Jesus rises from the grave, and sends his disciples forth to conquer the world for Him.

DISTICTIVE FEATURES:

1.   The Complete Genealogy of Christ. (**Chapter 1**:1-17)

2.   Incidents and Discourses found only in Matthew,

Chapter 2:

The visit of the Magi. (v. 1)

The flight into Egypt. (vs. 13, 14)

The slaughter of the innocents. (v. 16)

The return to Nazareth. (vs. 19-23)

Chapter 3:

The coming of the Pharisees and Sadducees to John the Baptizer. (v. 7)

Chapter 5-7:

The Sermon on the Mount (Complete).

Chapter 11:28:

"Come unto me, all ye that labor and are heavy laden, and I will give you rest."

Chapter 14:28-31:

Peter walking on the sea.

Chapter 23:

The denunciation of the Pharisees as an extended Discourse.

Chapter 26:15:

The thirty pieces of silver received by Judas.

Chapter 27:

The return of the thirty pieces of silver. (vs. 3-10)

The dream of Pilate's wife. (v. 19)

The appearance of resurrected saints. (v. 52)

The watch at the sepulcher. (vs. 64-66)

Chapter 28:

The bribing of the soldiers. (vs. 12, 13)

The earthquake. (v. 2)

The Great Commission. (vs. 19, 20)

3. **Miracles found only in Matthew**:

   Chapter 9:28-30, The two blind men healed.

4. **Chapter 17:24-27**, The tribute money.

5. **Parables found only in Matthew:**

   Chapter 13: The tares (v. 24), the hidden treasure (v 44), the goodly pearls (v. 45), the net (v. 47).

   Chapter 18: The unmerciful servant. (v. 23)

   Chapter 20: The laborers in the vineyard. (vs. 1-16)

   Chapter 21: The two sons. (vs. 28-32)

   Chapter 22: The marriage of the King's son. (vs. 1-14)

   Chapter 25:

   The ten virgins. (vs. 1-13)

   The talents. (vs. 14-30)

   The sheep and the goats. (vs. 31-46)

SYNOPSIS

I. LINEAGE AND BIRTH. (Chapter 1)

1. **Genealogy of Christ**. (vs. 1-17)

2. **Birth of Jesus**. (vs. 18-25)

   a. Conceived by the Holy Spirit, and born of the Virgin Mary.

   b. Prophetic name, "God with us." (v. 23: Isaiah 7:14)

II. SEARCH FOR CHRIST. (Chapter 2)

1. Wise men directed by the Star, edict of Herod and flight to Egypt. Herod slaughtered children under two years. Later, Jesus returned to Nazareth. Thirty silent years, except visit to Jerusalem at age twelve (Luke 2:46-52). Jesus a carpenter (Matthew 13:55).

III. JOH'S MINISTRY, BAPTISM AND TEMPTATION OF JESUS (Chapters 3, 4)

1. John the forerunner of the Messiah prophesied (Mal 4:5, 6; Isaiah 40:3). "Repent, for the kingdom of heaven is at hand."

2. John baptized Jesus.

3. Temptation of Jesus, three-fold:

    a. Through bodily appetite.

    b. Through his trust in God.

    c. Through his plans for dominion.

4. The proclamation of Christ. (Chapter 4:17)

5. Christ summoning followers. (Chapter 4:18-22)

IV. THE SERMON ON THE MOUNT (Chapters 5-7)

1. Laws and mandates of the kingdom (longest of Jesus' sermons)

V. WORDS AND WORKS OF JESUS (Chapters 8-13)

1. Miracles in Chapter 8: Cleanses the leper, healed centurion's servant, Peter's mother-in-law, and many others; stilled the tempest on the sea, drives demons out of two men, and permitted them to enter swine.

2. Miracles in Chapter 9: Heals sick of palsy, cures issue of blood, raised Jarius' daughter from the dead, gives sight to two blind men.

3. Christ sends twelve apostles with power to perform miracles. (Chapter 10)

4. John in prison, sends messengers to Christ asking if he is the Messiah. Jesus asked them to tell John of his works. (Chapter 11)

5. Jesus denounced Pharisees over Sabbath question, healed man blind and dumb, told of blasphemy against the Holy Spirit, spoke of idle words, and rebuked the unfaithful. (Chapter 12)

6. Parable in Chapter 13: The sower and the seed, the tares, the mustard seed, the leaven, the hidden treasure, the pearl, the net cast into the sea. (Likened to the kingdom.)

7. The murder of John. (Chapter 14:1-12)

8. Christ feeds the multitudes, walks on the sea and heals diseases. (Chapters 14:15- 15;1-39)

VI. <u>THE PERSON AND CHURCH OF CHRIST.</u> (Chapters 16-17)

1. Disciples rebuked for little faith. (Chapter 16:1-12)

2. The "Good Confession" of Christ's deity. (Chapter 16:13-17)

3. Promise of the Church. (Chapter 16:18-20)

4. His death foretold. (Chapter 16:21-28)

5. The transfiguration. (Chapter 17:1-8)

VII. <u>THE PERSON AND CHURCH OF CHRIST</u>. (Chapter 18-20).

1. Teaches disciples to be humble; the ninety and nine; how to deal with brethren and to forgive; parable of the unmerciful servant. (Chapter 18)

2. Heals the sick, teaches of marriage, blessed little children, Rich Young Ruler, asks people to leave all to follow him. (Chapter 19)

3. Parable of workers in vineyard, prophesies his passion, teaches disciples humility, and restores sight to two blind men. (Chapter 20)

VIII. THE LAST WEEK OF JESUS' MINISTRY

1. **SUNDAY: THE TRIUMPHAL ENTRY.** (Chapter 21:1-17)

   a. During the Passover week Jerusalem was crowded with strangers.

   b. Crowds gave Christ a great ovation, as He rode on a donkey, symbol of his reign, peace.

2. **MONDAY: BARREN FIG TREE: SECOND CLEANSING OF TEMPLE. (Chapter 21:12-19)**

    a. Jesus withered the barren of fig tree, symbol of city and nation.

    b. Cleansed the temple as he had done at the first Passover.

3. **TUESDAY: THE DAY OF QUESTIONS.** (Chapter 21:26-25:46)

    a. This was the last and greatest day in Jesus' ministry.

    b. Questioned by Sanhedrin about his authority; by Pharisees about the tribute; by Sadducees about resurrection; by Jesus himself about the Christ.

    c. Jesus matchless answers included three parables: The Two Sons, the Wicked Husbandmen, and the Marriage of the King's Son. Then he pronounced His seven-fold "woe unto you scribes and Pharisees, Hypocrites."

    d. Jesus gave disciples signs of His second coming and urged them to watch and be ready, illustrating with the parables of the Ten Virgins and the Talents.

    e. A description of the last judgment.

4. **WEDNESDAY: THE CALM BEFORE THE STORM**

    a. There seems to be no record of Wednesday's events.

5. **THURSDAY: THE LAST SUPPER.** (Chapter 26:17-35)

    a. The rulers conspire against Jesus, and Judas sells Him.

    b. Jesus institutes the Lord's Supper in the Upper Room.

    c. Prays in the Garden, is arrested and taken to Caiaphas.

    d. Peter denies Christ.

6. **FRIDAY: THE CRUCIFIXION**. (Chapter 27)

    a.   Christ is delivered bound to Pilate. Judas hangs himself.

    b.   Pilate, warned by his wife, washes his hands, released Barabbas and crucifies Jesus. He is buried, his tomb sealed and watched.

7. **SATURDAY: THE BODY IN THE TOMB**. (A dead Jesus – a live Devil)

IX. CHRIST'S RESURRECTION, APPEARANCES, AND COMMAND. Chapter 28)

1. An angel declared His resurrection.

2. Christ appeared to the women and to His disciples.

3. Disciples met Jesus on a mountain and worshipped Him.

4. Then, Jesus gave them the Great Command to evangelize and Christianize the nations of earth, and promised to be with them always, even to the end of the world.

GOOD NEWS BY MARK

AUTHOR: Mark, the son of Mary of Jerusalem (Acts 12:12). He is referred to as John Mark (Acts 12:25). He was a cousin of Barnabas (Colossians 4:10).

He was associated with Paul and Barnabas on their First Missionary Journey (Acts 12:25; 13:5). He went with them as far as Perga and Pamphylia when he deserted the work and went home. Paul was so displeased with Mark that he refused to take him along on the Second Missionary Journey when Barnabas urged it, and they separated. Barnabas took Mark with him to Cyprus, and Paul chose Silas with him to Syria and Celicia (Act. 13:13; 15:36-41).

Mark was later restored to Paul's friendship (II. Tim. 4:11). Ancient tradition states that Mark was a companion to Peter.

DATE: Possibly AD 60s, during the Roman persecution of Christians.

TO WHOM ADDRESSED:

Mark wrote his letter to the Romans, whose pact was power and action, and he presented Christ as the Son of God with Divine power and tireless action.

That it was not especially adapted to Jewish readers seems clear from the fact that it contains few references to the Old Testament prophecy. Also, the explanation of Jewish words and customs indicate the author had foreigners in mind when he wrote. (See Chapters 3:17; 5:41; 7:1-4; 11:34)

This is the earliest of our four letters and was probably written in Rome about AD 50.

MAIN THEME: Christ, the Son of God, with Divine Power and Tireless Action as the Servant of Man.

The life of Jesus is portrayed as crowded with benevolent deeds. His devotions interrupted (Chapter 1:35-37). No time to eat (Chapter 3:20). Accepting such perpetual calls for service that his friends said he was unbalanced (Chapter 3:21). Pursued when he sought rest. (Chapter 6:31-34).

KEY WORD: "Straightway," indicating immediate action, repeated throughout the book.

DISTINCTIVE FEATURES: It is the shortest of the Four Letters.

The style is vivid and picturesque. Much of the subject matter is found also in Matthew and Luke, but it is not a mere repetition for it contains many details not found in either of the others.

The Letter Mark opens, like that of John, with a declaration of the Deity of Jesus Christ, but unlike John, he does not enlarge upon the doctrine. There is nothing about the birth and childhood of Jesus, but a careful study of the Letter reveals the fact that the aim of the author is to let the wonderful works of Jesus testify to his Deity, rather than frequent statement of the writer.

MANY PERSONAL TOUCHES are found in this Letter as "was with wild beasts" (Chapter 1:13); "His surnames them Boanerges" (Chapter 3:17); "Jesus was much displeased" (Chapter 10:14); "The Common people heard him gladly" (Chapter 12:37); "Is not this the carpenter?" (Chapter 6:3), etc. **ALTHOUGH EMPHASIZING CHRIST'S DIVINE POWER**, the author often alludes to his human feelings: His disappointment (Chapter 3:5); his weariness (Chapter 4:38); his wonder (Chapter 6:6); his sighs (Chapter 7:34; 8:12); his affection (Chapter 10:21).

Matthew deals with the past, the Old Testament prophecies, to prove to the Jews that Jesus is the Promised Messiah. He also gives much space to the discourses of Christ.

Mark is more condensed; has little to say concerning prophecies; gives only a brief report of the discourses, but lays great stress upon the mighty works of Jesus.

NINETEEN MIRACLES are recorded in this short book, which demonstrate the supernatural power of the Master.
EIGHT, which prove his power over disease. (Chapters 1:31, 41; 2:3-12; 3:1-5; 5:25; 7:32; 8:23; 10:46)
FIVE, showing his power over nature. (Chapters 4:39, 6:41, 49; 8:8, 9; 11:13, 14)
FOUR, demonstrating his authority over demons. (Chapters 1:25; 5:1-13; 7:25-3-; 9:26)
SYNOPSIS
The book may be divided into six parts.

       PART I. THE INTRODUCTORY AND PRELIMINARY
       EVENTS leading up to the Public Ministry of Christ. (Chapter

1:1-13)

In this first chapter Mark plunges abruptly into his subject, and pours forth a torrent of description in the first thirteen verses.

He opens with the announcement that Jesus is the Son of God (v. 1). He then dwells upon the five preparatory steps for his work:

1. The coming of his herald, Joh the Baptist. (vs. 2-8)

2. The baptism of Jesus in the river Jordan. (v. 9)

3. The only manifestation of the Godhead (Trinity) ever to take place in human history
(v. 10). (The Son was baptized, the Holy Spirit descended as a dove, and the Father spoke. God never acknowledged Jesus as His Son until he was baptized.)

4. The divine witness of his Sonship. (v. 11)

5. His conflict of temptation with Satan. (vs. 12, 13)

PART II. THE EARLY GALILEAN MINISTRY (Chapter 1:14—Chapter 7:23)

Mark omits entirely the early Judean Ministry (See John Chapter 2:13 - Chapter 4:2). **Chapter 1:14-45** Christ preached, called Peter and others, and cures many people.

Chapter 2 Christ healed the man with the palsy who was let down through the roof, called Matthew, ate with publicans.

Chapter 3 Christ healed the withered hand, chose twelve apostles, refuted Pharisees claim that he performed miracles by the power of Beelzebub.

Chapter 4 Parables of the Sower, the Seed growing secretly, and the Mustard Seed.

Chapter 5 Christ cast out the unclean spirits from a Cardarene, and permitted them to enter swine; Jarius' daughter raised, also the woman with the issue of blood was healed.

GOOD NEWS BY LUKE

AUTHOR: Luke, the beloved physician (See Colossians 4:14). Also the author of Acts; both books being addressed to the same person, Theophilus (Luke 1:1-4; Acts 1:1).

Luke was a close friend and travelling companion of Paul as is shown in his personal allusions recording the journeys of the apostle. See in the book of Acts where the author changes the pronouns to "us" and "we," indicating that he himself was present at these times (Acts 16:10; 20:6; 27:1; 28:16).

DATE: Possibly the AD 70s – 80s as the good news was spreading throughout the Roman empire.

TO WHO ADDRESSED: The Letter of Luke was addressed to Theophilus, who Luke called "Most Excellent." And states that his reason was "that thou mightiest know the *certainty* concerning the things wherein thou was instructed" (Luke 1:4).

While addressed directly to Theophilus, Luke, himself a Greek, wrote to the Greek people. Their ideal was beauty, and Luke presents Jesus as the fulfillment of that ideal.

Luke wrote his Letter before he wrote the Acts, and after Mark wrote his Gospel. The Acts was probably written in Rome before 70-80s AD. It was probably written during the two years that Luke was with Paul in Caesarea (AD 57-59) when he had plenty of time to make the extended research of which he speaks in Luke 1:1-4.

PURPOSE: To give a connected and orderly narrative of the life of Christ as seen by eye witnesses. (Chapter 1:1-4)

KEY VERSE: Chapter 1:4.

IMPORTANT FACTS: Luke was a Greek, a physician, and a man of culture. He was the first scientist who confronted the facts of faith, and he shows the scientific temper and the historian's care, in his work combined with reverence and full acceptance of the mystery in Christ.

Luke portrays Jesus as the Christ and the Savior from the standpoint of the original sources.

Like Matthew he gives the birth-story but he gives it from the standpoint of Mary, from whom he probably obtained it directly.

Those who question or doubt the Virgin Birth of Jesus should learn that this supremely important fact was not reported by a lawyer, nor a scientist, nor a man ignorant of such things, but by Luke, the *physician*, and he accepted and vouched for the Virgin Birth of Jesus, together with all the other facts of the life of Christ, as he says after "having traced the course of all things accurately from the first." (Chapter 1:3)

Luke records the beautiful hymns of Elizabeth, Mary, and Zacharias, and through a Greek of the finest literary finish, he, in the first two chapters, preserves the Aramaic color of the story and style.

Luke was called a painter, and certainly drew the most wonderful pictures of the life of Jesus. Matthew is recognized as the most important book in the world, and Luke's Gospel is the most beautiful book in the world. It is the fullest story of Christ, and preserves a better balance for all the parts of his life.

Luke adds much new material for the last six months not found in Mark or Matthew. He gives us the most beautiful parables of Jesus that we have as in Chapter 14-18. He also records more of the miracles than any other of the Gospel writers, and is fond of medical terms and shows complete understanding and sympathy with the healing work of the Great Physician.

Luke also shows Christ's sympathy with sinners, Samaritans, and Gentiles, as the Savior of the whole world.

He pictures Christ as the friend of women and children and all the downtrodden and the poor.

The stories of the Good Samaritan (Chapter 10), and the Prodigal Son (Chapter 15) are the most beautiful and best loved stories in the world, and the walk to Emmaus, in Chapter 24, is the most wonderful experience in human history, and shows the charm and the power of the Risen Christ, the Son of God.

DISTINCTIVE FEATURES OF THE GOSPEL OF LUKE:

1. **GOOD NEWS OF THE IMMACULATE CONCEPTION AND VIRGIN BIRTH OF JESUS, THE CHRIST.** (Chapters 1:26-56; 2:1-20)

2. **GOOD NEWS OF ANGELS.** (Chapter 2:8-15)

3. **GOOD NEWS OF THE UNIVERSAL GRACE OF GOD.** (Chapters 2:32; 3:6; 24:47)

4. **GOOD NEWS OF "THE SON OF MAN."** It emphasizes Christ's sympathetic attitude toward the poor, the lowly, and the outcasts. The poor disciples (Chapter 6:20); the sinful woman (Chapter 7:37); Mary Magdalene (Chapter 8:2); the Samaritans (Chapter 10:33); publicans and sinners (Chapter 15:1); the deserted beggar (Chapter 16:20, 21); the lepers (Chapter 17:12); the dying thief (Chapter 23:43), etc.

5. **GOOD NEWS OF DEVOTION, ESPECIALLY EMPHASIZING PRAYER.**

    a. It contains three parables on prayer not found in other Gospels: The friend at midnight (Chapter 11:5-8); the unjust judge (Chapter 18:1-8); the Pharisee and the publican (Chapter 18:9-14).

    b. It contains Christ's prayers: At his baptism (Chapter 3:21); in the wilderness (Chapter 6:12); at the transfiguration (Chapter 9:29); before giving the Model Prayer (Commonly called the Lord's Prayer) (Chapter 11:1); for Peter (Chapter 22:32); in the garden of Gethsemane (Chapter 22:24); on the cross (Chapter 23:46), etc.

6. **GOOD NEWS OF JOY AND PRAISE, IN ITS EARLY CHAPTERS.**

    Some of the great Christian hymns are taken from the Gospel: "The Ave Maria," the words of the Angel to Mary (Chapter 1:28-33); "The Magnificent," Mary's song (Chapter 1:46-55); "The Benedictus," of angels (Chapter 2:13, 14); "The Nunc Dimittis," the rejoicing of Simeon (Chapter 2:29-32).

7. **GOOD NEWS GREATLY HONORING WOMANHOOD.**

    Women appear prominently Luke's narrative.

In Chapter One, Mary and Elizabeth; Mary and her sister Martha in Chapter Ten; the daughters of Jerusalem, Chapter 23:27; several widows are mentioned in Chapters 2:37; 4:26; 7:12; 18:3; 21:2.

8. **GOOD NEWS LIFE IN-SIGHTS FOUND ONLY IN LUKE.**

The Barren Fig Tree (Chapter 13); The Friend at Midnight (Chapter 11); The Good Samaritan (Chapter 10); The Great Supper (Chapter 14; The Pharisee and Publican (Chapter 18); The Piece of Money (Chapter 15); The Pounds (Chapter 19); The Prodigal Son (Chapter 15); The Rich Fool (Chapter 12); The Rich Man and Lazarus (Chapter 16); The Two Debtors (Chapter 7); The Unjust Judge (Chapter 18); The Unjust Steward (Chapter 16); The Unprofitable Servants (Chapter 17); The Wedding Feast (Chapter 12); The Wise Steward (Chapter 12).

9. **GOOD NEWS OF OTHER SAYINGS OF CHRIST FOUND ONLY IN LUKE.**

Christ weeping over Jerusalem (Chapter 19:41); reference to the conversation of Moses and Elijah on the Mount of Transfiguration (Chapter 9:30, 31); the bloody sweat (Chapter 22:44); Christ before Herod (Chapter 23:8); Christ's words to the women of Jerusalem (Chapter 23:28); the penitent thief (Chapter 23:40); the walk to Emmaus (Chapter 24:13-31).

10. **GOOD NEWS OF CHRIST'S BIOGRAPHY.**

The biography of Christ is more complete in Luke than in either of the other Gospels. About one half the material in this book is not in the others. Many of the most important utterances of Jesus, and striking incidents of his life are recorded in this one Gospel.

Examples of this are: The draught of fishes (Chapter 5:6); Raising the widow's son (Chapter 7:11-15); The ten lepers (Chapter 17:12); Malchus healed (Chapter 22:51), etc.

SYNOPSIS

(Since the events in the life of Christ have been given in full detail in the outlines of Matthew and Mark, a brief analysis is given here to complete the picture of our Lord.)

1. **THE INTRODUCTION**: Chapter 1:1-4. The birth of Jesus and incidents connected with his early life up to the time of his baptism and temptation (Chapter 1:5 to Chapter 4:13)

2. **THE BEGINNING OF HIS PUBLIC MINISTRY,** mainly in Galilee (Chapter 4:14 to Chapter 9:50).

3. **THE JOURNEY TOWARD JERUSALEM,** through Samaria and Perea; the ministry mainly in Perea (Chapter 19:29 to 23:55).

4. **THE LAST DAYS,** including the events of the Passion Week and the crucifixion (Chapter 19:29 to 23:55).

5. **EVENTS CONNECTED WITH THE RESURRECTION AND THE ASCENSION** (Chapter 24:1-

GOOD NEWS BY JOHN

AUTHOR: The Apostle John.

DATE: Around the AD 90s, as the last Good News (Gospel) written.

MAIN PURPOSE: To inspire faith in Jesus Christ as the Son of God.

KEY VERSE: 20:31 "But these are written, that ye may believe that Jesus is the Christ, the Son of God; and that believing ye may have life in his name."

DISTINCTIVE FEATURES:

1. Considered to be the deepest and most spiritual book in the Bible.

2. In it Christ gives a more complete revelation of himself and of God than in any other.

    a. Of his person and attributes see the "I am's."

    b. Of his divinity. (1:1; 10:30-38; 12:45; 14:7-9; 16:15)

    c. Of the work of the Holy Spirit.

    d. Of his own divine commission. (5:23; 24, 30, 36, 37, 38)

    e. Of the Fatherhood of God. Speaks of God as "The Father" over hundred times.

        1. Spiritual Father. (4:23)

        2. Life-giving Father. (5:21)

        3. Father's message. (7:16)

        4. Father greater than all. (10:29)

        5. Works of Father. (14:10)

        6. The indwelling Father. (14:23)

        7. Eternal Father. (17:5)

        8. The Holy Father. (17:11)

        9. The Righteous Father. (17:25), etc.

3. Over one half of the space in the Letter is given to events and sayings during Christ's last days.

4. Discourses and conversations found only in John.

a. Talk with Nicodemus. (3:1-21)

b. With the Woman of Samaria. (4:1-26)

c. Discourse to the Jews at the Feast of Tabernacles. (7:14-39; 8:3-58)

d. Parable of the Good Shepherd. (Chapter 10)

e. Series of private instructions to disciples, his comforting words and intercessory prayer. (Chapters 14-17)

f. Meeting with disciples at Sea of Galilee. (Chapter 21)

5. John records eight miracles of Christ to prove his Divinity. Six of these are found only in John:

a. Water made into wine. (2:1-11)

b. Healing Nobleman's son. (4:46-54)

c. Healing the man at the pool. (5:1-9)

d. The man born blind. (9:1-7)

e. Raising of Lazarus. (Chapter 11)

f. The second draught of fishes. (21:1-6)

6. There are two great currents of thought:

a. Faith. (3:16-18; 5:24; 6:29, 40; 7:38; 8:24; 10:37. 38; 11:25-27; 12:46; 14:12)

b. Eternal life. (3:15, 16, 36; 4:13; 5:24; 6:2; 11:26; 12:50; 17:3; 20:31)

SYNOPSIS

1. **THE PROLOGUE.** The eternal word incarnates. (1:1-18)

2. **MANIFESTATION OF CHRIST'S DIVINITY. Six-fold testimony:**

a. John the Baptist.

b. The Holy Spirit.

c.   The disciples.

d.   Christ's mighty works.

e.   The Father.

f.   The Scriptures. (1:10; 12:50)

3.   **PRIVATE REVELATION AND INSTRUCTION TO DISCIPLES.** (Chapters 13-17)

4.   **HIS HUMILATION AND INSTRUCTION TO DISCIPLES.** (Chapters 13-17)

5.   **THE EPILOGUE.** (Chapter 21:1-23)

GENERAL CHARACTERISTICS OF THE GOSPEL OF JOHN

1.   **Its relation to the Old Testament:**

a.   Matthew and others quote specific prophecies with external fulfillment.

b.   John quotes them to show their inner relation to Christ.

2.   **Revelation of character:**

a.   Types of personal belief and disbelief.

3.   **It is not a biography of Jesus:**

a.   John writes not of the actions, but the heart of Jesus.

4.   **The treatment of ordinances:**

a.   John does not deal with the Lord's supper and baptism directly.

5.   **It is the Good News of the Holy Spirit.**

6.   **It is the Good News of Christian unity.**

7.   **It is the Good News for Christians, and not for sinners.**

8.   **It is pre-eminently the Good News of Love:**

a.   Golden Text of the Bible is John 3:16.

JOHN, THE MAN AND THE APOSTLE

1.   Son of Zebidee and Silome.

2.   Cousin of Jesus and brother of James.

3. Youngest of all Apostles.

4. Was a fisherman, and had some property.

5. Was a Galilean.

6. Was one of Jesus' first disciples.

7. Was nicknamed Boanerges by the law.

8. His mother sought a place of honor in Christ's kingdom for him.

9. He followed Jesus to the Cross and cared for Mary.

10. After the ascension, he worked with Peter in Jerusalem.

11. Tradition says he went to Asia Minor and preached for many years.

12. He wrote Fourth Gospel, Three Letters and Revelation.

THE LETTER OF JOHN AS A PICTURE GALLERY

(This Letter presents a series of pictures, in each of which Christ is the central figure.)

Each of the twenty-one chapters contains a striking portrayal of some aspect of the character, or work, of the Savior.

In **Chapter 1** he is **THE SON OF GOD**, his deity is portrayed (v.1).

"In the beginning was the Word, and the Word was with God, and the Word was God" (v. 14) "and we beheld his glory, the glory as of the only begotten of the Father, full of grace and truth."

In **Chapter 2**, he is **THE SON OF MAN**.

Here we have a scene illustrating his perfect humanity. He appears as a guest at the marriage in Cana of Galilee. He mingles with men in their social activities.

In **Chapter 3**, he is **THE DIVINE TEACHER**, instructing a "master of Israel." Nicodemus says (v. 2), "We know that thou art a teacher come from God."

In **Chapter 4**, he is **THE SOUL-WINNER**.

Here we see the steps by which he led the darkened soul of the Samaritan woman out into the light.

In **Chapter 5**, he is **THE GREAT PHYSICIAN**, bending in compassion over the sufferers at the pool. He shows his divine power by the instantaneous cure of a hopeless case for thirty-eight years.

In **Chapter 6**, he is **THE BREAD OF LIFE** (v. 48).

"I am the bread of life." Without him the souls of men perish of hunger.

In **Chapter 7**, he is **THE WATER OF LIFE** (v. 37), satisfying the thirsty heart.

"Jesus stood and cried, saying, "If any man thirst, let him come unto me and drink."

In **Chapter 8**, he is **THE DEFENDER OF THE WEAK.**

Here we have a scene showing his gallant defense of a fallen woman taken in adultery and brought to him by the Pharisees (vs. 3-11).

In **Chapter 9**, he is **THE LIGHT OF THE WORLD** (v. 5).

"I am the light of the world." He demonstrates his right to this distinction by giving light to one who was born blind. (v. 11) He answered, "The man called Jesus made clay, and anointed my eyes, and said unto me, Go to the pool of Siloam, and wash: So I went and washed, and received my sight."

In **Chapter 10**, he is **THE GOOD SHEPHERD.** (v. 11)

He watches over "The Flock" with infinite care and gives his life for the sheep.

In **Chapter 11**, he is **THE RESURRECTION AND THE LIFE** (v. 25)

He proves his right to this title by calling Lazarus from the tomb. (vs. 43-44)

In **Chapter 12**, he is **THE KING.**

He rides into Jerusalem on Palm Sunday and is acclaimed king of Israel by the multitude. (vs. 12-15)

In **Chapter 13**, he **ASSUMES THE PLACE OF A SERVANT.**

Here we have the marvelous scene of his condescension, as he washes the disciples' feet. (vs. 4-5)

In **Chapter 14**, he is **THE CONSOLER.**

Although standing under the very shadow of his cross, in utter self-forgetfulness he comforts the sorrowing disciples. (v.1)

In **Chapter 15**, he is **THE TRUE VINE.**

(v. 1) "I am the true vine." Here we see him as the source of all spiritual fruit.

(v. 5) "I am the vine, ye are the branches: He that abideth in me, and I in him, the same beareth much fruit: for apart from me ye can do nothing." (This is used as a defense of denominationalism. Christ is the vine, and each individual is a branch – not churches)

In **Chapter 16**, he is **THE GIVER OF THE SPIRIT**.

On his departure, he promised to send the Comforter into the world. (v.7-15)

In **Chapter 17**, he is **THE GREAT INTERCESSOR**

He offers up his wonderful intercessory prayer for the unity of all his followers. (This 17th chapter is the real "Lord's Prayer.")

In **Chapter 18**, he appears as **THE MODEL SUFFERER**. (v. 11)

"Jesus therefore said unto Peter, Put up the sword into the sheath: the cup which the Father hath given me, shall I not drink it?" He submissively drinks the cup of woe pressed to his lips by the Father's hand.

In **Chapter 19**, he is **THE UPLIFTED SAVIOR**. (3:14)

"And as Moses lifted up the serpent in the wilderness, even so must the Son of man be lifted up." (v. 18) "Where they crucified him, and with him two others, on either side one, and Jesus in the midst." He becomes "obedient unto death, even the death of the cross".

In **Chapter 20**, he is **THE VICTOR OVER DEATH.**

Four times he met and conquered Death: First, at the bedside of the little maid (Matt. 9:24-

25). Second, at the bier of the widow's son (Luke 7:11-15). Third, at the tomb of Lazarus (John 11:43, 44). Fourth, he entered the very gates of death himself and came forth conqueror (John 20:11-17; Rev. 1:18)

In **Chapter 21**, he is **THE RESTORER OF THE PENITENT.**

He welcomes wandering Peter back to the fold and commissions him to feed the sheep and lambs (vs. 15-17).

ACTS OF THE APOSTLES

AUTHOR: Traditionally attributed to Luke, the beloved physician. He addressed both the third Letter and Acts to Theophilus (Luke 1:1-4; Acts 1:1).

DATE: Possibly written sometime between AD 60s – 80s.

FIRST BOOK OF THE NEW TESTAMENT: The four Letters are really a part of the Old Testament. Acts is really the first book of the New Testament because the Christian dispensation began with the events recorded in Acts.

MAIN THEME: History of the establishment and development of the Church from the Ascension of Christ to Paul's imprisonment at Rome, and the opening of his ministry there.

The departing Christ makes the announcement of a great campaign of world-wide missions, through human agency under the power and direction of the Holy Spirit. (Chapter 1:8)

SYNOPSIS:

THE BOOK MAY BE DIVIDED INTO TWO PARS:

1. The Period of Home Missions.

2. The Period of Foreign Missions.

I. THE PERIOD OF HOME MISSIONS, with Jerusalem as the center.

The work was mainly in Palestine among the Jews; the apostle Peter being the most prominent figure.

1. THE PREPARATORY EVENTS:

   a. The Divine Commission. (Chapter 1:4-8)

   b. The Ascending Lord. (Chapter 1:10-11)

   c. The Descending Spirit. (Chapter 2:1-4)

   d. The Workers' Equipment. (Chapters 2:4; 4:31)

2. THE MINISTRIES:

   a. Of Peter at Pentecost. (Chapter 2:14-40)

Peter's second sermon (Chapter 3:12-26)

   b. Of Stephen. (Chapter 7:1-60)

   c. Of Philip and Peter. (Chapter 8:5-25)

d. Of Philip. (Chapter 8:26-40)

3. FACTS CONCERNING THE CHURCH:

a. Established on Pentecost. (Chapter 2)

b. Growth of the church:

1. About three thousand charter members. (Chapter 2:41)

2. Daily additions. (Chapter 2:47)

3. Members increased by about five thousand men, not counting women. (Chapter 4:4)

4. Multitudes more added. (Chapter 5:14)

5. Great number of priests accepted Christ. (Chapters 6:7; 9:31)

6. Church established in Antioch with a great number as members (Chapter 11:21)

c. Characteristics of the church:

1. Christ founded it, built it. (Matt. 16:18)

2. Called the Body of Christ. (Rom. 12:5; 1 Cor. 12:27; Eph. 1:23; 4:12; Col. 1:24; 2:19)

3. Compared to a building. (1 Cor. 3:10; Eph. 2:21; I Peter 2:5)

4. Government of the church. (Acts 15:6, 28; 1 Cor. 7:17; 11:34; I Tim. 3:5; 5:1)

5. Christ, the Head of the church. (Eph. 1:22; 4:15; 5:23; Col. 1:18; 2:18)

6. Christ, the Bridegroom of the church. (Matt. 9:15; 25:1, 6; John 3:29; Rev. 21:2)

7. The Church as Bride of Christ. (Isa. 62:5; 2 Cor. 11:2; Rev. 19:7; 21:2; 22:17)

8. Members united with Christ in marriage. (Rom. 7:4; I Cor. 6:15; 2 Cor. 11:2; Eph. 5:30; I John 2:24)

9. Members compose the Family of God. (John 1:2; Rom. 8:5; 2 Cor. 6:18; Gal. 4:5, 6)

d. Special titles of members:

1. Children of God. (Matt. 5:9; Luke 20:36; Rom. 8:16, 21; 9:26; I John 3:10; 5:2)

2. Heirs of God. (Rom. 4:13; 8:17; Gal. 3:29; Titus 3:7; Heb. 1:14; 6:17; I Pet. 3:7)

3. Sons of God. (John 1:12; Rom. 8:14; Gal. 4:7; Phil. 2:15; I John 3:1)

4. Sons of Light. (Luke 16:8; John 12:36; Eph. 5:8, I Thess. 5:5)

e. The infilling of the church with the Holy Spirit. (Acts 4:31)

f. Unity and benevolence of the church. (Acts 4:32-37)

g. Spiritual power of the church. (Acts 5:12-16)

h. Appointment of deacons. (Acts 6:1-6)

4. **THE PERSECUTION OF THE CHURCH**

a. Acts 4:1-3, 17-22; 5:17, 18, 40; 6:8-15.

b. Persecutions under Saul of Tarsus. (Acts 8:1-3; 9:1)

II. THE PERIOD OF FOREIGN MISSIONS

Opening with Jerusalem as the center of operations, which was soon transferred to Antioch in Syria.

1. **PRELIMINARY EVENTS LEADING UP TO WORLD MISSIONS:**

a. The ministry of Philip in Samaria, in association with Peter and John. (8:5-25)

b. The conversion of Saul, who becomes the great missionary and the leading figure in the church during this period. (9:1-30)

c. The broadening of Peter's views by his vision at Joppa, resulting in his ministry among the Gentiles at Caesarea. (10:1-43)

d. The outpouring of the Holy Spirit upon the Gentiles at Caesarea and the vindication of Peter's ministry there. (10:44-11:8)

e. The sanction of the work at Antioch by Barnabas, the representative of the church at Jerusalem. (11:22-24)

f. The bringing of Paul from Tarsus to Antioch by Barnabas, and the cooperation of the two men in establishing the church in the place where the Christians were first called Christians. (11:25-26)

g. The persecution of the church at Jerusalem by Herod. The death of James and the imprisonment and deliverance of Peter. (12:1-19)

2. **THE EPOCHAL EVENTS IN THE HISTORY OF FOREIGN MISSIONS.**

a. Under the direction of the Holy Spirit, the sending forth of Paul and Barnabas as missionaries by the church at Antioch. John Mark accompanies them. (13:1-5)

3. **PAUL'S FIRST MISSIONARY JOURNEY.**

a. Missionaries: Paul, Barnabas, and John Mark. (13:4—14:26)

b. Places visited and outstanding events:

1. The island of Cyprus where the proconsul was converted and Saul's name was changed to Paul in the record. (13:4-12)

2. Perga in Pamphylia, where John Mark deserted the party. (13:13)

3. Antioch in Pisidia, Paul's great sermon in the synagogue. (13:14-41)

4. Opposition among the Jews and work among the Gentiles. (13:44-49)

5. Driven from the city by the Jews, the missionaries go to Iconium. Here they work for some time, but persecution arose, and they fled to Lystra and Debre. (14:6.)

6. The healing of the lame man at Lystra results in the people proposing to warn Paul and Barnabas, but the Jews stir up opposition and Paul is stoned.

7. Undaunted, the two heroes escape to Derbe, where they preach the gospel and teach many. (14:8-20)

8. From this point the missionaries retrace their steps, revisiting and organizing the churches, and return to Antioch in Syria, where they make a report of their journey. (14:21-28)

4. THE COUNCIL AT JERUSALEM

a. The question at issue. (15:5, 6)

b. Peter's argument in favor of Christian Liberty. (15:7-11)

c. Paul and Barnabas relate their experiences. (15:12)

d. The speech of James and the decision of the Council in favor of exempting the Gentiles from the rules of the ceremonial law (15:13-29). Judas and Silas are sent to Antioch to deliver the letter from the Council to the church (15:27-30).

5. PAUL'S SECOND MISSIONARY JOURNEY. (15:36-18:22)

a. PRELIMINARY EVENTS

1. Visitation of the churches of Syria and Cilicia. (Chapter 15:41)

2. At Lystra, Timothy joins the missionaries, and various cities of Asia Minor are visited, and the churches strengthened. (Chapter 15:41-16:5)

3. The Spirit guides them to Troas, where they are called into Europe by the Macedonian vision. (Chapter 16:7-10)

4. At Philippi, Paul and Silas are imprisoned and the jailor was converted, and a church established. (Chapter 16:12-34)

5. The next important event is the founding of a church at Thessalonica, where persecution arises and they depart for Berea. (Chapter 17:1-10)

   a. At Berea, the missionaries find some sincere students of the Word who become ready converts. (Chapter 17:11, 12)

6. The storm of persecution breaks out again and Paul goes on to Athens, leaving Silas as Timothy to establish the church in Berea. (Chapter 17:13-15)

7. At Athens Paul finds a city filled with idols, and preaches a sermon of Mars Hill, but secures only a few converts to the faith. (Chapter 17:15-34)

8. At Corinth Paul is soon joined by Silas ad Timothy, and a church is founded. The work is carried on in the midst of persecution for eighteen months. (Chapter 18:1-17)

9. After considerable time Paul bids the brethren farewell, and sets sail for Syria, making a brief stop at Ephesus, and closes his journey at Antioch. (Chapter 18:18-22)

6. **PAUL'S THIRD MISSIONARY JOURNEY.**
(18:23-21:15)

   a. PLACES VISITED AND OUTSTANDING EVENTS.

     1. Visitation of the churches in Galatia and Phrygia. (Chapter 18:23)

     2. Apollos at Ephesus. Knew only baptism of John, but was instructed by Priscilla and Aquila in the way of the Lord. (18:24-28)

     3. Paul returns to Ephesus and finds a group of John's disciples who knew only John's baptism. Paul preached to them Jesus, and they were baptized into the name of the Lord Jesus, and became Christians. (Chapter 19:1-7)

     4. Paul continues his work at Ephesus for two years. (Chapter 19:8-10)

     5. The Lord showed his approval of the work by bestowing upon Paul the gift of healing. (Chapter 19:11, 12)

     6. Sinners were confounded and burned their evil books. (Chapter 19:11-20)

     7. Then there arose a great uproar among the silver-smiths, fearing that Paul's doctrine would destroy their business of idol making. (Chapter 19:23-41)

     8. Paul leaves Ephesus, and after visiting the churches of Macedonia, comes to Greece. (Chapter 20:1, 2)

        a. He spends three months in Greece, then returns to Macedonia, and comes to Troas, and preaches. (Chapter 20:3-12)

     9. From Troas, Paul goes to Miletus, and sends for the Ephesian elders to come to him.

Here at Miletus he delivers his great farewell address to the elders. (20:17-38.)

10. From Miletus, Paul starts for Jerusalem, although warned by the Spirit of the sufferings awaiting him there. (21:1-17)

7. PAUL IN JERUSALEM AND CAESAREA:

a. He relates to the church the experiences of his ministry among the Gentiles. (21:18-20)

b. To silence suspicion, he is urged to take a Jewish vow, which he does . (Chapter 21:20-26)

c. Paul is seized by Jewish enemies in the Temple, and rescued from their fury by Roman soldier. (Chapter 21:27-40)

d. His defense before the multitude. (22:1-21)

e. He asserts his Roman citizenship to escape being scourged. (Chapter 22:25-30)

f. His appearance before the Sanhedrin. (23:1-10)

g. The Lord appears to him in the night with a message of cheer. (Chapter 22:11)

h. A conspiracy among the Jews to kill him leads to his being sent to Caesarea. (Chapter 23:12:33)

i. The accusation brought against Paul by the Jews, and his defense before the governor, Felix. (Chapter 24:1-21)

j. His speech before Felix concerning his faith in Christ. (Chapter 24:24-26)

k. His defense before Festus and his appeal unto Caesar. (Chapter 25:1-12)

l. His address before Agrippa. (Chapter 26:1-29)

8. PAUL'S JOURNEY TO ROME AS A PRISONER.
(27:1-28:16)

a. The first stage of the voyage. (Chapter 27:2-13)

b. The storm and the moral ascendency of Paul; his words of cheer and promise that none should be lost. (Chapter 27:14-36)

c. The shipwreck and the escape to land. (27:38-44)

d. The experiences on the Island of Melita: Paul bitten by a poisonous snake; Paul healed the father of Publius, the chief man on the island. (Chapter 28:1-10)

e. The arrival at Rome and Paul's ministry there: Paul was permitted to live alone under Roman guard; preached to Jews in Rome; some believed and others did not; he lived and preached there two years with all boldness. (Chapter 28:16-31)

ROMANS

AUTHOR: The Apostle Paul

ADDRESSED TO THE ROMAN CHRISTIANS:

The church in Rome was partly Jewish and partly Gentile. Paul takes occasion, since the Roman church had not heard his message, to give a fuller exposition of the gospel than he has done in any of his other epistles. Romans is the greatest of all his Letters.

It is not a treatise on theology and not a personal letter, but a powerful exposition, in argumentative form, of the great doctrine of the salvation of God.

His thesis is the revelation of God's righteousness with men in Christ by faith. He proves that both Jews and Gentiles fall short of God's standard of righteousness. He explains how Christ fulfilled the whole law and died for us as a propitiatory sacrifice, which is appropriated by us through that faith that obeys the will and commandments of Christ. He argues that Christ's work belongs to both Gentiles and Jews. He insists that we must be not merely legally righteous or justified, but actually righteous or sanctified (set apart) by the process of life Christ through the Holy Spirit. Paul admits that this is not possible in the flesh or by the law, but holds that the help of the Holy Spirit makes final likeness to Christ certain and sure. He says that the elect of God are those who believe in, and accept Christ, whether Jew or Gentile.

The doctrine of election or foreordination refers to classes and not to individuals. God foreordained his *plan of salvation*: That his son should be born of a virgin, live as a man, die as a sacrifice for all humanity, be buried and rise again, and ascend unto the Father: That all who accept Christ and live according to his teachings shall be saved, and their reward is heaven; that all who choose not to accept Christ and who live contrary to his teachings shall not enjoy eternal life. The decision is left to the individual.

Paul holds up the highest ethical standards of consecration and holy living (The 12th chapter). It is the greatest treatise in all of the Bible concerning human conduct, attitudes and relations.

He exhorts that the strong or more enlightened shall bear with the limitations of and prejudices of the enlightened, as in the matter of meats offered to idols and in the change from the seventh, or Sabbath day, to the first day of the week, or Lord's Day, as the day of worship.

DATE: Paul wrote this letter while he was in Corinth in the late winter or early spring of AD 57.

KEY VERSE: Chapter 1:16 "For I am not ashamed of the Good News: For it is the power (literally "dynamite") of God unto salvation to everyone that believes to the Jew first, and also to the Greek."

The Letter may be divided into two sections:

PART I. DOCTRINAL, Chapters 1-11.

PART II. PRACTICAL, Chapters 12-16.

MAIN THEME:

Part I. Salvation, justification and sanctification.

Part II.Exhortations concerning Christian living.

A MASTERLY ARGUMENT: In Part I, Paul points out three universals:
1. Universal guilt.
2. Universal tendencies to fleshly lusts.
3. Universal salvation offered to the human race.

KEY CHAIN: Showing the current of thought: Chapters 1:16; 3:22, 23, 28; 4:3; 5:1, 18; 9:31, 32; 10:3, 4, 6-9.

SYNOPSIS:

PART I. SALVATION THROUGH CHRIST
1. **THE NEED OF SALVATION**: Grounded in the universal guilt of mankind:

    a. Of the Gentile world. (Chapter 1:18-2:7) (This is the darkest picture of sinful humanity in all the Bible).

    b. Of the Jews under the condemnation of the Law. (Chapter 2:8 to 3:20)

    c. All alike are sinners (fall short of God's glory). (Chapter 3:23)

2. **THE METHOD OF SALVATION**: Righteousness by faith and obedience to Christ. (Chapter 3:21-28)

a. Universal. (Chapter 3:29, 30)

b. Honors from the law. (vs. 13-25)

3. **ILLUSTRATED IN THE LIFE OF ABRAHAM.** (Chapter 4)

a. Apart from works. (vs. 1-6)

b. Apart from ordinances. (vs. 9-12)

c. Apart from the law. (vs. 13-25)

4. **THE BLESSINGS OF SALVATION:** Made effective through the love of God as manifested in the sacrificial death of Christ. (Chapter 5:1-11)

5. **THE CONTRAST BETWEEN ADAM AND CHRIST.** (Chapter 5:12-21)

6. **THE MEANING OF SALVATION.** (Chapter 6:1-23)

a. The Christian must not continue in sin. (vs. 1, 2)

b. How one gets into Christ, and the description of New Testament baptism (burial). (vs. 4,5) (See Ephesians 4:5)

c. Union with Christ through baptism and the crucifixion of man's corrupt nature. (vs. 6-11)

d. A life of holy service to God. (vs. 12-23)

7. **THE STRUGGLE WITH SINFUL TENDECIES.** (Chapter 7)

a. Paul here vividly portrays the strife going on in the human heart constantly.

8. **THE SUPREME HAPPINESS, DIVINE COMPANIONSHIP, AND REWARD OF CHRISTIANITY.** (Chapter 8)

a. To those in Christ there is no condemnation. They enjoy a new spiritual life of liberty and righteousness.

b. This is one of the great spiritual chapters in the Bible. In it the Holy Spirit is referred to nineteen times.

c. This chapter closes with Christians as conquerors, and emphasizes that nothing can separate us from God's love.

9. **PARENTHESIS:** Paul's solicitude for his own people. (Chapter 9:1-5)

10. **GOD'S DEALINGS WITH ISRAEL.** (Chapter 9)

a. Special privileges of Israel. (Chapter 9:4, 5) (See also 3:1, 2)

b. The distinction between the natural and the spiritual seed of Abraham. (Chapter 9:6- 13)

c. The mystery of divine sovereignty. (Chapter 9:14-24)

d. The prophets predicted the failure of the Jews to live up to their privileges: The calling of the Gentiles and their acceptance of the divine plan of righteousness. (Chapter 9:25-33)

11. **THE MISAPPREHENSION OF THE JEWS.** (Chapter 10:1-3)

a. Their misunderstanding of God's plan resulted in their self-righteousness.

12. **THE UNIVERSAL OFFER OF SALVATION.** (Chapter 10:4-18)

a. Paul's passion for the lost. (v. 1)

b. God's righteousness through Christ. (vs. 2-7)

c. Faith and confession necessary to salvation. (vs. 8-11)

d. Christ is Lord of all, and must be preached. (vs. 12-18)

13. **GOD'S RELATION WITH ISRAEL.** (Chapter 10:19 to 11:12)

14. **THE GENTILES WARNED,** not to boast because of their privileges, but to take heed lest they fall under condemnation. (Chapter 11:13-22)

15. **THE RESTORATION OF ISRAEL**: Predicted and the mysteries of God's way were declared to be unsearchable. (Chapter 11:23-36)

PART II. PRACTICAL

Chiefly exhortations and instructions concerning Christian duties. (Chapters 12-16)

Chapter 12 This chapter presents the finest summary of Christian duties found in the Bible.

Chapter 13

1. Civic and social duties. (vs. 1-10)

2. The duty of living as "children of the day." (vs. 11-14)

Chapter 14 to 15:7 *Duties to the weak.*

1. Charitableness in judging. (Chapter 14:1-13)

2. Carefulness not to give offense to the weak. (Chapter 14:15-23)

3. Bearing the infirmities of the weak. (Chapter 15-7)

CLOSING THOUGHTS.

Mainly personal experiences and greetings.

Chapter 15, continued.

1. Reasons for thanksgiving on the part of the Gentiles and the Apostle's wide- spread ministry among them. (vs. 8-21)

2. Paul's desire to visit Rome and his greetings to the various Christian friends. (Chapter 15:22 to 16:16)

3. Final words and benedictions. (Chapter 16:17-27)

I CORINTHIANS

<u>**AUTHOR:**</u> Apostle Paul

This is the second of the four great doctrinal Letters and the fourth in the order in which the Letters were written. The first Letters being those to the Thessalonians followed by the Letter to the Galatians.

The group classified as the Doctrinal Letters consists of Galatians, I Corinthians, II Corinthians, Romans, and in that order.

The first letter to the Church at Corinth was written while Paul was at Ephesus. Corinth was the capital of the Roman province of Achaia. It was a commercial and wealthy city, and morally corrupt. Paul preached in this city for almost two years. The church consisted of Jews and Gentiles.

Paul had to contend with Judaizing teachers and tendencies in some of these churches. It will be remembered that he and Barnabas were sent as commissioners by the church at Antioch to the Council at Jerusalem, which was convened for the purpose of considering the standing of Gentiles and in the compromise he proposed. He had to deal with this same question in various churches and especially the Galatian.

The bigotry of the Jews and worldliness of the Gentiles of the Corinthian Church, disorders and dissensions called forth this letter. A denominational spirit had grown up in this church, the tendency being to select religious leaders, some choosing Paul, some Apollos, some Cepheus, and some clinging to Christ. This Epistle was designed to correct this error, which Paul does by declaring that there should be no divisions among them, but that they should all be one in Christ. (I Cor. 1:10-15)

Paul received word concerning disturbing matters related to marriage, eating of meat offered to idols, the Lord's Supper, the wrong attitude to spiritual gifts and the doctrine of the resurrection. These things are handled in Paul's masterly manner in this epistle. He puts the matter of eating meat on the high plane of Christian example and service. Mistaken views of the resurrection call forth the one great treatment of that essential doctrine. To those aspiring to certain gifts he points out what is far greater in the line of Christian graces, and the preeminence of Love, the greatest of all things.

<u>**DATE:**</u> Approximately AD 55 – 57.

HISTORICAL OCCASION:

The Church at Corinth was founded by Paul on his second missionary journey. It had become infected with the evils that surrounded it in a licentious city.

SYNOPSIS:

PART ONE: Main purpose: TO CLEANSE THE CHURCH.

1. **The salutation. (Chapter 1:1-9)**

2. **The need of cleansing the church. (Chapter 1:10-31)**

    a. From denominationalism, and divisions.

    b. From Man-worship (Paul, Apollos, Cepheus).

    c. From glorying in worldly wisdom.

3. **Paul's exemplary ministry.**

    a. There was no attempt on his part to display worldly wisdom but to declare the wisdom of God in a message revealed to him by the Holy Spirit. (Chapter 2:1-16)

4. **Divisions - a mark of carnality.**

    a. Strife and divisions over leaders is a mark of immaturity and carnality. (Chapter 3:1-8)

5. **The true view of the ministry.** Ministers should be regarded:

    a. As dispensers of the Truth. (Chapter 3:1, 2)

    b. As gardeners. (Chapter 3:6-8)

    c. As Co-laborers with God. (Chapter 3:9)

    d. As character builders. (Chapter 3:10)

    e. As stewards of the mysteries of God. ((Chapter 4:1, 2)

    f. As sufferers for Christ's sake. (Chapter 4:9-13)

    g. As examples for others. (Chapter 4:16, 17)

    h. As administrators of discipline. (Chapter 4:18-21)

6. **The duty of cleansing the church:**

    a.   From immorality. (Chapter 5:1-13)

    b.   From lawsuits before unbelievers. (Chapter 6:1-8)

    c.   Believers as members of Christ's Body, (the Church) and temples of the Holy Spirit, should purify themselves from all sensuality. (Chapter 6:9-20)

7. **Paul's opinions on marriage**. (Chapter 7)

    a.   Marriage should not be lightly dissolved.

    b.   Relations between husbands and wives.

    c.   Marriage of virgins.

8. **The right use of Christian ideals**. (Chapter 8)

    a.   Christian ideals demand the sacrifices of certain rights and privileges for the sake of the ignorant and weak.

    b.   We must not abuse our Christian liberty to the offense of people.

    c.   The eating of meat that has been offered to idols.

9. **Paul's personal sacrifice of material things**. (Chapter 9)

    a.   Surrendered certain rights and privileges in order to win men to Christ.

    b.   The minister should live by the gospel, but he ministered without worldly gain.

10. **Israel's example of infidelity**.

    a.   Their idolatry, fornication and temptation of God a warning to the church. (Chapter 9:1- 15)

11. **Fellowship at the Lord's Supper**.

    a.   Demands separation from evil associations.

    b.   Cannot be partakers of the Lord's cup and the devil's cup at the same time. (Chapter 10:16-21)

12. **The problem of Christian influence**. (Chapter 10:23-33)

    a.   Related to eating and conscience.

    b.   Christian influence to be guarded.

13. Social customs to be observed in matters of dress.
(Chapter 11:1-16)

14. Cleansing the church related to Lord's Supper.

    a.   Should show proper respect for house of God.
(Chapter 11:17-22)

    b.   Reviewed beginning of Lord's Supper. (Chapter 11:23-27)

    c.   Neither "open" nor "close" communion, but each must examine herself. (Chapter 11:28-34)

PART TWO: DOCTRINAL INSTRUCTIONS AND ADVICES.

1. Concerning the diversity of spiritual gifts. (Chapter 12)

    a.   Many gifts but all come from God.

    b.   Church is Christ's body and each disciple is a member of that body.

2. The pre-eminence of Love. (Chapter 13)

    a.   Greatest treatise on Love in all literature.

    b.   All gifts which men have is nothing without love in the heart.

    c.   Description of love and its characteristics.

3. The pre-eminence of prophecy over the gift of tongues, and the importance of maintaining proper order in church assemblies. (Chapter 14)

    a.   Prophecy is commended and preferred before speaking in tongues.

    b.   All speaking in tongues must be interpreted.

    c.   Concerning women speaking in church.

4. The doctrine of the resurrection. (Chapter 15)

    a.   The foundation of the Christian system.

    b.   Christ stands or falls by the resurrection.

5. **Closing instructions and salutations**. (Chapter 16)

    a.   Systematic, and individual giving.

    b.   Salutations.

II CORINTHIANS

AUTHOR: Apostle Paul

MAIN THEME: This is somewhat hidden, but it is quite apparent that Paul had prominently in mind the *vindication of his apostleship* when he was writing this book.

Both Letters to the Corinthians indicate that there was an element in this church, which tended to discredit his ministry and authority. This tendency is shown in the texts of the Key Chain below.

DATE: Approximately AD 55 – 57, shortly after his writing of 1 Corinthians.

CONTENTS: This is one of the most personal of all of Paul's Letters. He swells largely upon his own ministry. He opens his heart and discloses his motives, his spiritual passion, and his tender love for the church.

SYNOPSIS:

There are no definite division of thought in the Letter but the subject matter may be arranged under three headings.

1. **THE CHARACTERISTICS OF THE APOSTLE'S MINISTRY**

    a. Comforting. (Chapters 1:4-7; 7:7, 13)

    b. Suffering. (Chapters 1:5-9; 4:8-12; 5:4; 6:4-10; 7:5; 11:24-28; 12:7-10)

    c. Sincere. (Chapters 1:12; 2:17; 4:2; 7:2)

    d. Steadfast. (Chapters 1:17-19; 4:1, 16)

    e. Solicitous. (Chapters 2:3, 4; 7:7, 8; 11:2, 3; 12:20, 21)

    f. Triumphant. (Chapters 2:14; 4:8. 9:12, 10)

    g. Self-sacrificing. (Chapters 4:5, 11, 15; 5:13; 11:7, 9)

    h. h. Love of Christ the controlling motive. (Chapters 4:11; 5:14)

    i. Spiritual. (Chapters 4:18; 5:16, 10:4)

    j. Persuasive. (Chapters 5:11, 20; 6:1; 10:1, 2)

    k. Reconciling. (Chapter 5:19-21)

  l. Demonstrated by earnestness, afflictions, and good works. (Chapters 5:13; 6:4-10; 12:12)

  m. Authoritative, (Chapter 10:1-11)

  n. Self-supporting. (Chapter 11:9)

 2. Exhortations and Instructions concerning Benevolence. (Chapter 8.9)

 3. The Apostleship of Paul.

  a. **Discredited by one element** in the church. (Chapters 10, 1-10; 12:11; 13:3)

  b. **The authority of**, (Chapters 2:9; 13:2)

  c. **Authenticated**:

   1. By the Lord. (Chapters 1:1, 21, 22; 3:5; 6:4, 6)

   2. By unparalleled sufferings for the cause. (Chapters 6:4-10; 11:23-27)

   3. By wonderful revelations received. (Chapter 12:1-5)

   4. By mighty deeds performed. (Chapter 12:12)

CHOICE SELECTIONS:

 1. The ideal ministry. (Chapter 4:1-18)

 2. The triumph over death. (Chapter 5:1-9)

 3. The call to separation from the world. (Chapter 6:14-18)

 4. The list of sufferings endured by Paul. (Chapter 11:24-33)

GALATIANS

<u>AUTHOR:</u> Apostle Paul.

<u>DATE:</u> It is probable that the Letter was written from Ephesus in AD 49 as one of the Apostle Paul's earliest letters.

<u>TO WHOM ADDRESSED:</u> To the churches in Galatia, a district in Asia Minor, the exact boundaries of which are uncertain.

<u>MAIN THEMES:</u> A Defense of the Doctrine of Justification by Faith in an Obedience to Christ, warnings against Reversion to Judaism, and a Vindication of Paul's Apostleship.

<u>THE MAGNA CARTA OF THE CHURCH:</u> This Letter has been so called by some writers. The main argument is in favor of Christian Liberty in opposition to the teachings of the Judaizes. These false teachers insisted that the observance of the ceremonial law was an essential part of the plan of salvation.

<u>KEY TEXT:</u> Chapter 5:1 "For freedom did Christ set us free: Stand fast therefore, and be not entangled again in the yoke of bondage."

<u>KEY CHAIN:</u> Chapters 1:6; 2:11-16; 3:1-11; 4:9-11; 5:1-7; 6:15.

<u>EMPHATIC WORDS:</u> "Faith," "Grace," "Liberty," "The Cross."

<u>SYNOPSIS:</u>

THE EPISTLE MAY BE DIVIDED INTO FOUR PARTS:

PART I. The Salutation and Introduction. (Chapter 1:1-9)

PART II. A Narrative of Paul's Experiences in Support of his claim to true Apostleship.

1. The Good News that he preached came directly by revelation from Christ while he himself was a zealous Jew persecuting the church. (Chapter 1:10-16)

2. For years, he was away from the church at Jerusalem and labored independently of the other apostles. (Chapter 1:17-23)

3. He was under divine direction in his work among the Gentiles, and in the case of Titus, the Greek, had insisted that he could be free from the observation of the ceremonial law. (Chapter 2:1-5)

4. The church at Jerusalem indorsed his apostleship and worked among the Gentiles. (Chapter 2:7-10)

5. He had not hesitated to rebuke Peter, Barnabas and other Christian Jews when he saw that they were yielding to ritualistic tendencies. (Chapter 2:11-14)

Summary of Part I:

This Letter was written because of two serious defections that caused great disturbance in these churches. Judaizing teachers contended that the Gentile believers should submit to certain forms of Jewish legalism, and were thus alienating them from the true principles of the gospel. This was contrary to the teachings of Paul, and to undermine his influence they asserted that he was inferior to the other apostles in his assumed apostleship. That he was not one of the Twelve, and claimed that their doctrines were supported by the other apostles.

Paul vindicates his apostleship, declaring that he received his apostolic appointment directly from Christ. In support of this and as opposed to their contention is the fact that the Twelve, and especially Peter, John and James, the brother of Jesus, acknowledged his apostleship to be fully equal to theirs, and that he was the divinely accredited apostle to the Gentiles.

To save these Christians from the demoralizing influence of this Judaizing legalism, Paul announces and establishes the necessity of faith and liberty in Christ, and urges them not to be misled by these false teachers. He sets before them Christ and His redemption as the only way of salvation and urges them to stand fast in the liberty of the gospel.

PART III. Paul's Defense of the Doctrine of Faith and Obedience apart from the Works of the Law.

1. By showing the folly of Christian Jews abandoning their new faith and light, and returning to the old legalism. (Chapter 2:15-21)

2. By appealing to the former spiritual experience of the Galatians. (Chapter 3:1-5)

3. By showing that Abraham was an example of faith. (Chapter 3:3-9)

4. By showing that the law had no redeeming power but brought a curse upon the disobedient, from which Christ redeemed believers. (Chapter 3:10-14)

5. By proving that the law could not disannul the covenant of Christ, and relapse into legalism.

6. By indicating the purpose of the law as a tutor to bring us to Christ, and since He has come we are no longer under the tutor. (Chapter 3:19-25)

7. By showing the losses of those who surrender their faith in Christ, and relapse into legalism:

   a. They lost the blessing of their inheritance and Children of God, and return to the bondage of ceremonialism. (Chapter 3:26 to Chapter 4:11)

   b. They have lost the sense of appreciation for the labors performed on their behalf. (Chapter 4:11-16)

   c. They are in danger of becoming the children of Abraham after the flesh, instead of children of promise. (Chapter 4:19-31)

   d. They not only lose their spiritual liberty, but make Christ's sacrifice of no avail for them. (Chapter 5:1-6)

PART 1V. Warnings, Instructions, and Exhortations.

1. Warnings in regard to false teachers, and the misuse of liberty. (Chapter 5:7-13)

2. Exhortations concerning the spiritual life:

   a. The conflict between the flesh and the Spirit. (Chapter 5:17, 18)

   b. The works of the flesh, which exclude from the kingdom of God. (Chapter 5:19-21)

   c. The fruits of the Spirit, which should be manifest in Christian life. (Chapter 5:22-26)

3. The characteristics of the spiritual life:

    a.   The conflict between the flesh and the Spirit. (Chapter 5:17, 18)

    b.   The works of the flesh, which exclude from the kingdom of God. (Chapter 5:19-21)

    c.   The law of sowing and reaping holds good in the moral realm; that God is not mocked; that what we sow we also reap – to the flesh, corruption – to the Spirit, eternal life. (Chapter 6:7-9)

4.   The contrast between the doctrine of the false teachers and that of Paul. The former, glory in ceremonial rites and the marks in the flesh; the later, in the cross, and the marks of the Lord Jesus. (Chapter 6:12-17)

CONCLUSION: Paul's benediction of Christ's grace upon the brethren. (Chapter 6:18)

LETTER TO THE EPHESIANS

AUTHOR: The Apostle Paul.

DATE: Written at Rome between AD 60–64, toward the end of the Apostles life.

PAUL'S MINISTRY AT EPHESUS:

> His first visit. (Acts 18:12-21)
>
> On his second visit, the Holy Spirit is given to believers. (Acts: 19:27)
>
> His continuance of the work with remarkable success. (Acts. 19:9-20)
>
> His conflict with the silver smiths. (Acts. 19:23-41)
>
> His address to the Ephesian elders. (Acts. 20:17-35)

HISTORICAL OCCASION OF THE WRITING:

> The converted Jews in the early churches were inclined to be exclusive, and to separate themselves from their Gentile brethren. This condition of affairs in the church at Ephesus probably led to the writing of this epistle, the keynote of which is CHRISTIAN UNITY.

KEY VERSE: 4:13 "Till we all attain unto the unity of the faith, and of the knowledge of the Son of God, unto a full-grown man, unto the measure of the stature of the fullness of Christ."

MAIN THEME: THE UNITY OF THE CHURCH.

1. **The word "Together."**

   a. 1:10 "gathered together."

   b. 2:5 "quickened together."

   c. 2:6 "raised up together, sitting together."

   d. 2:22 "builded together."

2. **The word "One," indicating unity:**

   a. 2:5 "one new man."

   b. 2:16 "one body."

   c. 2:18 "one Spirit."

   d. 4:4 "one hope."

   e. 4:5-6 "one Lord, one faith, one baptism, one God and Father of all."

3. God's platform of unity. (4:3-6)

OTHER RECURRENT WORDS AND PHRASES:

1. "In Christ,." (1:1, 3, 6, 12, 15, 20; 2:10, 13; 3:11; 4:21)

2. "In heavenly places." (1:3, 20; 2:6; 3:10)

3. "Riches"

    a. Of grace. (1:7; 2:7)

    b. Of glory. (1:18; 3:16)

    c. Of Christ. (3:8)

SYNOPSIS:

PART ONE: SALVATION

Chapter 1

1. The salutation. (vs. 1, 2)

2. The divine origin of the church. (vs. 3-6)

3. Salvation:

    a. Through the redemptive work of Christ. (vs. 7, 8)

    b. Universal in its scope. (vs. 9, 10)

    c. Insuring a rich spiritual inheritance. (vs. 11-14)

    d. Prayer that believers might be fully enlightened as to the riches of its provisions. (vs. 15-23)

Chapter 2

1. Salvation provides for a spiritual resurrection from sin and the exaltation of the believer into heavenly places. (1-6)

2. Salvation is the gift of God; not of men. (7-10)

3. It embraces the Gentiles who were far from God, but were brought near by the blood of Christ. (11-13)

4. It removes all barriers between Jews and Gentiles and unites them into one body for the indwelling of the Holy Spirit. (14-22)

Chapter 3

1. The mysteries of the divine purpose revealed to Paul, and his appointment as apostles to the Gentiles. (1-12)

2. Paul's second prayer for the spiritual fullness of the church and her enlightenment concerning the matchless love of Christ. (14-21)

PART TWO: PRACTICAL APPLICATION
What the divine plan calls for on the part of the church.
Chapter 4

1. **The Unity of Believers**

   a. In Spirit. (vs. 1-3)

   b. God's seven unities. (vs. 4-6)

   c. Diversity of gifts but unity in the one Body of Christ. (vs. 7-16)

2. **Consistent Christian Life and Walk:**

   a. Not as sinful people. (vs. 17-21)

   b. In newness of life, abandoning old sins. (vs. 22-32)

Chapter 5

   c. Walking in love and purity. (vs. 1-7)

   d. Walking in the light. (vs. 8-14.)

   e. Walking circumspectly, filled with the Spirit. (vs. 15-21)

3. **The Home Life.**

   a. Duties of husbands and wives. (vs. 22-33)

Chapter 6

   b. Duties of children, fathers, servants and masters. (vs. 1-9)

4. **The Spiritual Warfare**

   a. Source of strength, the Lord. (vs. 10)

   b. The armor and the foes. (vs. 11-18)

5. **Concluding words and benediction.** (vs. 19-24)

CHOICE SELECTIONS:

1. Paul's prayers for the church. (1:16-23; 3:14-21)

2. God's plan for Christian Unity. (4:3-6)

3. The Spiritual Armor. (6:10-17)

LETTER TO THE PHILLIPPIANS

AUTHOR: The Apostle Paul.

DATE: Written at Rome between AD 60–64.

THE CHURCH:

Philippi was the first European city that heard Christian preaching, and the Philippian Church was an ideal one in many respects. It was very appreciative and benevolent.

It was founded by Paul on his second missionary journey, in the midst of a storm of persecution. The beginnings of the work were small, among a few women at the riverside. Lydia, a seller of purple, was the first in Europe to become a Christian. She was soon joined by the Philippian jailor and his family. These and perhaps a few others became the nucleus of the Church. (Acts 16:12-40)

CHARACTERISTICS OF THE LETTER:

It is a spiritual love letter to the church.

It contains outbursts of warm affection and gratitude. Written under hard circumstances while Paul was a prisoner. He strikes the keynotes of victory and joy.

SYNOPSIS:

THINGS IN WHICH PAUL REJOICED:

1. In prayer. (1:4)

2. In the gospel. (1:18)

3. In Christian fellowship. (2:1, 2)

4. In sacrifices for the cause. (2:17, 18)

5. In the Lord. (3:1)

6. For the loving care of the Church. (4:10)

CENTRAL MESSAGE: JESUS CHRIST.

Chapter 1

1. As the Source of spiritual fruit. (vs. 11)

2. As the theme of preaching. (vs. 18)

3. As the highest motive of Christian service. (vs. 20, 21)

Chapter 2

1. As exhibiting the only perfect spirit and example. (vs. 5-11)

Chapter 3

1. The knowledge of whom is the supreme prize for which to struggle in life. (vs. 7- 14)

2. At whose appearing believers' bodies shall be fashioned anew. (vs. 20, 21)

Chapter 4

1. Whose power is limitless in Christian lives. (vs. 13)

2. Who is the channel of divine supplies for every need. (vs. 19)

LETTER TO THE COLOSSIANS

<u>AUTHOR:</u> The Apostle Paul

<u>DATE:</u> Possibly early AD 60s.

<u>TO WHOM ADDRESSED:</u> The Church at Colosse, a city in Asia Minor.

PURPOSE:

1. General: A message of good will, to exhort and strengthen the believers.

1. Special: To counteract doctrinal errors growing out of the mixture of Judaistic teaching, combined with oriental and philosophic speculation. These heresies tended to obscure the divine glory of Christ.

<u>CHARACTERISTICS:</u>

The letter resembles Paul's letter to the Ephesians both in language and thought, yet has a distinct message of its own. In Ephesians Paul swells upon the thought of the *Church and the Body of Christ* while in Colossians he emphasizes *Christ as the Head of the Church.*

The warning against trusting in worldly wisdom, which appears in I Corinthians, reappears in Colossians.

<u>SYNOPSIS:</u>

<u>PART I:</u>

Chapter 1

1. The apostolic greeting and commendation. (vs. 1-8)

2. The prayer for the church.

   a. That it might be filled with wisdom, fruitful in good works, and strengthened with divine power. (vs. 9-11)

   b. Thanksgiving for the spiritual inheritance, the great deliverance and redemption from sins. (vs. 12-14)

PART II. THE DOCTRINAL SECTION.

Main Theme: The glory of the person and work of Christ.

Chapter 1

1. **His glorious preeminence**.

    a. As the image of God. (vs. 15)

    b. The creator of all things. (v. 16)

    c. His pre-existence. (vs. 17)

    d. As head of the church. (vs. 18)

    e. His divine fullness. (vs. 19)

    f. His reconciling work. (vs. 20-23)

    g. The mystery of his indwelling in believers proclaimed by Paul's ministry. (vs. 24-29)

Chapter 2

2. **Paul's anxiety about the state of the church.**

    a. That the members might be united in love, having a fuller understanding of the spiritual mysteries of the Father and of Christ. (vs. 1-3)

    b. He warns against false doctrine and urges steadfast faith in Christ.
(vs. 4-7)

PART III. DOCTRINAL ARGUMENTS

Chapter 2.

1. **The peril of worldly philosophy and legalism.**

FIRST LETTER TO THE THESSALONIANS

AUTHOR: The apostle Paul, joined in his salutation by Silvanus and Timothy (1:1), and with specific mention of his name again later in the epistle (2:18). Early sources in church history that attribute this letter to Paul include: Clement of Alexandria (200 AD), Tertullian (200 AD), and Irenaeus (200 AD).

DATE: It appears that the Apostle Paul wrote this letter soon after arriving in Corinth on his second journey. This would put it early AD 50s.

THE CHURCH AT THESSALONICA:

The establishment of the church is recorded in Act 17:1-9. On his second missionary journey, Paul and his companions (Silas and Timothy) had just left Philippi and passed through Amphipolis and Apollonia to arrive at Thessalonica. As was his custom, Paul immediately located the synagogue and reasoned with the Jews for three Sabbaths concerning Jesus Christ. While some of them were persuaded, including a great number of devout Greeks and leading women, the unbelieving Jews became jealous and created an uproar in the city. Therefore, it became necessary to send Paul and Silas away secretly by night to Berea. Despite such ominous beginnings, a strong church was established in Thessalonica (cf. 1:2-10). Mostly Gentile (cf. 1:9), its members Included Jason (Act 17:9), Aristarchus, and Secundus (Act 20:4).

HISTORICAL OCCASION OF THE WRITING:

The abrupt departure from Thessalonica so soon after the beginning of the church naturally left Paul anxious about the condition of the brethren. When Timothy joined Paul at Athens (cf. Act 17:14-16), his concern prompted Paul to send Timothy at once back to Thessalonica to encourage and ground the new disciples in the faith, and to learn how they were enduring persecution (cf. 3:1-5).

When Timothy returned to Paul in Corinth (cf. Act 18:5), the news was mostly encouraging (cf. 3:6-7). Despite persecution they had remained strong (2:13-16), and even proved themselves to be an example to others (1:6-8). Yet, as with any young church, they needed further instruction concerning holy living (cf. 4:1-12). They also needed to be reassured that their loved ones who died in Christ would not miss out on the blessings involving the coming of our Lord (cf. 4:13-18). Therefore, we can summarize by saying that Paul's purpose in writing was:

   * To instruct the congregation on what disciplinary action to take toward those who refused to work.

THEME OF LETTER: In correcting their misunderstanding about the return of Christ, Paul explains that the Lord will not come right away.

SYNOPSIS:

Chapter I

PART I:

A. **SALUTATION** (1)

1. From Paul, Silvanus, and Timothy. (1a)

2. To the church of the Thessalonians in God the Father and the Lord Jesus Christ. (1b)

3. Grace and peace from God and Jesus. (1c)

B. **THANKSGIVING** (2-4)

1. 1. Offered to God on their behalf, making mention of them in his prayers. (2)

2. Mindful always of their:

   a. Work of faith.

   b. Labor of love.

   c. Patience of hope in the Lord Jesus Christ ... in the sight of our God and Father. (3)

3. Knowing their election by God. (4)

II. **REFLECTIONS REGARDING THEIR CONDITION** (1:5-10)

A. **THEIR RECEPTION OF THE GOSPEL** (5-7)

1. The gospel came to them not only in word, but ...

   a. In power,

   b. In the Holy Spirit,

   c. In much assurance,

   ... for they knew what kind of men Paul and his

companions had been for their sakes while with them. (5)

2. They had become followers of Paul and of the Lord, having received the word ...

    a. In much affliction (6a),

    b. With joy of the Holy Spirit (6b).

3. They had become examples to the believers in Macedonia and Achaia. (7)

B. **THEIR REPUTATION IN EVERY PLACE** (8-10)

1. For them the word of the Lord had sounded forth in Macedonia, Achaia, and beyond. (8a)

2. Their faith toward God had gone out, so Paul did not need to say anything (8b)

3. Others were telling Paul ...

    a. What manner of entry Paul had to them (9a),

    b. How they had turned from idols to serve the living and true God (9b),

    c. How they were waiting for the resurrected Jesus to return from heaven, who delivers from the wrath to come (10).

Chapter 2

I. REFLECTIONS REGARDING HIS CONDUCT (1-12)

A. THE MANNER OF HIS PREACHING (1-8)

1. Not in vain, but with boldness in the midst of abuse. (1-2)

2. Not in deceit, impurity, or guile, but as pleasing God. (3-4)

3. Not with flattery, covetousness, nor seeking glory from men by making demands as apostles of Christ. (5-6)

    4.   As a nursing mother, with gentleness and affection he imparted   not only the gospel but his own life as well. (7-8)

B. THE MANNER OF HIS LIFE (9-12)

    1.   Worked night and day, so as not to be burdened while preaching the gospel. (9)

    2.   Behaved in a devout, just, and blameless manner. (10)

    3.   As a father would his own children, he exhorted and comforted them, encouraging them to walk worthy of God who calls them into His kingdom. (11-12)

II. REFLECTIONS REGARDING HIS CONCERN (13-20)

A. THANKFUL FOR THEIR RECEPTION OF THE WORD (13-16)

    1.   They received his message as it was in truth, the word of God, which works effectively in those who believe. (13)

    2.   They became imitators of the churches in Judea. (14-16)

        a.   Suffering persecution from their ow countrymen. (14a)

        b.   Just as those in Judea received from the Jews. (14b)

            (1) Who killed the Lord Jesus and their own prophets. (15a)

            (2) Who persecuted the apostles, forbidding them to speak to the Gentiles. (15b-16a)

            (3) Who are piling up their sins, and upon whom wrath has come. (17)

B. CONCERNED FOR THEIR WELFARE (17-20)

1. He is eager to see them again. (17)

2. He had wanted to come to them, but Satan hindered him. (18)

3. Because they are his hope, joy, and crown of rejoicing in the presence of the Lord Jesus Christ at His coming. (19-20)

Chapter 3
I. PAUL'S CONCERN FOR THEIR FAITHFULNESS (1-10)

A. TIMOTHY'S MISSION (1-5)

1. When he could endure it no longer, Paul remained in Athens alone. (1)

2. He sent Timothy ...

    a. To establish and encourage them in the faith. (2)

    b. That they not be shaken by their afflictions (3a)

        (1) To which they had been appointed (3b)

        (2) As Paul told them before (4).

    c. To know of their faith ...

        (1) Whether they had been tempted. (5a)

        (2) Whether his labor might be in vain. (5b)

B. TIMOTHY'S REPORT (6-10)

1. Timothy's return brought good news ...

    a. Of their faith and love (6a),

    b. Of their fond memories of Paul (6b),

    c. Of their desire to see him, just as he desires to see them (6c),

2. Such news brought comfort to Paul in his affliction. (7-8).

      a.   He was comforted, knowing of their faith. (7)

      b.   He felt alive, knowing of their steadfastness in the Lord. (8)

  3.   He is thankful beyond words. (9-10)

      a.   Thankful to God for them, for the joy they bring to him. (9)

      b.   Praying night and day that he may soon see them and perfect   what is lacking in their faith. (10)

II. <u>PAUL'S CONCERN FOR THEIR CONTINUED GROWTH</u> (11-13)

A. HIS PRAYER FOR HIMSELF (11)

  1.   A request made to both God the Father, and the Lord Jesus Christ (11a)

  2.   That he may come to the Thessalonians again (11b).

B. HIS PRAYER FOR THEM (12-13)

  1.   That the Lord make them increase and abound in love ...

      a.   To one another and to all (12a)

      b.   Just as Paul does toward them (12b).

  2.   So that the Lord might establish their hearts blameless in holiness ...

      a.   Before our God and Father (13a)

      b.   At the coming of our Lord Jesus Christ with all His saints (13b).

<u>Chapter 4</u>
I. <u>WALK IN HOLINESS</u> (1-8)

A. TO PLEASE GOD (1-2)

1. An exhortation in the Lord Jesus to abound more and more. (1)

2. According to the commandments, Paul gave them through the Lord Jesus. (2)

B. **TO ABSTAIN FROM SEXUAL IMMORALITY** (3-8)

1. For this is the will of God, their sanctification (3)

2. That each one know how to possess his own vessel (4-5)

   a. In sanctification and honor (4)

   b. Not in passion of lust, like the Gentiles who do not know God. (5)

3. That no one take advantage of and defraud his brother in this matter (6)

   a. Because the Lord is the avenger of such things (6a)

   b. As Paul forewarned and testified (6b).

4. For God called us in holiness, not to uncleanness (7)

5. To reject this is to reject God, who has also given us His Holy Spirit (8).

II. <u>WALK IN LOVE</u> (9-10)

A. **AS TAUGHT BY GOD** (9)

1. Concerning brotherly love, Paul really did not need to write anything (9a)

2. For they were taught by God to love one another (9b).

B. **TO INCREASE MORE AND MORE** (10)

1. Indeed, their love was manifest toward all the brethren throughout Macedonia. (10a)

2. Yet, Paul urges them to increase in their love even more. (10b)

III. <u>WALK IN DILIGENCE</u> (11-12)

A. **TO WORK WITH THEIR HANDS** (11)

1. They should aspire to lead quiet lives, to mind their own business. (11a)

2. Working with their own hands, as Paul commanded them. (11b)

B. **TO WALK PROPERLY TOWARD OUTSIDERS** (12)

1. Conducting themselves properly toward those outside. (12a)

2. So that they may lack nothing. (12b)

IV. <u>WALK IN HOPE</u> (13-18)

A. **WITH NO SORROW CONCERNING THOSE WHO HAVE DIED** (13-14)

1. Paul does not want them to be ignorant (13)

   a. Concerning those who have fallen asleep. (13a)

   b. Lest they sorrow as others who have no hope. (13b)

2. For if we believe that Jesus died and rose again, even so God will bring with Him those who sleep in Jesus. (14)

B. **FOR WE SHALL BE REJOINED WITH THEM WHEN CHRIST RETURNS** (15-18)

1. Those who are alive when Christ comes will not precede those who are asleep. (15)

   a. The Lord Himself will descend from heaven (16)

      (1) With a shout,

      (2) With the voice of an archangel,

(3) With the trumpet of God,

    b.   And the dead in Christ will rise first (16b).

2.   Then we who are alive and remain ... (17)

    a.   Shall be caught up together with them in the clouds to meet the Lord (17a),

    b.   And thus, we shall always be with the Lord (17b).

3.   Therefore, comfort one another with these words (18).

Chapter 5

I. WALK IN LIGHT (1-11)

A. FOR THE DAY OF THE LORD WILL COME AS A THIEF IN THE NIGHT (1-4)

1.   Concerning times and seasons, Paul did not need to write to them. (1)

2.   They understood that the day of the Lord will come as a thief in the night. (2)

3.   It will come unexpectedly upon many, and such will not escape. (3)

4.   But they are not in darkness, so that day would overtake them as a thief. (**4**)

B. FOR WE ARE TO BE SONS OF LIGHT AND SONS OF THE DAY (5-8)

1.   We are not to be of the night or of darkness. (5)

2.   herefore, we must watch and be sober, unlike those who sleep and get drunk. (6-7)

3.   Those of the day are to be sober, and properly attired by putting on ... (8)

    a.   The breastplate of faith and love,

      b.   The hope of salvation as a helmet.

C. FOR GOD HAS APPOINTED US TO SALVATION (9-11)

1. He did not appoint us to wrath, but to obtain salvation through Jesus Christ (9),

2. Who died for us, that whether dead or alive, we should live together with Him. (10)

3. Therefore, we need to comfort and edify one another (11).

II. WALK IN OBEDIENCE (12-22)

A. WITH RESPECT TOWARD THOSE OVER US (12-13)

1. To recognize those ...

    a.   Who labor among us (12c),

    b.   Who are over us in the Lord (12b),

    c.   Who admonish us (12c).

2. To esteem them highly in love for their work's sake. (13a)

3. To be at peace among ourselves. (13b)

B. WITH CONCERN FOR ONE ANOTHER (14-15)

1. Exhorted to ...

    a.   Warn those who are unruly (14a),

    b.   Comfort the fainthearted (14b),

    c.   Uphold the weak (14c),

    d.   Be patient with all (14d).

2. To not rendering evil for evil to anyone. (15a)

3. To always pursue what is good for yourselves and for all. (15c)

C. WITH JOY, PRAYER AND THANKSGIVING (16-18)

1. Rejoicing always (16),

2. Praying without ceasing (17),

    3.   Giving thanks in everything (18a),

    4.   Which is God's will for us in Christ Jesus (18b).

D. NOT QUENCHING THE SPIRIT, BUT STILL TESTING ALL THINGS (19-22)

    1.   They were not to quench the Spirit, nor despise prophesies. (19-20)

    2.   Yet they were to test all things; holding fast to that which is good, and abstaining from all forms of evil. (21-22)

III. CONCLUDING REMARKS (23-28)

A. A PRAYER FOR THEM (23-24)

    1.   That the God of peace sanctify them completely. (23a)

    2.   That their whole spirit, soul, and body be preserved blameless at the coming of the Lord Jesus Christ. (23b)

    3.   Reminding them that the One who calls them is faithful, who will also do it. (24)

B. REQUEST FOR PRAYER ON HIS BEHALF (25)

C. FINAL CHARGES (26-27)

    1.   To greet all the brethren with a holy kiss. (26)

    2.   That this epistle be read to all the brethren. (27)

D. FINAL BENEDICTION OF GRACE FROM THE LORD JESUS (28)

SECOND LETTER TO THE THESSALONIANS

AUTHOR: The Apostle Paul, joined in his salutation by Silvanus and Timothy (1:1), and with a reference to his own signature at the end of the epistle (3:17). Early sources in church history that attribute this letter to Paul include: Clement of Alexandria (200 AD), Tertullian (200 AD), and Irenaeus (200 AD).

DATE: Second Thessalonians appears to have been written just a few months, possibly a year, after First Thessalonians. Early AD 50s.

THE CHURCH AT THESSALONICA:

The establishment of the church is recorded in Act 17:1-9. On his second missionary journey, Paul and his companions (Silas and Timothy) had just left Philippi and passed through Amphipolis and Apollonia to arrive at Thessalonica. As was his custom, Paul immediately located the synagogue and reasoned with the Jews for three Sabbaths concerning Jesus Christ. While some of them were persuaded, including a great number of devout Greeks and leading women, the unbelieving Jews became jealous and created an uproar in the city. Therefore, it became necessary to send Paul and Silas away secretly by night to Berea. Despite such ominous beginnings, a strong church was established in Thessalonica (cf. 1:2-10). Mostly Gentile (cf. 1:9), its members included Jason (Act 17:9), Aristarchus, and Secundus (Act 20:4). It had already been the recipient of an earlier letter (First Thessalonians).

HISTORICAL OCCASION OF THE WRITING:

The first epistle to the Thessalonians had been written in response to news brought back by Timothy who had made a quick trip there while Paul was in Athens (cf. 1Th 3:1-3,6). Encouraged by their steadfastness in the face of persecution, Paul had exhorted them to holiness in view of the Lord's coming (cf. 1Th 3:12-13; 5:23). From the second letter, it appears that they remained strong in the Lord despite persecution (cf. 1:3-4). But it is apparent from this letter that misunderstandings about the Lord's coming was present in the church. Some of the members were being troubled by false reports (cf. 2:1-2); others had stopped working, perhaps assuming that the Lord's imminent return meant one did not need to work anymore (cf. 3:11-12). Paul's purpose in writing this epistle, therefore, is three-fold:

* **To encourage them in their steadfastness under persecution.**

* To correct their misunderstanding about the imminence of the Lord's return.

* To instruct the congregation on what disciplinary action to take toward those who refused to work.

MAIN THEME OF LETTER:

In correcting their misunderstanding about the return of Christ, Paul explains that the Lord will not come right away (cf. 2:1-3). Therefore, they need to continue with steadfastness and patience for which they had been commended. A suggested theme of this epistle might therefore be: **"STEADFASTNESS WHILE WAITING FOR THE COMING OF CHRIST."**

KEY VERSES:

2 Thessalonians 2:15-17 **"Therefore, brethren, stand fast and hold the traditions which you were taught, whether by word or our epistle. Now may our Lord Jesus Christ Himself, and our God and Father, who has loved us and given us everlasting consolation and good hope by grace, comfort your hearts and establish you in every good word and work."**

SYNOPSIS:

Chapter 1

I. INTRODUCTION (1-2)

    A. SALUTATION (1a)

        1.   From Paul.

        2.   Also Silvanus and Timothy.

II. GREETINGS (1b-2)

        1.   To the church of the Thessalonians in God our Father and the Lord Jesus Christ. (1b)

        2.   Grace and peace from God and Jesus. (2)

II. ENCOURAGEMENT IN PERSECUTIONS (3-12)

A. THANKFUL FOR THEIR SPIRITUAL GROWTH (3-4)

        1.   Such thanksgiving is fitting in view of:

           a.   Their faith growing exceedingly. (3a)

           b.   Their love abounding toward each other. (3b)

2. Paul and his companions even boast of them among the churches of God (4a)

   a. For their patience and faith. (4b)

   b. In all the persecutions and tribulations they endured. (4c)

B. ENCOURAGEMENT IN TRIAL IN VIEW OF CHRIST'S RETURN (5-10)

1. Their persecutions are evidence of God's righteous judgment to come (5-7a)

   a. In which they shall be counted worthy of the kingdom of God. (5)

   b. In which God will repay with tribulation those who trouble them. (6)

   c. In which they will receive rest. (7a)

2. Such judgment will occur when Jesus is revealed from heaven (7b-9)

   a. With His mighty angels, in flaming fire taking vengeance (7b-8a)

      (1) On those who do not know God. (8b)

      (2) On those who do not obey the gospel of our Lord Jesus Christ. (8c)

   b. Punishing such with everlasting destruction (9a)

      (1) From the presence of the Lord. (9b)

      (2) From the glory of His power. (9c)

3. Jesus will come in that Day ... (10a)

   a. To be glorified in His saints. (10b)

   b. To be admired among all those who believe. (10c)

4. Because Paul's testimony among them was believed. (10d)

C. HIS PRAYER FOR THEM (11-12)

1. That God would ...

    a. Count them worthy of His calling. (11a)

    b. Fulfill all the good pleasure of His goodness and the work of faith with power. (11b)

2. That according to the grace of God and the Lord Jesus Christ ...

    a. The name of the Lord Jesus Christ may be glorified in them. (12a)

    b. And they may be glorified in Him. (12b)

Chapter 2

I. ENLIGHTENMENT ABOUT THE COMING OF THE LORD (1-12)

A. DO NOT BE TROUBLED (1-2)

1. Concerning the coming of the Lord, and our gathering to Him. (1)

2. By false reports, as though the day of Christ has come. (2)

B. THE APOSTASY MUST COME FIRST (3-12)

1. The Day of Christ will not come until ...

    a. A falling away comes first. (3a)

    b. The man of sin (lawlessness) is revealed (3-4)

        (1) The son of perdition (3c)

        (2) Who opposes and exalts himself above all that is called God and that is worshipped (4a)

        (3) He sits as God in the temple of God, showing himself that he is God (4b)

      (4) As Paul told them while he was with them (5).

2. The man of sin is being restrained. (6-7)

    a. They knew what it was that was restraining him. (6a)

    b. He will be revealed in his own time. (6b)

    c. The mystery of lawlessness is already at work. (7a)

    d. But the one who restrains will do so until taken out of the way. (7b)

3. When the lawless one is revealed (8-12)

    a. The Lord will ...

        (1) Consume him with the breath of His mouth. (8a)

        (2) Destroy him with the brightness of His coming. (8b)

    b. The coming of the lawless one ...

        (1) Will be according to the working of Satan (9a),

        (2) With all power, signs, and lying wonders (9b),

        (3) With all unrighteous deception among those who perish (10a)

            a. Because they did not receive the love of the truth (10b)

            b. That they might be saved (10c).

    c. For this reason ...

        (1) God will send them a strong delusion (11a)

            a. That they should believe the lie (11b)

   b. That they may be condemned (12a).

  (2) Because they did not believe the truth but had pleasure in unrighteousness (12b).

II. STEADFASTNESS ENCOURAGED (13-17)

A. THANKSGIVING AND A CALL TO STEADFASTNESS (13-15)

  1. Bound always to give thanks to God (13a)

   a. Who from the beginning chose them for salvation (13b)

    (1) Through sanctification by the Spirit (13c)

    (2) And belief in the truth (13d).

   b. To which He called them (14a)

    (1) By the gospel (14b)

    (2) For the obtaining of the glory of the Lord Jesus Christ (14c)

  2. Stand fast and hold the traditions, which they were taught (15a),

   a. Whether by word (15b)

   b. Or by his epistle (15c).

B. PAUL'S PRAYER FOR THE THESSALONIANS (16-17)

1. May the Lord Jesus Himself, and our God and Father (16a)

   a. Who loved us (16b),

   b. Who has given us ... (16c)

    (1) Everlasting consolation,

    (2) Good hope by grace,

2. Comfort your hearts (17a),

3. Establish you in every good word and work (17b).

Chapter 3
I. A REQUEST FOR PRAYER, AND A PRAYER FOR THEM (1-5)
A. PAUL REQUESTS THEIR PRAYERS (1-2)

1. That the word of the Lord may have free course and be glorified, as it was in their case. (1)

2. That Paul and his companions be delivered from unreasonable and wicked men, for not all are believers. (2)

B. AN EXPRESSION OF CONFIDENCE (3-4)

1. In the faithfulness of the Lord (3)

    a. Who would establish them. (3a)

    b. Who would guard them from the evil one. (3b)

2. In them (4)

    a. That they do the things he commands them. (4a)

    b. That they will do the things he commands them (4b)

C. A PRAYER FOR THEM (5)

1. That the Lord direct their hearts (5a)

2. Into the love of God and the patience of Christ (5b).

II. A CHARGE TO DISCIPLINE THE DISORDERLY (3:6-15)
A. WITHDRAW FROM THOSE WHO ARE DISORDERLY (6-9)

1. Commanded in the name of the Lord Jesus Christ (6a)

2. To be administered toward those ...

a. Who do not walk according to apostolic tradition. (6b)

b. Who do not follow apostolic example (7a)

(1) For Paul was not disorderly among them. (7b)

(2) For Paul was not a burden to them, but gave them an example (8-9).

B. ESPECIALLY THOSE WHO WILL NOT WORK (10-12)

1. They had been commanded: If anyone will not work, neither shall he eat. (10)

2. Yet there were some not working at all, but were busybodies. (11)

3. Such are commanded and exhorted to work in quietness and eat their own bread. (12)

C. SUMMATION CONCERNING CHURCH DISCIPLINE (13-15)

1. Do not grow weary in doing good. (13)

2. For those who do not obey the apostolic teaching in this letter ... (14a)

a. Note that person. (14b)

b. Do not keep company with him. (14c)

c. That he may be ashamed. (14d)

3. Count him not as an enemy, but admonish him as a brother. (15)

III. CONCLUDING REMARKS (16-18)

A. ANOTHER PRAYER ON THEIR BEHALF (16)

1. May the Lord of peace give them peace always in every way. (16a)

2. May the Lord be with them all. (16b)

B. CONFIRMATION OF HIS AUTHORSHIP (17)

1. His own salutation with his own hand (17a)

2. As he writes in every epistle (17b).

C. FINAL BENEDICTION (18)

1. he grace of the Lord Jesus Christ be with them all.

2. Amen (so be it).

FIRST LETTER TO TIMOTHY

AUTHOR: The Apostle Paul, as stated in the salutation (1:1). The internal evidence certainly supports Paul as the author, especially references to his earlier life (1:13), and the close relationship between the author and Timothy (1:2; cf. Php 2:22). Early sources in church history that attribute this letter to Paul include: Eusebius (300 AD), Origen (250 AD), Clement of Alexandria (200 AD), Tertullian (200 AD), Irenaeus (200 AD), the Muratorian Fragment (180 AD). References to the epistle are also found in the writings of Theophilus of Antioch (180 AD), Justin Martyr (160 AD), Polycarp (135 AD), and Clement of Rome (90 AD).

DATE: Some believe that Paul may have written 1st Timothy after his extended stay at Ephesus and departure to Macedonia on his third missionary journey (cf. Acts 19:1-41; 20:1-3). This would place its composition around AD 63–65.

INSIGHT TO LETTER: Paul had left Timothy behind at Ephesus with an awesome responsibility: To charge some not to teach anything contrary to the "sound doctrine," which was according to the "glorious gospel of the blessed God" (1:3-11). Fulfilling this charge was made difficult by Timothy's youth and natural timidity (4:11-12; cf. 2Ti 1:7-8). While Paul hoped to come himself, he writes Timothy to guide him in the meantime (1Ti 3:14-15). Therefore, Paul writes:

> *** To instruct Timothy on how to conduct himself while administering the affairs of the church. (3:14-15)**
>
> *** To encourage Timothy by providing counsel concerning his own spiritual progress. (4:12-16)**

KEY VERSES:

1 Timothy 3:14-15 "These things I write to you, though I hope to come to you shortly; but if I am delayed, I write so that you may know how you ought to conduct yourself in the house of God, which is the church of the living God, the pillar and ground of the truth."

SYNOPSIS:

> **Chapter 1**
>
> **I. INTRODUCTION** (1-2)
>
> > **A. THE AUTHOR (1)**
> >
> > > 1.   Paul, an Apostle of Jesus Christ. (1a)

2. By the commandment of God our Savior and Jesus Christ our hope. (1b)

B. THE RECIPIENT (2)

1. Timothy. (2a)

2. Paul's true son in the faith. (2b)

C. GREETINGS (2c)

1. Grace, mercy, and peace.

2. From God our Father and Jesus Christ our Lord.

II. <u>TEACHING SOUND DOCTRINE</u> (3-11)

A. PAUL'S CHARGE TO TIMOTHY (3-7)

1. Remain in Ephesus and charge some ... (3a)

    a. To teach no other doctrine (3b),

    b. Nor give heed to fables and endless genealogies (4a)

        (1) Which cause disputes (4b)

        (2) Rather than godly edification, which is in faith (4c).

2. The purpose of the commandment is ... (5a)

    a. Love from a pure heart (5b),

    b. A good conscience (5c),

    c. Sincere faith (5d).

3. For some have strayed ... (6a)

    a. Having turned aside to idle talk (6b).

    b. Desiring to be teachers of the law (7a)

        (1) Not understanding what they say (7b),

        (2) Nor the things they affirm (7c).

B. THE PROPER USE OF THE LAW (8-11)

1. It is good if one uses it lawfully. (8)

2. The law is not made for the righteous (9a), a. But for all sorts of sinners (9b-10a),

   a. And anything else that is contrary to sound doctrine (10b),

      (1) According to the glorious gospel of the blessed God (11a),

      (2) Which was committed to Paul's trust (11b).

III. THANKSGIVING FOR THE LORD'S GRACE AND MERCY (12-17)

A. THANKFUL TO CHRIST JESUS (12-14)

1. For enabling him (12a)

   a. Because He counted him faithful (12b)

   b. Putting him into the ministry (12c).

2. Though he had formerly been ... (13a)

   a. A blasphemer (13b),

   b. A persecutor (13c),

   c. An insolent man (13d), but he obtained mercy because he did it ignorantly in unbelief (13e).

3. The grace of the Lord was exceedingly abundant, with faith and love in Christ Jesus. (14)

B. THE MERCY SHOWN TO HIM IS A PATTERN FOR OTHERS (15-17)

1. Christ came to save sinners, and Paul was one of the worst. (15)

2. But he received mercy, that Christ might demonstrate His long suffering to others who believe on Him for everlasting life. (16)

3. 3. Paul desires that honor and glory be given forever and ever ... (17c)

   a. To the King eternal, immortal, invisible. (17a)

   b. o God who alone is wise. (17b)

IV. TIMOTHY'S RESPONSIBILITY (18-20)

A. TO WAGE THE GOOD WARFARE (18)

1. This is the charge Paul commits to his son Timothy (18a)

2. In accordance to prophecies made concerning him (18b).

B. TO HAVE FAITH AND A GOOD CONSCIENCE (19-20),

1. Which some have rejected, and concerning the faith have suffered shipwreck. (19)

2. Such as Hymenaeus and Alexander (20a)

   a. Whom Paul delivered to Satan (20b)

   b. That they may learn not to blaspheme (20c).

Chapter 2

I. THE PRACTICE OF PRAYER (1-8)

A. THE SCOPE OF PRAYER (1-7)

1. Supplications, prayers, intercessions, and giving of thanks are to be made for all. (1)

   a. For kings and all who are in authority. (2a)

   b. That we may lead quiet and peaceable lives in all godliness and reverence. (2b)

2. This is good and acceptable in the sight of God our Savior (3)

   a. Who desires all men to be saved and know the truth. (4)

b. For there is one Mediator between God and men (5a)

    (1) The Man Christ Jesus, who gave Himself a ransom for all (5b-6a)

    (2) To be testified in due time, for which Paul was appointed a preacher and an apostle (6b-7a)

        a. Paul speaks the truth in Christ and is not lying (7b)

        b. A teacher of the Gentiles in faith and truth (7c).

B. **A CALL TO PRAYER** (8)

1. For men to pray everywhere. (8a)

2. Lifting up holy hands, without wrath and doubting. (8b)

II. <u>INSTRUCTIONS FOR WOMEN</u> (9-15)

A. **THEIR ADORNMENT** (9-10)

1. With modest apparel. (9a)

    a. With propriety and moderation. (9b)

    b. Not with braided hair, gold, pearls, or costly clothing. (9c)

2. With good works, which is proper for women professing godliness. (10)

B. **THEIR SUBMISSION** (11-15)

1. To learn in silence with all submission. (11)

2. Not permitted to teach or have authority over a man, but to be in silence (12)

    a. For Adam was formed first, then Eve (13)

    b. And Adam was not deceived, but the woman being deceived fell into transgression (14).

3. A woman will be saved in childbearing if they continue in ...

   a. Faith,

   b. Love,

   c. Holiness,

4. With self-control (15).

Chapter 3

I. THE QUALIFICATIONS FOR BISHOPS (1-7)

A. THE NATURE OF THE WORK (1)

1. It is a position, or office. (1a)

2. It is a good work for a man to desire. (1b)

B. WHAT A BISHOP MUST BE (2-7)

1. Positive qualifications:

   a. Blameless (2a),

   b. The husband of one wife (2b),

   c. Temperate (2c),

   d. Sober-minded (2d),

   e. Of good behavior (2e),

   f. Hospitable (2f),

   g. Able to teach (2g),

   h. Gentle (3d),

   i. One who rules his own house well (4a)

      (1) Having his children in submission with all reverence (4b)

      (2) For if he can't rule his own house, how will he take   care of the church? (5)

   j. A good testimony among those outside (7a)

(1) Lest he fall into reproach (7b)

(2) And into the snare of the devil (7c).

1. Negative qualifications:

   a. Not given to wine (3a),

   b. Not violent (3b),

   c. Not greedy for money (3c),

   d. d. Not quarrelsome (3e),

   e. e. Not covetous (3f),

   f. f. Not a novice (6a)

     (1) Lest he be puffed up with pride (6b),

     (2) And fall into the same condemnation as the devil (6c).

II. THE QUALIFICATIONS FOR DEACONS (8-13)

A. WHAT A DEACON MUST BE (8-12)

1. Positive qualifications:

   a. Reverent (8a),

   b. Holding the mystery of the faith with a pure conscience (9),

   c. Proven (10a),

   d. Found blameless (10b),

   e. The husband of one wife (12a),

   f. Ruling his children and house well (12b).

2. Negative qualifications:

   a. Not double-tongued (8b),

   b. Not given to much wine (8c),

   c. Not greedy for money (8d).

3. Their wives:

   a. Reverent (11a),

   b. Not slanderers (11b),

      c.   Temperate (11c),

      d.   Faithful in all things (11d).

B. THE HONOR OF THEIR WORK (13)

    1.   Those who serve well obtain a good standing (13a).

    2.   Also great boldness in the faith, which is in Christ Jesus (13b).

III. PAUL'S PURPOSE IN WRITING (14-16)

A. WHY PAUL IS WRITING THIS LETTER (14-15)

    1.   He hopes to come shortly, but writes in case he is delayed (14-15a).

    2.   That Timothy might know how to conduct himself in the house of God (15b),

      a.   Which is the church of the living God. (15c)

      b.   Which is the pillar and ground of the truth. (15d)

B. THE MYSTERY OF GODLINESS (16)

    1.   Without controversy, it is great. (16a)

    2.   In summation, it's key elements are these: God was ...

      a.   Manifested in the flesh (16b),

      b.   Justified in the Spirit (16c),

      c.   Seen by angels (16d),

      d.   Preached among the Gentiles (16e),

      e.   Believed on in the world (16f),

      f.   Received up in glory (16g).

Chapter 4

I. THE COMING APOSTASY (1-5)

A. THE DEPARTURE FORETOLD (1-2)

    1.   Foretold expressly by the Spirit. (1a)

    2.   In latter times some will depart from the faith (1b-2)

        a.   Giving heed to deceiving spirits and doctrines of demons. (1b)

        b.   Speaking lies in hypocrisy. (2a)

        c.   Having consciences seared with a hot iron. (2b)

B. THE DEPARTURE DESCRIBED (3-5)

    1.   Some will forbid to marry. (3a)

    2.   Some will command abstention from certain foods (3b),

        a.   Which God created to be received with thanksgiving (3c),

        b.   For every creature of God is good, and nothing is to be refused (4a):

           (1) If it is received with thanksgiving (4b),

           (2) For it is sanctified by the word of God and prayer (5).

II. A GOOD SERVANT OF JESUS CHRIST (6-16)

A. IN REGARDS TO DOCTRINE (6-7a):

    1.   Instruct the brethren in regards to such things as the apostasy. (6a)

    2.   You will be a good minister of Jesus Christ. (6b)

    3.   You will be nourished in the words of faith and good doctrine. (6c)

    4.   But reject profane and old wives' fables. (7a)

B. IN REGARDS TO GODLINESS (7b-10):

1. Exercise yourself to godliness, for bodily exercise profits a little (7b-8a).

2. But godliness is profitable for all things, having promise ...

    a. Of the life that now is (8b),

    b. And of that which is to come (8c).

3. Such is a faithful saying, and worthy of all acceptance (9)

4. And to this end we labor and suffer reproach (10a)

    a. Because we trust in the living God (10b)

    b. Who is the Savior of all men, especially of those who believe (10c).

C. COUNSEL FOR A YOUNG PREACHER (11-16)

1. Command and teach such things as previously described. (11)

2. Let no one despise your youth. (12a)

3. Be an example to the believers (12b):

    a. In word, in conduct, in love.

    b. In spirit, in faith, in purity.

4. Give attention to reading, to exhortation, to doctrine. (13)

5. Do not neglect the gift in you (14a):

    a. Given by prophecy (14b)

    b. With the laying of hands of the presbytery (14c).

6. In order that your progress may be evident to all ...

    a. Meditate on these things. (15a)

    b. Give yourself entirely to them. (15b)

7. Take heed to yourself and to the doctrine. (16a)

    a. Continue in them. (16b)

    b. b. In doing this, you will save both your-self and those who hear you. (16b)

Chapter 5
I. <u>INSTRUCTIONS CONCERNING THE MEMBERS</u> (1-20)

A. EXHORTING THE MEMBERS (1-2):

1. Older men as fathers, younger men as broth-ers. (1)

2. Older women as mothers, younger women as sisters, with all purity. (2)

B. HONORING WIDOWS (3-16)

1. Honor those who are truly widows. (3)

2. Widows with children or grandchildren should be taken care of by them (4),

    a. That they may learn to show piety at home and repay their   parents.

    b. This is good and acceptable before God.

3. Contrast between a true widow and one who is not (5-6)

    a. A true widow (5):

        (1) One who is left alone. (5a)

        (2) One who trusts in God. (5b)

        (3) One who continues in supplications night and day. (5c)

    b. The one who lives in pleasure is dead while she lives. (6)

4. Command these things that people may be blameless. (7)

5. One who does not provide for his own, especially his household ... (8)

    a. Has denied the faith.

    b. Is worse than an unbeliever.

6. Regarding the church support of widows (9-16):

    a. Qualifications for those who can be taken into the number (9-10):

        (1) Not under sixty years of age.

        (2) The wife of one man.

        (3) Well reported for good works.

        (4) Has brought up children.

        (5) Has lodged strangers.

        (6) Has washed the saints' feet.

        (7) Has relieved the afflicted.

        (8) Has diligently followed every good work.

    b. Reasons to reject younger widows (11-13):

        (1) When they begin to grow wanton against Christ, they desire to marry.

        (2) Casting off their first faith, they have condemnation.

        (3) They learn to be idle, wandering about from house to house as busybodies and gossip.

    c. Counsel for younger widows (14-15):

        (1) To marry, bear children, manage the house.

        (2) To give no opportunity for the adversary to speak reproachfully.

(3) 3) For some have already turned aside after Satan.

d. Those widows with believing children (16):

(1) The children should relieve them.

(2) Do not burden the church, that it may relieve those who are truly widows.

C. TREATMENT OF ELDERS (17-20)

1. Those who rule well (17-18):

a. They are counted worthy of double honor.

b. Especially those who labor in word and doctrine.

c. Scriptural basis for supporting elders:

(1) "You shall not muzzle an ox while it treads out the grain."

(2) "The laborer is worthy of his wages."

2. Those who don't rule well (19-20):

a. Don't receive an accusation against an elder except from two or three witnesses. (19)

b. Elders who are sinning (20):

(1) Should be rebuked in the presence of all,

(2) So that the rest may fear.

II. FURTHER INSTRUCTIONS RELATED TO TIMOTHY (21-25)

A. THE CHARGE GIVEN TO HIM BY PAUL (21):

1. Given before God, the Lord Jesus Christ, and the elect angels,

2. To observe these things without prejudice, doing nothing without partiality.

B. **WARNINGS AGAINST HASTY RECOMMENDATIONS** (22):

    1.   Don't lay hands hastily on anyone.

    2.   Don't share in other people's sins.

    3.   Keep yourself pure.

C. **COUNSEL FOR ALLEVIATING HIS STOMACH PROBLEMS** (23):

    1.   No longer drink only water.

    2.   Use a little wine for the sake of the stomach and frequent infirmities.

D. **REMINDER CONCERNING SIN AND GOOD WORKS** (24-25):

    1.   Some sins are clearly evident, others we learn after the judgment. (24)

    2.   The same is true regarding good works. (25)

<u>Chapter 6</u>

I. <u>**INSTRUCTIONS CONCERNING SERVANTS**</u> (1-2)

A. **HOW THEY SHOULD REGARD THEIR MASTERS (1):**

    1.   As worthy of all honor (1a),

    2.   So that God and His doctrine might not be blasphemed (1b).

B. **HOW THEY SHOULD REGARD BELIEVING MASTERS** (2):

    1.   Not to be despised because they are brethren. (2a)

    2.   But to serve them, remembering that those who are benefited are believers and beloved. (2b)

II. <u>**INSTRUCTIONS CONCERNING TEACHERS MOTIVATED BY GREED**</u> (3-10)

A. **SUCH TEACHERS DESCRIBED** (3-5):

1. Anyone who does not consent to the wholesome words of our Lord, and to the doctrine according to godliness. (3)

2. He is proud, knowing nothing. (4a)

3. He is obsessed with disputes and arguments over words (4b):

    a. From which come envy, strife, reviling, evil suspicions. (4c)

    b. From which come useless wrangling's of men of corrupt minds and destitute of the truth. (5a)

4. Who supposes that godliness is a means of gain. (5b)

B. THE IMPORTANCE OF CONTENTMENT (6-8):

1. Godliness with contentment is great gain (6)

    a. For we brought nothing into this world (7a),

    b. And it is certain we can carry nothing out (7b).

2. Thus, we should be content with food and clothing (8).

C. THE DANGERS FACING THOSE WHO DESIRE TO BE RICH (9-10):

1. Those who desire to be rich fall ...

    a. Into temptation and a snare. (9a)

    b. Into many foolish and harmful lusts (9b), which drown men in destruction and perdition. (9c)

2. For the love of money is a root of all kinds of evil (10a)

    a. For which some have strayed from the faith in their greediness (10b),

b.   And have pierced themselves with many sorrows (10c).

III. <u>INSTRUCTIONS CONCERNING THE MAN OF GOD HIMSELF</u> (11-16)

A. **GENERAL EXHORTATIONS** (11-12):

1.   Flee the things described before, such as the desire to be rich. (11a)

2.   Pursue righteousness, godliness, faith, love, patience, gentleness. (11b)

3.   Fight the good fight of faith. (12a)

4.   Lay hold on eternal life (12b):

    a.   To which you were called. (12c)

    b.   To which you have confessed the good confession in the presence of many. (12d)

B. **A SOLEMN CHARGE** (13-16):

1.   Urged by Paul in the sight of ...

    a.   God, who gives life to all things. (13a)

    b.   Jesus Christ, who witnessed the good confession before

    c.   Pontius Pilate. (13b)

2.   To keep the commandment without spot, blameless until the Lord's appearing (14),

    a.   Which He will manifest in His own time. (15a)

    b.   Who is then described as:

        (1) The blessed and only Potentate, the King of kings and Lord of lords. (15b)

        (2) He who alone has immortality, dwelling in unapproachable light, whom no man has seen or can see. (16a)

    c.   To whom be honor and everlasting power. (16b)

IV. INSTRUCTIONS CONCERNING THE RICH (17-19):

A. WHAT TO COMMAND THEM (17):

1. Not to be haughty, nor trust in uncertain riches. (17a)

2. But to trust in the living God, who gives us richly all things to enjoy. (17b)

B. WHAT TO ENCOURAGE THEM (18-19)

1. To do good, to be rich in good works, ready to give, willing to share. (18)

2. Storing up for themselves a good foundation for the time to come, that they may lay hold on eternal life. (19)

V. CONCLUDING CHARGE TO TIMOTHY (20-21)

A. A FERVENT PLEA TO TIMOTHY (20-21a):

1. To guard what was committed to his trust. (20a)

2. To avoid the profane and vain babbling and contradictions of what is falsely called knowledge. (20b)

3. For by professing such, some have strayed concerning the faith. (21a)

B. FINAL BENEDICTION: "GRACE BE WITH YOU. AMEN" (21b)

THE SECOND LETTER TO TIMOTHY

AUTHOR: Apostle Paul.

The Apostle begins this letter to his "beloved son" with a prayer for grace, mercy and peace on his behalf. Thankful to God for the unceasing memories that he has of Timothy in his prayers night and day, Paul greatly desires to see the young man. Seeing him again will bring great joy as Paul is mindful of Timothy's tears and his unfeigned faith (1-5). Paul's purpose in writing begins in earnest with a series of exhortations toward steadfast service. He encourages Timothy to stir up the gift of God, which was in him, by the laying on of Paul's hands, to not be ashamed of the testimony of the Lord nor of Paul His prisoner, and to hold fast the pattern of sound words, which he had then reminded of those who had forsaken Paul, but also how Onesiphorus had proven to be a true friend and brother by virtue of his courage, diligence, and service (6-18).

DATE: Probably the mid-60s AD.

INSIGHT TO LETTER: Second Timothy may be the last known letter of the Apostle Paul. The letter warns the young pastor against false teaching and urges him to live a life of purity before his congregation. The Apostle tell us that: "All scripture is given by inspiration of God" (3:16)

SYNOPSIS:

Chapter 1

I. INTRODUCTION (1-5)

A. SALUTATION (1-2a)

1. From Paul, an apostle of Jesus Christ (1)

   a. By the will of God.

   b. According to the promise of life in Christ Jesus.

2. To Timothy, his beloved son. (2a)

3. Grace, mercy, and peace from God the Father and Christ Jesus our Lord. (2b)

B. THANKSGIVING (3-5)

1. Thanks offered to God by Paul (3)

    a.   Whom he serves with pure conscience, as did his forefathers.

    b.   For without ceasing he remembers Timothy in his prayers night and day.

2.   Greatly desiring to see Timothy (4-5)

    a.   For he is mindful of Timothy's tears.

    b.   For Paul himself desires to be filled with joy.

    c.   For he remembers the genuine faith that is in Timothy,

       (1) Which dwelt first in his grandmother Lois and his mother Eunice,

       (2) And which Paul is persuaded is in Timothy also.

II. <u>EXHORTATION TO ZEAL AND COURAGE</u> (6-12)

A. STIR UP THE GIFT OF GOD (6-7),

1.   Which was in him through the laying on of Paul's hands. (6)

2.   For God has given a spirit, not of fear, but of power, love and a sound mind. (7)

B. DON'T BE ASHAMED (8-12)

1.   Of the testimony of our Lord, nor of Paul His prisoner. (8a)

2.   Share with Paul in the suffering of the gospel according to the power of God (8b-12)

    a.   Who saved us and called us with a holy calling (9-10)

       (1) Not according to our works,

       (2) But according to His own purpose and grace.

   a. Given to us in Christ before time began

   b. But has now been revealed by the appearing of our Savior Jesus Christ:

    (1) Who abolished death,

    (2) And brought light and immortality to light through the gospel.

  b. For the gospel, Paul was appointed a preacher, apostle and teacher (11-12):

   (1) For such things, he suffers.

   (2) But he not ashamed:

    a. For he knows Whom he has believed,

    b. And is persuaded that He is able to keep what Paul has committed to Him until that Day.

III. EXHORTATION TO STEADFASTNESS AND LOYALTY (13-18)

A. BE STEADFAST (13-14)

 1. Hold fast the pattern of sound words (13),

  a. Which he had heard from Paul.

  b. In faith and love which are in Christ Jesus.

 2. Keep that good thing (14),

  a. Which was committed to you.

  b. Keep it by the Holy Spirit who dwells is us.

B. BE LOYAL (15-18)

1. All in Asia have turned away from Paul, including Phygellus and Hermogenes. (15)

2. In contrast, the example of Onesiphorus (16-18):

   a. May the Lord grant mercy to the household of Onesiphorus:

      (1) For he often refreshed Paul.

      (2) He was not ashamed of Paul's chains.

      (3) Arriving in Rome, he sought Paul diligently and found him.

      (4) He also ministered to Paul in many ways at Ephesus.

   b. May the Lord grant mercy to Onesiphorus in that Day.

Chapter 2

I. EXHORTATION TO TRANSMIT THE TRUTH TO OTHERS (1-2)

A. A PLEA TO BE STRONG (1)

1. Directed to Timothy as his son. (1a)

2. To be strong in the grace that is in Christ Jesus. (1b)

B. COMMIT WHAT HE HAS HEARD TO FAITHFUL MEN (2)

1. Those things he heard from Paul among many witnesses. (2a)

2. Commit to faithful men who will be able to teach others. (2b)

II. EXHORTATION TO ENDURE HARDSHIP (3-13)

A. AS A SOLDIER, ATHLETE, AND FARMER (3-7)

1. Endure hardship as good soldier of Jesus hrist (3),

      a.   Not entangled with the affairs of this life. (4a)

      b.   That he might please the One who enlisted him. (4b)

  2.   As an athlete, follow the rules of competition in order to win. (5)

  3.   It is the hard-working farmer who will be the first to partake of his crops. (6)

  4.   May the Lord give him understanding as he considers what Paul is saying. (7)

B. THE EXAMPLE OF PAUL HIMSELF (8-13)

  1.   Remember that Jesus was raised from the dead, according to the gospel (8):

      a.   For which Paul suffered trouble as an evil-doer, even to the point of chains. (9a)

      b.   Yet the word of God was not chained. (9b)

  2.   Paul endured all things for the sake of the elect (10a)

      a.   That they might obtain the salvation in Christ Jesus with eternal glory. (10b)

      b.   A faithful saying to encourage us to endure hardship (11-13):

         (1) If we died with Christ, we shall live with Him.

         (2) If we endure, we shall also reign with Him.

         (3) If we deny Him, He will also deny us.

         (4) If we are faithless, He remains faithful for He cannot deny Himself.

III. EXHORTATION TO DILIGENCE AS A SERVANT OF THE LORD (14-26)

A. INSTRUCTIONS RELATED TO HIS WORK (14-19):

1. Remind others, charging them not to strive about words. (14)

    a. Words that do not profit.

    b. Words that only produce ruin of the hearers.

2. Be diligent to present yourself approved to God. (15)

    a. As a worker who does not need to be ashamed.

    b. As a worker who rightly divides the word of truth.

3. Shun profane and vain babblings. (16-18)

    a. For they only increase to more ungodliness. (16)

    b. For their message will spread like cancer. (17a)

        (1) Hymenaeus and Philetus are examples (17b),

        (2) Who have overthrown the faith of some by saying the resurrection is already past. (18)

4. God's solid foundation stands, having this seal:

    a. The Lord knows those who are His. (19a)

    b. Let those who name the name of Christ depart from iniquity   (19b).

B. INSTRUCTIONS FOR BEING USEFUL TO THE MASTER (20-26):

1. A great house has all kinds of vessels, some for honor and some for dishonor. (20)

2. If anyone cleanses himself from things of dishonor, he will be a vessel of honor (21),

   a. Sanctified and useful for the Master.

   b. Prepared for every good work.

3. Instructions that will make one a servant useful to the Master:

   a. Flee youthful lusts. (22a)

   b. Pursue righteousness, faith, love, peace with those who call on the Lord out of a pure heart. (22b)

   c. Avoid foolish and ignorant disputes that generate strife. (23)

   d. Do not quarrel, but be gentle to all, able to teach, patient. (24)

   e. In humility correct those in opposition. (25-26)

      (1) Perhaps God will grant them repentance, so that they may know the truth. (25)

      (2) Perhaps they may come to their senses and escape the snare of the devil who has taken them captive to do his will. (26)

Chapter 3
I. PERILOUS TIMES TO COME (1-9)

A DESCRIPTION OF THESE PERILOUS TIMES (1-5a):

1. They will come in the last days. (1)

2. There will be perilous times because of the condition of men (2-5a):

    a. Lovers of themselves, lovers of money.

    b. Boasters, proud, blasphemers, disobedient to parents.

    c. Unthankful, unholy, unloving, unforgiving.

    d. Slanderers, without self-control, brutal, despisers of good.

    e. Traitors, headstrong, haughty.

    f. Lovers of pleasure rather than lovers of God.

    g. Having a form of godliness but denying its power.

B. REASONS TO TURN AWAY FROM SUCH PERILOUS PEOPLE (5b-9):

    1. A warning to turn away from such people. (5b)

    2. Reasons to do so (6-9):

        a. For such lead gullible people astray.

        b. For such are always learning but never able to come to the knowledge of the truth.

        c. Just like Jannes and Jambres who resisted Moses ...

            (1) These resist the truth.

            (2) They are men of corrupt minds, disapproved concerning the faith.

            (3) They will not progress, and their folly will become manifest to all.

II. A REMINDER OF PAUL'S EXAMPLE (10-13)

A. TIMOTHY HAD CAREFULLY FOLLOWED PAUL'S DOCTRINE AND LIFE (10-11):

1. His doctrine, manner of life, purpose, faith, love, perseverance. (11)

2. Even his persecutions and afflictions at Antioch, Iconium and Lystra. (11a)

3. Yet the Lord delivered him out of them all. (11b)

B. **EXPECT PERSECUTION** (12-13)

1. For those who live godly in Christ Jesus will suffer persecution. (12)

2. Evil men and impostors will grow worse, deceiving and being deceived. (13)

III. **EXHORTATION TO ABIDE IN THE SCRIPTURES** (14-17)

A. **CONTINUE IN THE THINGS HE HAD LEARNED** (14-15):

1. Things he had been assured of, knowing from whom he had learned them. (14)

2. In particular that which he learned from childhood, the Holy Scriptures. (15a)

3. For they are able to make him wise for salvation through faith in Christ. (15b)

B. **THE ALL-SUFFICIENCY OF THE SCRIPTURES** (16-17):

1. All scripture is given by inspiration of God. (16a)

2. It is profitable for doctrine, reproof, correction, instruction in righteousness. (16b)

3. So the man of God can be complete, thoroughly complete for every good work. (17)

Chapter 4

I. **EXHORTATION TO PREACH THE WORD** (1-5)

A. **SOLEMN CHARGE** (1-2)

1. Before God and the Lord Jesus Christ (1):

   a. Who will judge the living and the dead,

    b.   At His appearing and His kingdom.

2.   To preach the word! (2)

    a.   Be ready in season and out of season.

    b.   Convince, rebuke, exhort.

    c.   With all long suffering and teaching.

B. THE REASON FOR THIS CHARGE (3-4)

1.   The time is coming when people will not endure sound doctrine (3):

    a.   According to their own desires, they will heap up for themselves teachers.

    b.   For they will have itching ears.

2.   They will turn their ears away from the truth, and be turned aside to fables. (4)

C. RELATED EXHORTATIONS (5):

1.   Be watchful in all things.

2.   Endure afflictions.

3.   Do the work of an evangelist.

4.   Fulfill your ministry.

II. EXHORTATION TO COME QUICKLY (6-18)

A. HIS TIME IS COMING TO AN END (6-8):

1.   Already being poured out like a drink offering, his departure is at hand. (6)

2.   Expressions of his faithfulness (7):

    a.   He has fought the good fight.

    b.   He has finished the race.

    c.   He has kept the faith.

3.   His confidence concerning the future (8):

    a.   A crown of righteousness is laid up for him,

b. Which will be given by the Lord, the righteous Judge:

(1) Given to him on that Day (of judgment).

(2) Given to all who have loved His appearing.

B. A PLEA TO COME QUICKLY (9-16):

1. For Demas has forsaken him, having loved this present world. (9-10a)

2. Crescens and Titus have left, having gone to various places. (10b)

3. Only Luke is with him. (11a)

4. Bring Mark, for he is useful to Paul for ministry. (11b)

5. Tychicus has been sent to Ephesus. (12)

6. Bring the cloak and the books, especially the parchments. (13)

7. A warning against Alexander the coppersmith. (14-15)

8. He was forsaken at his first defense, but prays it will not be charged against them. (16)

C. THE FAITHFULNESS OF THE LORD (17-18)

1. The Lord stood with him and strengthened him (17),

a. So that the message was preached fully by him to the Gentiles,

b. And he was delivered out of the mouth of the lion.

2. The Lord will deliver and preserve him (18):

a. Deliver him from every evil work.

b. Preserve him for His heavenly kingdom.

3. For which glory belongs to the Lord!

III. <u>CONCLUDING REMARKS</u> (19-22)

A. MISCELLANEOUS GREETINGS AND FINAL INSTRUCTIONS (19-21):

1. Greet Prisca and Aquila, and the household of Onesiphorus. (19)

2. Erastus stayed in Corinth, Trophimus was left sick in Miletus. (20)

3. Timothy is to do his best to come before winter. (21a)

4. Greetings from Eubulus, Pudens, Linus, Claudia, and all the brethren. (21b)

B. BENEDICTION (22)

1. The Lord Jesus Christ be with his spirit.

2. Grace be with him. Amen.

LETTER TO TITUS

AUTHOR: **The Apostle Paul**

During Apostle's third missionary journey, Titus became his personal emissary to the church at Corinth, seeking to learn how they received his first letter. When Titus did not return to Troas as expected, Paul anxiously went on to Macedonia (2 Co 2:12-13). It was there that Paul and Titus finally connected, much to the relief and comfort of Paul when Titus reported how well he was received by the Corinthians (2 Co 7:5-7,13-15). Paul then sent Titus and two others back to Corinth, bearing the letter we call Second Corinthians, and exhorting the brethren to complete their collection for the needy saints in Jerusalem (2 Co 8:16-9:5). At the time of the epistle to Titus, he had been left on the island of Crete by Paul to "set in order the things that are lacking, and appoint elders in every city" (Tit 1:5). If Paul's plans as expressed in this epistle materialized, then Titus left soon after the arrival of Artemas or Tychicus, and met Paul at Nicopolis in northwest Greece (cf. Ti 3:12). We last read of Titus that he had gone to Dalmatia (in modern day Yugoslavia) during the final days of Paul's life (2 Ti 4:10).

DATE: It cannot be established with certainty, but it possible that the Apostle Paul wrote this letter from Corinth, sometime around 63-66 AD.

INSIGHT INTO LETTER: Like his first letter to Timothy, this letter is written to a young preacher assigned a difficult task. Evidently, the churches on the island of Crete were in need of maturation, and this letter is designed to assist Titus in that work. Therefore, Paul wrote to encourage Titus.

KEY VERSE: Titus 3:8 "This is a faithful saying, and these things I want you to affirm constantly, that those who have believed in God should be careful to maintain good works. These things are good and profitable for men."

SYNOPSIS:

Chapter 1

I. INTRODUCTION (1-4)

A. FROM PAUL (1-3)

    1. A servant of God and apostle of Jesus Christ. (1a)

  2. According to ... (1b)

    a. The faith of God's elect.

    b. The acknowledgment of the truth which is according to godliness.

  3. In hope of eternal life, which God, who cannot lie ... (2-3)

    a. Promised before time began.

    b. In due time has manifested His Word:

      (1) Through preaching,

      (2) Which was committed to him according to the commandment of God.

B. **TO TITUS** (4)

  1. His true son in their common faith. (4a)

  2. Grace, mercy and peace from God the Father and Jesus Christ our Savior. (4b)

II. <u>CONCERNING ELDERS</u> (5-9)

A. **THE REASON TITUS WAS LEFT IN CRETE** (5):

  1. To set in order the things that are lacking. (5a)

  2. To appoint elders in every city as Paul commanded him. (5b)

B. **QUALIFICATIONS OF ELDERS** (6-9)

  1. Positive qualifications:

    a. Blameless,

    b. The husband of one wife,

    c. Having faithful children not accused of dissipation or insubordination,

    d. Blameless as a steward of God,

    e. Hospitable,

    f. A lover of what is good,

    g. Sober-minded,

      h.   Just,

      i.   Holy,

      j.   Self-controlled,

      k.   Holding fast the faithful word as he has been taught,

      l.   Able by sound doctrine to exhort and convict those who contradict.

   2.   Negative qualifications:

      a.   Not self-willed,

      b.   Not quick-tempered,

      c.   Not given to wine,

      d.   Not violent,

      e.   Not greedy for money.

III. CONCERNING FALSE TEACHERS (10-16)

A. THEIR CHARACTER (10-13a):

   1.   Insubordinate (10a),

   2.   Idle talkers and deceivers, especially those of the circumcision (10b-11):

      a.   Whose mouths must be stopped.

      b.   For they subvert whole households.

      c.   For they teach things which they ought not, for the sake of dishonest gain.

   3.   They live up to the estimation of one of Crete's own prophets:

      "Cretans are always liars, evil beasts, lazy gluttons." (12-13a)

B. THEIR CONDEMNATION (13b-16)

   1.   They are to be rebuked sharply (13b-14):

      a.   That they may be sound in the faith.

b. That they not give heed to Jewish fables and commandments of men.

2. To the pure all things are pure ... (15)

    a. But to those who are defiled and unbelieving, nothing is pure.

    b. But even their mind and conscience are defiled.

3. They profess to know God ... (16)

    a. But in works they deny Him.

    b. Being abominable, disobedient, and disqualified for every good work.

Chapter 2

I. <u>INSTRUCTIONS CONCERNING CHRISTIAN CONDUCT</u> (1-10)

A. THE OLDER MEN (1-2)

1. Titus is to speak things proper for sound doctrine. (1)

2. The older men are to be ... (2)

    a. Sober, reverent, temperate,

    b. Sound in faith, love, patience.

B. THE OLDER WOMEN (3-4a)

1. In similar way they are to be reverent in behavior (3a):

    a. Not slanderers,

    b. Not given to much wine.

2. They are to be teachers of good things, and admonish the young women. (3b-4a)

C. THE YOUNG WOMEN (4b-5):

1. They are to love their husbands and their children. (4b)

    2. They are to be... (5)

       a. Discreet, chaste, homemakers,

       b. Good, obedient to their own husbands that the word of God may not be blasphemed.

D. **THE YOUNG MEN** (6-8):

    1. In a similar way they are to be sober-minded. (6)

    2. In all things Titus is to be a pattern of good works. (7a-8)

       a. In doctrine showing integrity, reverence, incorruptibility,

       b. With sound speech that cannot be condemned:

         (1) So that any opponent may be ashamed,

         (2) Having nothing evil to say of him.

E. **THE SERVANTS** (9-10):

    1. They are to be ... (9-10a)

       a. Obedient to their masters.

       b. Well pleasing in all things, not answering back.

       c. Not pilfering, but showing fidelity in all things.

    2. So they can adorn the doctrine of God in all things. (10b)

II. <u>THE INSTRUCTION OF THE GRACE OF GOD</u> (11-15)

A. **THE GRACE OF GOD HAS APPEARED** (11)

    1. That which brings salvation. (11a)

    2. It has appeared to all men. (11b)

B. **THE GRACE OF GOD TEACHES US** (12-14)

1. To deny ungodliness and worldly lusts. (12a)

2. To live soberly, righteously, and godly in the present age. (12b)

3. To look for the blessed hope and glorious appearing of our great God and Savior Jesus Christ (13),

   a. Who gave Himself for us. (14a)

   b. That He might ...

      (1) Redeem us from every lawless deed. (14b)

      (2) Purify for Himself, His own special people zealous for good works. (14c)

C. **TITUS' RESPONSIBILITY** (15)

1. Speak these things, exhort, and rebuke with all authority. (15a)

2. Let no one despise him (15b).

Chapter 3

I. <u>**INSTRUCTIONS FOR THE BRETHREN IN GENERAL**</u> (1-11)

A. **CONCERNING PROPER CONDUCT** (1-2)

1. Toward those in authority (1):

   a. Be subject to and obey rulers and authorities.

   b. Be ready for every good work.

2. Toward all men (2):

   a. Speak evil of no one.

   b. Be peaceable, gentle, showing humility to all.

B. **REASONS TO HEED SUCH EXHORTATIONS** (3-11)

1. In view of our past conduct (3):

   a. We were once foolish, disobedient and deceived.

   b. We served various lust and pleasures.

   c. We lived in malice and envy, hateful and hating one another.

2. In view of our salvation (4-7):

   a. We were saved according to God's kindness, love and mercy, not by works of righteousness, which we have done. (4-5)

   b. We were saved through the washing of regeneration and renewing of the Holy Spirit (5-7),

     (1) Whom God poured out abundantly through Jesus our Savior.

     (2) That being justified by grace we should become heirs according to the hope of eternal life.

3. In view of what is good and profitable (8):

   a. Those who have believed in God should be careful to maintain good works.

   b. This is a faithful saying, and should be affirmed constantly.

4. In view of what is unprofitable and useless (9-11):

   a. Foolish disputes, genealogies, contentions, and strivings about the law are to be avoided. (9)

   b. A divisive man is to be rejected after two admonitions (10-11)

     (1) For such is warped and sinning,

     (1) And is self-condemned.

II. <u>CONCLUDING REMARKS</u> (12-15)

A. **FINAL INSTRUCTIONS** (12-14):

1. To meet him at Nicopolis, after the arrival of Artemas or Tychicus. (12)

2. To send Zenas and Apollos on their journey with haste, lacking nothing. (13)

3. To aid others in learning to maintain good works, meeting urgent needs, so as not to be unfruitful. (14)

B. **FINAL GREETINGS, AND A PRAYER** (15)

1. Greetings from those with Paul.

2. Greetings to those who love the brethren in the faith.

3. Grace be with you all. Amen.

LETTER TO PHILEMON

<u>AUTHOR:</u> Apostle Paul

<u>DATE:</u> If the letter to Philemon was written about the time Colossians and the other "prison letters" (Ephesians and Philippians) were written, during Apostles imprisonment at Rome, sometime during the period of 61-63 AD.

<u>INSIGHT INTO LETTER:</u> Philemon was a member of the church at Colosse (cf. 1,2, with Col 4:17), and a very hospitable one at that (1,2,5,7). It is possible that he was one of the Apostles own converts (19). Onesimus had been one of Philemon's slaves (16), who had run away (15).

It appears that he somehow traveled to Rome where he found Paul and was converted to Christ (10). He had become very dear to Paul, and was proving to be very useful (11-13). However, Paul did not think it right to keep Onesimus in Rome, and was sending him back to Philemon (12-14). This letter to Philemon is an appeal for him to receive Onesimus now as a brother in Christ, and for him to forgive Onesimus, if he had done any wrong (15-21).

<u>KEY PASSAGE:</u> "I appeal to you for my son Onesimus, whom I have begotten while in my chains, who once was unprofitable to you, but now is profitable to you and to me." (10,11)

<u>SYNOPSIS:</u>

Chapter 1

I. SALUTATION (1-3)

A. **FROM ...** (1a)

    1. Paul, a prisoner of Christ Jesus.

    2. Timothy, a brother.

B. **TO ...** (1b-2)

    1. Philemon, a beloved friend and fellow laborer.

    2. Apphia.

    3. Archippus, a fellow soldier.

    4. The church in their house.

C. **GREETINGS** (3)

    1. Grace and peace.

2. From God the Father and the Lord Jesus Christ.

II. <u>THANKSGIVING AND PRAYER</u> (4-7)

A. PAUL'S THANKFULNESS (4-5)

1. Expressed in frequent prayers to God.

2. For Philemon's love and faith toward Jesus and all the saints.

B. PAUL'S PRAYER (6-7)

1. That the sharing of Philemon's faith might be effective.

2. Through the acknowledgment of every good thing in Philemon.

3. For example, the joy and comfort experienced by Paul from Philemon's love, as Paul hears of how he refreshed the hearts of the saints.

III. <u>THE PLEA FOR ONESIMUS</u> (8-21)

A. AN APPEAL, NOT A COMMAND (8-9)

1. Paul had the authority to command what is fitting.

2. He chose instead to make an appeal based upon ...

   a. Love itself,

   b. Paul's "age,"

   c. His imprisonment.

B. PAUL'S PLEA (10-20)

1. Concerns Onesimus (10-11):

   a. Who was converted by Paul while in chains, and is now like a son to him.

   b. Who though once was unprofitable to Philemon, is now profitable to both him and Paul.

2. Paul is now sending Onesimus back to Philemon (12-14):

   a. Though he is very dear to Paul.

   b. Though Paul wished to keep him and have him work in Philemon's behalf in the gospel.

   c. But Paul did not want to do anything without Philemon's whole-hearted consent.

3. Paul's desire is that Philemon receive Onesimus as a brother in Christ (15-17).

   a. Perhaps his running away was for this purpose that he might become a beloved brother in the Lord.

   b. So, if Philemon considered himself a partner of Paul, Paul asks that he receive Onesimus as he would Paul himself.

4. Paul offers to repay Philemon (18-19)

   a. For any wrong that Onesimus might have done.

   b. Of course, Philemon already owed Paul his own life.

5. By receiving Onesimus in this way, Philemon could give Paul joy and a refreshed heart in the Lord. (20)

C. PAUL'S CONFIDENCE IN PHILEMON (21)

1. In Philemon's obedience.

2. That Philemon will do even more than what Paul is asking for.

IV. CONCLUDING REMARKS (22-25)

A. A REQUEST FOR LODGING (22):

1. That Paul might be able to stay with Philemon.

2. For Paul is confident that through the prayers of Philemon he will soon be able to come to him.

B. **GREETINGS FROM OTHERS** (23-24):

1. Epaphras, a fellow prisoner in Christ Jesus.

2. Mark, Aristarchus, Demas, and Luke, fellow laborers with Paul.

A **CLOSING PRAYER** (25)

LETTER TO THE HEBREWS

The letter to the Hebrews is a unique book in the New Testament. It begins as an essay (He 1:1-2), progresses as a sermon (He 2:1-4), and ends as a letter (He 13:23-25). Its contents are deep and challenging. Many Christians find it difficult; some equate its difficulty with the book of Revelation.

AUTHOR: The author does not identify himself. Many believe it to be the Apostle Paul (e.g., Clement of Alexandria) and have offered arguments in his favor (cf. Commentary on Hebrews, Robert Milligan, p. 5-19). Yet it seems unlikely when you consider the author's statement, " ... was confirmed to us by those who heard Him" (He 2:3). This suggests the author received the gospel message second-hand, while Paul declared that he had not received the gospel from or through men (Ga 1:11-12).

DATE: Approximately between 63–65 AD.

INSIGHT INTO LETTER:

The author wrote this epistle to prevent his readers from abandoning their faith in Christ (He 2:1-4). To encourage his Jewish brethren not to go back to the Old Law, he endeavored to show the superiority of Christ and His Covenant (He 8:1-2,6). A key word found throughout the epistle is "better:"

> * Christ is "better than the angels" - He 1:4
> * We enjoy "the bringing in of a better hope" - He 7:19
> * Jesus has become "the surety of a better covenant" - He 7:22
> * He is also "the Mediator of a better covenant, which was established on better promises" - He 8:6
> * The heavenly things benefit from "better sacrifices" - He 9:23

The Superiority Of Christ and The New Covenant

KEY WARNINGS

A unique feature of the letter **warnings.**

1. **The warning against drifting** (He 2:1-4)

   a. Through neglect we can easily drift away.

   b. The solution is to give the more earnest heed to the things we have heard.

2. **The warning against departing** (He 3:12-15)

a. Through sin's deceitfulness we can become hardened and develop a lack of faith by which we can depart from the living God.

b. The solution is to exhort one another daily and remain steadfast.

3. **The warning against disobedience** (He 4:11-13)

a. Like Israel in the wilderness, we can fail to enter our rest through disobedience.

b. The solution is diligence and heeding the Word of God.

4. **The warning against dullness** (He 5:11-6:6)

a. Dullness of hearing can make it difficult for us to appreciate the extent of our blessings in Christ, and even falling away to the point of crucifying the Son of God afresh!

b. The solution is grasping the first principles of the oracles of God, and then pressing on to spiritual maturity and perfection.

5. **The warning against despising** (He 10:26-39)

a. It is possible to so despise God's grace as to no longer have a sacrifice for sins, but only a certain fearful expectation of judgment.

b. b. The solution is to hold unto our confidence in Christ, and believe with endurance.

6. **The warning against defying** (He 12:25-29)

a. It is possible to refuse to listen to the One who now speaks from heaven!

b. The solution is to look diligently to the grace of God, receiving it in such a way so we may serve Him acceptably with reverence and godly fear.

SYNOPSIS:
Chapter 1

Dispensing with greetings and salutations typical of letters at that time, the epistle to the Hebrews begins like a sermon, with the author immediately declaring the superiority of Jesus. While God spoke in times past to the fathers by the prophets, He now speaks to us through His Son (1-3). Jesus is also demonstrated to be much better than angels (4-14).

Chapter 2

The author interrupts his comparison of Christ with angels with his *first* of six warnings in this epistle: A warning against *drifting* by neglecting our great salvation (1-4). He then illustrates Jesus' superiority to angels by being made lower than the angels, whereby He became the perfect captain of our salvation and a merciful and faithful High Priest (5-18).

Chapter 3

Having demonstrated Jesus' superiority to prophets and angels, the author now compares Jesus to Moses (1-6). The comparison is followed with a reference to Israel's unfaithfulness in wilderness, which leads to the *second* of six warnings in this epistle: A warning against *departing* from the living God by developing an evil heart of unbelief (7-19).

Chapter 4

Since many Israelites failed to enter their Canaan rest because of unbelief, the author says we should fear lest we come short of our promised rest: Heaven (1-10). Diligence is also required, and the *third* of six warnings is given: A warning against *disobedience* in view of God's living and powerful Word (11-13). A positive motivation is then given: Our great High Priest, Jesus, who enables us to obtain mercy and grace as needed (14-16).

Chapter 5

How Jesus is superior to prophets, angels, and Moses has been discussed. Now comes Jesus' superiority to Aaron as High Priest. Qualities necessary to be high priest are reviewed, ably met by Jesus (1-10). Before proceeding further, the author finds it necessary to extend the *fourth* warning, this one against dullness due to spiritual immaturity (11-14).

Chapter 6

The interruption of the discussion regarding Jesus as High priest continues with a solemn warning regarding spiritual progress, and the need for diligence, faith and patience in order to inherit the promises (1-12). The certainty of God's promises upon which our hope is based serves as an anchor of the soul that reaches into heaven itself, where Christ is now our High Priest according the order of Melchizedek (13-20).

Chapter 7

Resuming the discussion of Jesus as High Priest, the superiority of Melchizedek to Abraham and Levi is first demonstrated (1-10). Reasons are then given why a new priest after the order of Melchizedek was necessary, which also required a change in the Law (11-19). Finally, the greatness of Jesus as our new High Priest is explained (20-28).

Chapter 8

Having demonstrated Jesus' superiority to prophets, angels, Moses, and Levi, the author summarizes: We have a High Priest at God's right hand who is Minister and Mediator of a better covenant established on better promises (1-6). Our attention is then directed toward that New Covenant, which has replaced the Old Covenant (7-13).

Chapter 9

To appreciate the difference between the two covenants, their respective sanctuaries and divine services are compared. First, the earthly sanctuary and the limitations of its divine services are reviewed (1-10); then, the greater and more perfect heavenly sanctuary with emphasis on its better sacrifice, the blood of Christ Himself (11-28).

Chapter 10

The animal sacrifices of the Law (the first covenant) are shown to be insufficient, while the death of Christ fulfills the will of God and perfects those who are being sanctified (1-18). A three-fold exhortation based on what Christ has done (19-25) is followed by the *fifth* of six warnings, this one against despising God's grace with

willful sin (26-39).

Chapter 11

Having stressed the importance of faith for salvation (He 10:39), the author defines faith (1-3) and then illustrates faith's role in the lives of many Old Testament saints (4-40).

Chapter 12

With the "heroes of faith" like a cloud of witness cheering us on, we are to run the race of faith, looking to Jesus' example for endurance and to

God's loving discipline lest we fall short of His grace (1-17). Coming not to Mt. Sinai but to glorious Mt. Zion (18-24), we are given the *sixth* warning: Not to refuse or defy Him who speaks from heaven (25-29).

<u>Chapter 13</u>

The epistle concludes with miscellaneous moral and religious exhortations regarding their conduct as Christians (1-19), followed by a benediction, a final exhortation, and a farewell that mentions Timothy along with greetings from those who are from Italy (20-25).

LETTER OF JAMES

AUTHOR: James, who identifies himself as "a bondservant of God and of the Lord Jesus Christ" (1:1). There are five men who bear this name in the New Testament:

James, son of Zebedee and brother of John - A fisherman called by Christ (Mt 4:17-22) who later became an apostle (Mt 10:2). Together with John, they were nicknamed "Sons of Thunder" because of their impulsiveness (cf. Mk 3:17 with Lk 9:51-56). He was killed by Herod in 44 AD (Act 12:1-2).

James, son of Alphaeus - Another one of the apostles (Mt 10:3; Act 1:12), about whom very little is known. He may be "James the younger," whose mother, Mary, was among the women at Jesus' crucifixion and tomb (Mt 27:56; Mk 15:40; 16:1; Lk 24:10). In Jn 19:25, this Mary is called the wife of Cleophas, perhaps to be identified with Alphaeus.

James, father of Judas the Apostle - Even more obscure, one of the few references to him is Lk 6:16.

James, the brother of our Lord - A half-brother of our Lord (Mt 13:55), who did not believe in his brother at first (Jn 7:5). He became a disciple following the resurrection (1 Co 15:7; Act 1:14) and gained prominence in the church at Jerusalem (Ga 2:9). As evidence of his prominence, Peter sent him a special message following his own release from prison (Act 12:17). James also played an important role in the conference at Jerusalem (Act 15:13-33), and Paul brought him greetings upon arriving at Jerusalem (Act 21:18-19).

"James, the Lord's brother" (Ga 1:19) is most likely the author of this epistle. Tradition describes James as a man of prayer, which may explain the emphasis on prayer in his letter. It was said that he prayed so much, his knees were as hard as those on a camel. He was martyred in 62 AD, either by being cast down from the temple, or beaten to death with clubs. It is reported that as he died, he prayed as did Jesus, "Father, forgive them, for they know not what they do."

DATE: With no mention of the Jerusalem conference recorded in Acts 15 (AD 49), and the use of the word "synagogue" (assembly, 2:2), AD 48–50 is the date commonly given for this letter. This would make it the first book of the New Testament written. If James, the Lord's brother, is the author, then he probably wrote it in Jerusalem.

INSIGHT INTO LETTER:

The epistle deals with a variety of themes, with an emphasis upon practical aspects of the Christian life. Some of the subjects include handling trials and temptations, practicing pure religion, understanding the relation between faith and works, the proper use of the tongue and display of true wisdom, being a friend of God rather than a friend of the world, and the value of humility, patience and prayer. While these may appear unrelated, they are crucial to the growth and development of the Christian. For this reason, I suggest that James' purpose was:

KEY VERSE: James 1:22 "But be doers of the word, and not hearers only, deceiving yourselves."

SYNOPSIS:

Chapter 1

SALUTATION (1)

I. TRUE RELIGION ENDURES TRIALS AND TEMPTATIONS (2-18)

A. WITH JOY AND PATIENCE (2-4)

1. Knowing that the testing of your faith produces patience.

2. Letting patience produce its perfect work:

   a. That you may be perfect and complete.

   b. That you may lack nothing.

B. WITH WISDOM FROM GOD (5-8)

1. If you lack wisdom, ask God,

   a. Who gives to all liberally and without reproach?

   b. It will be given to you.

2. But ask in faith, with no doubting; for he who doubts ...

   a. Is like a wave of the sea driven and tossed by the wind.

    b.   Should not suppose that he will receive anything from the Lord.

    c.   Is a double-minded man, unstable in all his ways.

C. WITH A PROPER PERSPECTIVE (9-11)

1.   If a lowly brother, glory in your exaltation.

2.   If rich, glory in your humiliation:

    a.   For as the flower of the field you will pass away, as the grass withers with the burning heat of the rising sun.

    b.   So, the rich man will fade away in his pursuits.

D. WITH AN UNDERSTANDING OF TEMPTATION (12-15)

1.   The man who endures temptation will be blessed:

    a.   For he will receive the crown of life when he is proven,

    b.   Which the Lord has promised to those who love Him.

2.   Temptations do not come from God:

    a.   God cannot be tempted by evil.

    b.   He does not tempt anyone.

3.   The source of temptations:

    a.   One is tempted when drawn away by his own desires and is enticed.

    b.   When desire has conceived, it gives birth to sin.

    c.   in, when full-grown, brings forth death.

E. WITH AN AWARENESS OF THE FATHER'S GOODNESS (16-18)

1.   Do not be deceived, beloved brethren.

2. Every good and perfect gift is from above:

    a. Coming down from the Father of lights,

    b. With whom there is no variation or shadow of turning.

3. Of His own will He brought us forth:

    a. By the word of truth,

    b. That we might be a kind of first fruits of His creatures.

II. TRUE RELIGION CONSISTS OF DOING, NOT JUST HEARING (19-27)

A. ONE SHOULD BE SWIFT TO HEAR (19-20)

1. Let everyone be swift to hear, slow to speak, slow to wrath.

2. For the wrath of man does not produce the righteousness of God.

B. ONE SHOULD NOT BE HEARERS ONLY, BUT DOERS (21-27)

1. What to lay aside, and what to receive

    a. Lay aside all filthiness and overflow of wickedness.

    b. Receive with meekness the implanted word, which is able to save your souls.

2. Be doers of the word, and not hearers only:

    a. Otherwise you deceive yourselves.

    b. You are like a man who after looking in the mirror soon forgets what he looked like.

3. One who looks into the perfect law of liberty and continues in it ...

    a. Is not a forgetful hearer, but a doer of the work.

b. Will be blessed in what he does.

4. Your religion is useless …

    a. If you think you're religious, but do not bridle your tongue.

    b. You deceive only your heart.

5. Pure and undefiled religion before God and the Father is this …

    a. To visit orphans and widows in their trouble.

    b. To keep oneself unspotted from the world.

Chapter 2

I. TRUE RELIGION DOES NOT SHOW PARTIALITY (1-13)

A. SUCH AS SHOWING PREFERENCE TO THE RICH (1-3)

1. The faith of our Lord Jesus Christ, the Lord of glory, is not to be held with partiality.

2. A case in point: Showing preference with seating arrangements in the assembly.

B. REASONS NOT TO SHOW PARTIALITY TOWARD THE RICH (4-13):

1. It makes one a judge with evil thoughts.

2. Has not God chosen the poor to be rich in faith and heirs of the kingdom?

3. Have not the rich oppressed and blasphemed you?

4. Does not the royal law call upon us to love our neighbor?

5. Partiality will convict us as transgressors, even if we stumble in only one point.

6. We shall be judged by the law of liberty, in which judgment without mercy is given to those who show no mercy.

II. <u>TRUE RELIGION SHOWS FAITH THROUGH WORKS</u> (14-26)

A. FAITH WITHOUT WORKS CANNOT SAVE ONE (14-19)

1. What profit is there in faith without works?

   a. Can such faith save one?

   b. Is there any profit to tell a naked and destitute person to be warm and filled, and not give them what they need?

   c. Thus, faith by itself, without works, is dead.

2. Faith is shown by one's works:

   a. It is not enough to claim to have faith.

   b. The devils believe in God, and tremble.

B. FAITH WITHOUT WORKS IS DEAD (20-26)

1. As exemplified by Abraham, the friend of God,

   a. Who was justified by works when he offered his son Isaac on the altar.

   b. His faith was working with his works, and by them perfected his faith.

   c. By his works the Scripture was fulfilled that declared him faithful and righteous.

2. As exemplified by Rahab, the harlot,

   a. Who was justified by works when she hid the spies.

   b. Thus, faith without works is dead, just as the body without the spirit is dead.

Chapter 3
I. <u>TRUE RELIGION CONTROLS THE TONGUE</u> (1-12)

A. CAUTION AGAINST BECOMING TEACHERS (1-2)

1. Teachers shall receive a stricter judgment.

    2.   Maturity and self-control are required not to stumble in word.

B. **THE POWER OF THE TONGUE** (3-4)

    1.   Like a bit, which controls the horse.

    2.   Like a small rudder, which directs the ship.

C. **THE DANGER OF THE TONGUE** (5-6)

    1.   A little member, which boasts great things.

    2.   Like a little fire, which kindles a great forest fire.

    3.   Indeed, the tongue can be a fire, a world of iniquity:

        a.   Capable of defiling the whole body.

        b.   Capable of setting on fire the course of nature, being set on fire by hell.

D. **THE DIFFICULTY OF TAMING THE TONGUE** (7-12)

    1.   Man can control creatures of land and sea, but not the tongue.

    2.   It is an unruly evil, full of deadly poison.

    3.   With it we bless God, and then curse man made in His image.

        a.   Thus, blessing and cursing proceed from the same mouth.

        b.   Something which should not be so:

           (1) For no spring sends forth both fresh and salt water.

           (2) Neither does a fig tree bear olives, nor a grapevine bear figs.

II. <u>TRUE RELIGION DISPLAYS HEAVENLY WISDOM</u> (13-18)

A. THE TRUE DISPLAY OF WISDOM AND UNDERSTANDING (13)

    1.   To be seen in one's conduct.

    2.   With works done in meekness.

B. THE DISPLAY OF EARTHLY WISDOM (14-16)

    1.   Full of bitter envy, self-seeking, boasting and lying.

    2.   A wisdom not from above, but is earthly, sensual, demonic.

    3.   Producing confusion and every evil thing.

C. THE DISPLAY OF HEAVENLY WISDOM (17-18)

    1.   Wisdom from above is first pure, then it is ...

       a.   Peaceable, gentle, willing to yield, full of mercy and good fruits.

       b.   Without partiality and without hypocrisy.

    2.   The fruit of righteousness is produced by peacemakers who sow in peace.

Chapter 4

I. TRUE RELIGION DOES NOT BEFRIEND THE WORLD (1-6)

A. THE SOURCE OF WARS AND FIGHTS (1-3)

    1.   From within, from desires that war in one's members.

    2.   Such as lust (envy), murder (hate), coveting, which do not give what one seeks.

    3.   Leading to unanswered prayers due to selfishness.

B. FRIENDSHIP WITH THE WORLD IS ENMITY WITH GOD (4-6)

    1.   Whoever wants to be a friend of the world becomes an enemy of God.

    2.   Even as the Scripture warns, and not in vain.

    3.   While God resists the proud, He is willing to give grace to the humble.

II. TRUE RELIGION DRAWS NEAR TO GOD (7-17)

A. **BY SUBMITTING TO GOD'S AUTHORITY** (7-12)

1. Submit to God, resist the devil and he will flee.

2. Draw near to God and He will draw near to you:

   a. Cleanse your hands, sinners.

   b. Purify your hearts, double-minded.

   c. Mourn and weep for your sins.

   d. Humble yourself before God, and He will lift you up.

3. Let God be the Lawgiver and Judge:

   a. Do not speak evil of one another and judge one another:

      (1) Otherwise you speak evil of the law and judge the law.

      (2) Otherwise you are not a doer of the law, but a judge.

   b. When there is really only one Lawgiver who is able to save and destroy.

B. **BY SUBMITTING TO GOD'S WILL** (13-17)

1. We should be careful in making plans for the future:

   a. We do not know what will happen tomorrow.

   b. Life is but a vapor that appears for a little while and then vanishes.

2. Therefore, we should acknowledge "If the Lord wills" in our plans,

   a. Otherwise we boast in arrogance, which is evil.

  b. For one to know to do good and not do it, that is sin.

Chapter 5

I. TRUE RELIGION DISPLAYS PATIENCE UNDER OPPRESSION (1-12)

A. GOD'S ANGER AT RICH OPPRESSORS (1-6)

  1. The rich are called to weep and howl for the miseries to come upon them:

    a. Their riches are corrupted.

    b. Their garments are moth-eaten.

    c. Their gold and silver are corroded,

      (1) Which will be a witness against them.

      (2) Which will eat their flesh like fire.

    d. They have heaped up treasure in the last days.

  2. The reasons for God's anger against the rich:

    a. They have defrauded the laborers who mowed their fields:

      (1) Keeping back wages owed to them.

      (2) he cries of the reapers have been heard by the Lord of Sabaoth (Hosts).

    b. They have lived in pleasure and luxury, fattening their hearts in a day of slaughter.

    c. They have condemned and murdered the just who does not resist them.

B. A CALL FOR PATIENCE UNDER OPPRESSION (7-12)

  1. Be patient until the coming of the Lord:

    a. Consider the patience of the farmer.

    b. Establish your hearts, for the coming of the Lord is at hand.

  2. Do not grumble against one another:

      a.   Lest you be condemned.

      b.   The Judge is standing at the door.

3.   Remember the examples of suffering and patience:

      a.   Such as the prophets who spoke in the name of the Lord and are blessed for their endurance.

      b.   Such as the perseverance of Job, to whom the Lord proved very compassionate and merciful at the end.

4.   Above all, do not swear (make rash oaths):

      a.   Either by heaven or by earth or with any other oath.

      b.   Let your "Yes" mean "Yes," and your "No" mean "No."

      c.   Lest you fall into judgment.

II. TRUE RELIGION BLESSED THROUGH PRAYER, SINGING, AND CONCERN <u>FOR THE ERRING</u> (13-20)

A. THE BLESSING OF PRAYER AND SONG (13-18)

1.   If anyone is suffering, let him pray.

2.   If anyone is cheerful, let him sing psalms.

3.   If anyone is sick, let him call for the elders of the church:

      a.   Let them pray over him, anointing him with oil in the name of the Lord.

      b.   The prayer of faith will save (heal) the sick, and the Lord will raise him up.

      c.   If he has committed sins, he will be forgiven.

      d.   Confess your trespasses to one another and pray for one another:

(1) That you may be healed.

(2) For the effective, fervent prayer of a righteous man avails much:

    a.   The example of Elijah, a man with a nature like ours.

    b.   He prayed that it would not rain, and no rain fell for three years.

    c.   He prayed again, the heaven gave rain, and the earth produced its fruit.

B. THE BLESSING OF LOVE FOR ERRING BRETHREN (19-20)

1.   He who turns back one who wanders from the truth will save a soul from death.

2.   He who turns a sinner from the error of his way will cover a multitude of sins.

FIRST LETTER OF PETER

AUTHOR: The Apostle Peter, as stated in the salutation (1:1).

DATE: A common view is the epistle was written on the eve of the Neronian persecution (perhaps alluded to in 4:12-19), placing its composition around 63–64 AD.

INSIGHT INTO LETTER:

The Apostle Peter refers to the recipients of his letter as "pilgrims of the Dispersion" (1:1). The term "Dispersion" is found in Jn 7:35 and was used to describe Israelites who had been "scattered" following the Assyrian and Babylonian captivities (Ca. 700–500 BC). This leads many to suppose that the letter was written to Jewish Christians, as was the case of James' letter (cf. Jn 1:1). However, there is indication some of his readers were Gentile converts who had come to believe in God through Jesus (cf. 1:21), and that Peter applies the term "dispersion" to Christians in general, just as he applied other designations to the church that were formerly applied to the nation of Israel (cf. 2:9-10). It is apparent from the letter that Christians in Asia Minor had experienced persecution (1:6), and more suffering was on the way (4:12-19). Throughout the letter Peter encourages them to remain steadfast (1:13; 4:16; 5:8,9). He reminds them of their blessings and duties that are incumbent upon them as God's "elect" (1:2), "His own special people" (2:9).

KEY VERSES:

1 Peter 2:11-12 "Beloved, I beg you as sojourners and pilgrims, abstain from fleshly lusts, which war against the soul, having your conduct honorable among the Gentiles, that when they speak against you as evildoers, they may, by your good works, which they observe glorify God in the day of visitation."

SYNOPSIS:

Chapter 1

I. INTRODUCTION (1-2)

A. THE AUTHOR (1a)

    1.   Peter.

    2.   An Apostle of Jesus Christ.

B. **THE RECIPIENTS** (1b-2b)

   1.   Pilgrims of the Dispersion.

   2.   In Pontus, Galatia, Cappadocia, Asia, and Bithynia.

   3.   Elect (chosen) ...

      a.   According to the foreknowledge of God the Father.

      b.   In sanctification of the Spirit.

      c.   For obedience and sprinkling of blood of Jesus Christ.

C. **GREETINGS** (2c)

   1.   Grace and peace,

   2.   Be multiplied.

II. OUR SALVATION IN CHRIST (3-12)

A. **BORN AGAIN TO A LIVING HOPE** (3-5)

   1.   Because of God's abundant mercy.

   2.   Because Jesus has been raised from the dead.

   3.   Because of our wonderful inheritance:

      a.   Incorruptible, undefiled, and that does not fade away.

      b.   Reserved in heaven.

   4.   Because of being safely kept:

      a.   By the power of God through faith.

      b.   b. For salvation ready to be revealed in the last time.

B. **PRODUCING JOY IN THE MIDST OF SUFFERING** (6-9)

   1.   Great joy, though for a little while grieved by various trials.

   2.   The genuineness of faith tested by fire:

    a.   Proving more precious than gold that perishes.

    b.   May be found to praise, honor, and glory at the revelation of Jesus Christ.

3.   Rejoicing with joy inexpressible and full of glory:

    a.   For loving Him whom you have not seen.

    b.   For believing Him whom you have not seen.

4.   Receiving the end of such faith - the salvation of your souls.

C. SERVED BY PROPHETS AND APOSTLES (10-12)

1.   Regarding our salvation the prophets inquired and searched diligently:

    a.   Wondering what and when the Spirit of Christ in them was indicating,

    b.   When He testified beforehand of the sufferings of Christ and the glories to follow.

2.   They were ministering such things not to themselves, but to us:

    a.   Things now reported by those who preached the gospel by the Holy Spirit,

    b.   Things which angels desire to look into.

III. OUR DUTY IN CHRIST (13-25)

A. HOLY CONDUCT (13-21)

1.   Gird up the loins of your mind:

    a.   Be sober,

    b.   Rest your hope fully upon the grace to be brought at the revelation of Jesus Christ.

2.   Be holy in all your conduct:

    a.   As obedient children,

     b.   Not conforming to former lusts done in ignorance,

     c.   As He who called you is holy, just as it is written.

  3.   Conduct yourselves during your stay in fear,

     a.   Since you call on the Father who judges each one without partiality.

     b.   Knowing that you redeemed:

       (1) Not with corruptible things like silver and gold.

       (2) From your aimless conduct received by tradition from your fathers.

       (3) With the precious blood of Christ:

          a.   As of a lamb without blemish and without spot.

          b.   Foreordained before the foundation of the world.

          c.   Manifest in these last times for yo

          d.   Through whom you believe in God:

             1] Who raised Him from the dead and gave Him glory,

             2] So that your faith and hope are in God.

B. **FERVENT AND PURE LOVE** (22-25)

  1.   Since you have purified your souls:

     a.   In obeying the truth through the Spirit.

     b.   In sincere love of the brethren.

  2.   Having been born again, not of corruptible seed but incorruptible:

a. Through the word of God which lives and abide forever:

(1) All flesh is as grass, all the glory of man as the flower of the grass.

(2) The grass withers, its flower falls away.

(3) The word of the Lord endures forever.

b. The word which by the gospel was preached to you.

Chapter 2

I. A CALL TO SPIRITUAL GROWTH (1-3)

A. WHAT TO LAY ASIDE (1):

1. All malice, all deceit.

2. Hypocrisy, envy, and all evil speaking.

B. WHAT TO DESIRE (2-3):

1. The pure milk of the word:

   a. As newborn babes,

   b. That you may grow thereby.

2. If indeed you have tasted that the Lord is gracious.

II. OUR PRIVILEGE IN CHRIST (4-10)

A. AS LIVING STONES (4-8)

1. Coming to Christ as to a living stone,

   a. Who was rejected by men.

   b. Who is chosen by God and precious.

2. We as living stones are being built up as a spiritual house:

   a. To be a holy priesthood.

      b.   To offer spiritual sacrifices acceptable to God through Jesus Christ.

   3.   Christ is the precious cornerstone,

      a.   As foretold in Isaiah 28:16:

         (1) God would lay in Zion a chief cornerstone, elect, precious.

         (2) He who believes on Him will by no means be put to shame.

         (3) Precious to those who believe.

      b.   As foretold in Psalms 118:22 and Isaiah 8:14:

         (1) A stone rejected by the builders, which has become the chief cornerstone.

         (2) A stone of stumbling and rock of offense to those who are disobedient.

         (3) To which they were appointed.

B. AS PEOPLE OF GOD (9-10)

   1.   They are now:

      a.   A chosen generation.

      b.   A royal priesthood.

      c.   A holy nation.

      d.   His own special people.

   2.   They are now:

      a.   To proclaim the praises of God, who called them:

         (1) Out of darkness.

         (2) Into His marvelous light.

      b.   The people of God, who once were not the people of God

(1)   Who had not obtained mercy.

(2)   But now have obtained mercy.

III. <u>OUR DUTIES IN CHRIST</u> (11-25)

A. **AS SOJOURNERS** (11-12)

1.   To abstain from fleshly lusts, which war against the soul.

2.   To have conduct honorable among the Gentiles:

    a.   That when they speak against you as evildoers.

    b.   They may glorify God in the day of visitation.

    c.   Because of your good works they observe.

B. <u>**AS CITIZENS**</u> (13-17)

1.   Submit yourselves to every ordinance of man for the Lord's sake:

    a.   To the king as supreme.

    b.   To governors as those sent by the king:

        (1) For the punishment of evildoers.

        (2)   For the praise of those who do good.

2.   For this is the will of God, as bondservants of God:

    a.   That by doing good you may put to silence the ignorance of foolish men.

    b.   As free, yet not using liberty as a cloak for vice.

3.   Therefore:

    a.   Honor all,

    b.   Love the brotherhood,

    c.   Fear God,

       d.   Honor the king.

C. AS SERVANTS (18-25)

1. Submissive to your masters with all fear:

   a. Not only to the good and gentle,

   b. But also to the harsh.

2. For this is commendable before God:

   a. If because of conscience before God one endures grief, suffering wrongfully,

   b. What credit is there when beaten for your faults, you take it patiently?

   c. If when you do good and suffer, yet take it patiently, that is commendable.

3. For we were called to Follow in the steps of Jesus our example:

   a. Who committed no sin, nor was deceit found in His mouth (Isaiah 53:9):

      (1) When He was reviled, did not revile in return.

      (2) When He suffered, He did not threaten.

      (3) He committed Himself to Him who judges righteously.

   b. Who bore our sins in His own body on the tree:

      (1) That we, having died to sins, might live for righteousness.

      (2) By whose stripes, you were healed.

      (3) You were like sheep going astray, but have now returned to the Shepherd and Overseer of your souls.

Chapter 3

I. <u>OUR DUTIES AS WIVES AND HUSBANDS</u> (1-7)

A. THE DUTIES OF WIVES (1-6)

    1.   Be submissive to your husbands:

        a.   That you might win those who are not believers.

        b.   As they observe your chaste conduct accompanied by fear.

    2.   Adorn yourselves properly:

        a.   Not merely outward - arranging the hair, wearing gold, putting on of fine apparel.

        b.   With the incorruptible beauty of a gentle and quiet spirit, precious in God's sight.

        c.   As holy women in the past who trusted God:

            (1) Adorned themselves,

            (2) Submitted to their husbands.

        d.   As Sarah obeyed Abraham, calling him lord:

            (1) Whose daughters you are.

            (2) If you do good, and are not afraid with any terror.

B. <u>THE DUTIES OF HUSBANDS (7)</u>

    1.   Dwell with your wives with understanding.

    2.   Give honor to your wives:

        a.   As to the weaker vessel.

        b.   As being heirs together of the grace of life.

        c.   So, your prayers may not be hindered.

II. <u>OUR DUTIES AS BRETHREN</u> (8-12)

A. <u>OUR DUTIES TO EACH OTHER (8-9):</u>

1. Be of one mind.

2. Have compassion for one another.

3. Love one another as brethren.

4. Tenderhearted, courteous.

5. Not returning evil for evil, or reviling for reviling:

   a. On the contrary, respond with a blessing.

   b. Knowing that you were called to this, that you might inherit a blessing.

B. MOTIVATION TO FULFILL SUCH DUTIES (10-12)

1. If you would love life and see good days,

   a. Refrain your tongue from evil and lips from speaking deceit.

   b. Turn from evil and do good.

   c. C. Seek peace and pursue it.

2. If you would desire the Lord's favor,

   a. For His eyes are on the righteous.

   b. For His ears are open to their prayers.

   c. But His face is against those who do evil.

III. OUR DUTIES AS SUFFERERS FOR RIGHTEOUSNESS' SAKE (13-22)

A. THINGS TO REMEMBER (13-17)

1. Who will harm you if you do what is good?

   a. Even if you should suffer for righteousness' sake, you are blessed.

   b. So, don't be afraid of threats, nor be troubled.

2. Sanctify the Lord God in your hearts.

3. Always be ready to give a defense:

       a.   To everyone who asks.

       b.   For a reason for the hope that is in you.

       c.   With meekness and fear.

4.   Maintain a good conscience:

       a.   That when others may defame you as evildoers,

       b.   Those who revile your good conduct in Christ may be ashamed.

5.   It is better, if it is the will of God ...

       a.   To suffer for doing good,

       b.   Than to suffer for doing evil.

B. REASONS TO REMEMBER (18-22)

1.   Christ also suffered once for sins:

       a.   The just for the unjust.

       b.   That He might bring us to God.

2.   He was put to death in the flesh, but made alive by the Spirit:

       a.   By whom He went and preached to the spirits in prison who were formerly disobedient:

          (1) During the longsuffering of God.

          (2) In the days of Noah, while the ark was being prepared:

              a.   In which eight souls were saved through water,

              b.   Which was a type of baptism which now saves us:

                 1] Not the removal of the filth of the flesh,

                 2] But the answer of a good conscience toward God

    3] Through the resurrection of Christ.

b. Who has gone in to heaven:

    (1) And is at the right hand of God,

    (2) Where angels, authorities, and powers have been made subject to Him.

SECOND LETTER OF PETER

AUTHOR: The Apostle Peter, as stated in the salutation (1:1). The writer claims to have had special revelation from the Lord concerning his demise (1:14; cf. Jn 21:18-19), and to have been present when the Lord was transfigured on the mountain (1:16-18; cf. Mt 17:1-9). He also alludes to the first epistle (3:1), and acknowledges acquaintance with the Apostle Paul (3:15).

DATE: Since Nero committed suicide in 68 AD, most believe the letter dated before then. The letter was therefore probably written sometime during 67 AD. The letter is addressed to those "who have obtained like precious faith with us by the righteousness of our God and Savior Jesus Christ" (1:1). The author notes this is the second letter he has written to them (3:1). If it is indeed the second letter written to the same audience as First Peter, then the recipients were those Christian "pilgrims" (cf. 1Pe 1:1; 2:11) who were living in Pontus, Galatia, Cappadocia, Asia, and Bithynia, provinces in what is now Turkey.

INSIGHT INTO LETTER: Peter states His purpose very clearly in writing this letter: **To stir up his brethren by way of reminder** (1:12-15; 3:1).

Knowing his death is imminent (1:13-14), Peter wanted to ensure that his readers remain established in the truth (1:12), and be mindful of both the words spoken before by the prophets and the commandments given by the Apostles, especially in regards to the promise of the Lord's return (3:1-4). He warns Christians to beware lest they fall from their steadfastness, being led away by error. At the same time he exhorts them to grow in the grace and knowledge of Jesus Christ. After the opening salutation, virtually every verse of the letter is either an encouragement to grow or a warning against false teachers (including those who scoff at the idea of the Lord returning).

KEY VERSES: 2 Peter 3:17-18 "You therefore, beloved, since you know this beforehand, beware lest you also fall from your own steadfastness, being led away with the error of the wicked; but grow in the grace and knowledge of our Lord and Savior Jesus Christ. To Him be the glory both now and forever. Amen."

SYNOPSIS:

Chapter 1

I. **INTRODUCTION** (1-2)

A. **THE AUTHOR** (1a)

1. Peter.

2. A bondservant and Apostles of Jesus Christ.

B. **THE RECIPIENTS** (1b)

1. Those who have obtained like precious faith.

2. By the righteousness of our God and Savior Jesus Christ.

C. **GREETINGS** (2)

1. Grace and peace be multiplied,

2. In the knowledge of God and of Jesus our Lord.

II. <u>**GROW IN GRACE AND KNOWLEDGE**</u> (3-21)

A. **WITH PRECIOUS GIFTS FROM GOD** (3-4)

1. His divine power has given us all things that pertain to life and godliness:

   a. Through the knowledge of Him,

   b. Who called us by glory and virtue.

2. His glory and virtue has given us exceedingly great and precious promises:

   a. Through which we may be partakers of the divine nature,

   b. Having escaped the corruption that is in the world through lust.

B. **ABOUNDING IN THE KNOWLEDGE OF CHRIST** (5-11)

1. Diligent to add to our faith:

   a. Virtue, knowledge, self-control, perseverance,

   b. Godliness, brotherly kindness, love.

2. Diligent to make our call and election sure:

    a. Abounding in these graces, neither barren nor unfruitful in the knowledge of Christ.

    b. Not lacking in these graces, neither short-sighted nor forgetful of our cleansing.

    c. Ensuring that we do not stumble, but have an abundant entrance into the everlasting kingdom of our Lord Jesus Christ.

C. STIRRED UP BY CAREFUL REMINDER (12-21)

1. By one who knows his death is imminent:

    a. Who desires not to be negligent in reminding them.

    b. Even though they know and are established in the present truth.

    c. Who thinks it right to stir them up by way of reminder.

    d. Knowing he will shortly put off his tent, as Jesus showed him.

    e. To ensure they will always have a reminder of these things after his death.

2. Whose eyewitness testimony along with the prophetic Word we should heed:

    a. He did not offer cunningly devised fables:

        (1) When proclaiming the power and coming of the Lord,

        (2) But was an eyewitness of His majesty,

        (3) Such as when Christ received honor and glory from God the Father on the Mount of Transfiguration.

    b. We also have the prophetic word confirmed,

        (1) Which we do well to heed:

      a. As a light in a dark place.

      b. Until the day dawns and the morning star rises in our hearts.

   3. Knowing the prophetic nature of Scripture:

      a. It was not of private interpretation (origin), or by the will of man,

      b. But holy men of God spoke as they were moved by the Holy Spirit.

Chapter 2

I. **THE DESTRUCTIVENESS OF FALSE TEACHERS** (1-3)

A. THEIR DESTRUCTIVE HERESIES (1-2)

   1. Just as there were false prophets, so there will be false teachers.

   2. They will bring in destructive heresies, even denying the Lord who bought them.

   3. Many will follow their destructive ways, and the truth will be blasphemed.

B. THEIR DESTRUCTIVE METHODS (1,3)

   1. They bring in their heresies secretly.

   2. They will exploit through covetousness and deceptive words.

C. THEIR DESTRUCTIVE END (1,3)

   1. They will bring swift destruction on themselves.

   2. Their judgment is not idle, their destruction does not slumber.

II. **THE DOOM OF FALSE TEACHERS** (4-9)

A. THE EXAMPLE OF ANGELS WHO SINNED (4)

   1. God did not spare the angels who sinned.

2. He cast them down to hell (Tartarus).

3. Delivered them to chains of darkness, reserved for judgment.

B. THE EXAMPLE OF THE FLOOD (5)

1. God did not spare the ancient world, bringing the flood on the ungodly.

2. He saved Noah and his family of eight, a preacher of righteousness.

C. THE EXAMPLE OF SODOM AND GOMORRAH (6-8)

1. God turned the cities into ashes, condemning them to destruction.

2. He made them an example to those who would live ungodly.

3. He delivered righteous Lot:

   a. Who was oppressed by the filthy conduct of the wicked.

   b. Who was tormented daily by seeing and hearing their lawless deeds.

D. GOD WILL DELIVER THE GODLY, PUNISH THE UNJUST (9)

1. The Lord knows how to deliver the godly out of temptations.

2. He will reserve the unjust under punishment for the day of judgment.

III. THE DEPRAVITY OF FALSE TEACHERS (10-17)

A. REVILING AGAINST AUTHORITY (10-13a)

1. They walk according to the flesh in the lust of uncleanness.

2. They despise authority, are presumptuous, self-willed.

3. They are not afraid to speak evil of dignitaries, unlike angels:

    a. Who are greater in power and might.

    b. Who do not bring reviling accusations before the Lord.

4. They are like natural brute beasts made to be caught and destroyed:

    a. Speaking evil of things they do not understand.

    b. Who will utterly perish in their own corruption.

    c. Who will receive the wages of unrighteousness.

B. REVELING WITH GREAT PLEASURE (13b-14)

1. They count it pleasure to carouse in the daytime.

2. Spots and blemishes, they carouse in their own deceptions while feasting with Christians.

3. They have eyes full of adultery that cannot cease from sin, beguiling unstable souls.

4. They have hearts trained in covetous practices, and are accursed children.

C. REVOLTING AGAINST THE RIGHT WAY (15-17)

1. They have forsaken the right way and gone astray.

2. Like Balaam, who loved the wages of unrighteousness,

    a. Who was rebuked for his iniquity.

    b. His madness restrained by donkey speaking with a man's voice.

3. They are wells without water, clouds carried by a tempest.

4. For who the gloom of darkness is reserved forever.

IV. THE DECEPTIONS OF FALSE TEACHERS (18-22)

A. DECEPTIVE IN THEIR METHODS (18)

1. They speak great swelling words of emptiness.

2. They allure those who have escaped through the lusts of the flesh, through licentiousness.

B. DECEPTIVE IN THEIR PROMISES (19)

1. They promise liberty, while they themselves are slaves of corruption.

2. For by whom a person is overcome, by him also he is brought into bondage.

C. WHOSE LATTER END IS WORSE THAN THE BEGINNING (20-22)

1. Having become entangled and overcome by the pollutions of the world, which they had escaped through the knowledge of the Lord and Savior Jesus Christ.

2. It would have been better not to have known the way of righteousness than having known it, to turn from the holy commandment delivered to them.

3. t has happened to them according to the proverb:

   a. "A dog returns to his own vomit."

   b. "A sow, having washed, to her wallowing in the mire."

Chapter 3

I. THE SCOFFERS WILL COME (1-9)

A. REMEMBER THE WORDS SPOKEN BEFORE (1-4)

    1. Peter writes this second letter to stir up his readers by way of reminder.

    2. To be mindful of the prophets' words and the apostles' commandments.

    3. That scoffers will come in the last days, walking according to their own lusts:

        a. Questioning the promise of the Lord's coming.

        b. Declaring that all things continue as they were since creation.

B. <u>**REMEMBER THE WORLD WAS DESTROYED BEFORE**</u> (5-7)

    1. Which the scoffers willfully forget.

    2. That the world once perished being flooded with water.

    3. The same word that brought destruction by water now promises judgment by fire:

        a. The heavens and the earth, which now exists, are reserved for fire.

        b. When comes the day of judgment and perdition of ungodly men.

C. REMEMBER THE LORD'S TIMELESSNESS AND LONG SUFFERING (8-9)

    1. Do not forget that time means nothing to the Lord:

        a. One day is as a thousand years.

        b. A thousand years is as one day.

    2. The Lord is not slack concerning His promise, but long suffering:

        a. Not willing that any perish,

        b. But that all should repent.

II. <u>**THE DAY OF THE LORD WILL COME**</u> (10-18)

A. UNEXPECTED WITH CATACLYSMIC DESTRUCTION (10-12)

1. The day of the Lord will come as a thief in the night.

2. The heavens and the earth be dissolved:

   a. The heavens will pass away with a great noise.

   b. The elements will melt with fervent heat.

   c. The earth and its works will be burned up.

   d. The heavens will be dissolved being on fire.

3. Since all these things will be dissolved ...

   a. What manner of persons ought we to be in holy conduct and godliness?

   b. Looking for and hastening the coming of the day of God?

B. EXPECTED BY THOSE WHO ARE LOOKING (13-18)

1. According to His promise, we look forward:

   a. To new heavens and a new earth,

   b. In which righteousness dwells.

2. Looking forward to these things, we should be diligent

   a. To be found by Him in peace.

   b. To be without spot and blameless.

3. We thus consider the long suffering of the Lord to be salvation,

   a. Of which the beloved brother Paul has written, according to the wisdom given to him.

    b.   In which are some things hard to understand, which the unstable and untaught twist to their own destruction.

4.   Knowing such things beforehand, we should beware and grow:

    a.   Beware lest we fall from our own steadfastness, led away with the error of the wicked.

    b.   Grow in the grace and knowledge of our Lord and Savior Jesus Christ.

5.   To Him be the glory both now and forever. Amen.

FIRST LETTER OF JOHN

AUTHOR: Not stated but according to church tradition, the Apostle John, the beloved disciple of Jesus (Jn 13:23; 19:26-27; 20:2; 21:7, 20).

DATE: Most Bible scholars place the writing around 95 AD.

INSIGHT INTO LETTER:

In his letter, John frequently states why he was writing:

> * "these things we write to you that your joy may be full" (1 Jn 1:4).
> * "these things I write to you, that you may not sin" (1 Jn 2:1).
> * "these things I have written to you ... that you may know that you have eternal life" (1 Jn 5:13).
> * "these things I have written to you ... that you may continue to believe in the name of the Son of God" (1 Jn 5:13).

The Apostle John address a strange heresy that claimed Jesus has been on earth only in spirit, not in body (4:3). John wrote that he knew Jesus personally, as one who looked upon him, and his hands have touched (1:1), and that knowledge leads to a saving belief in Jesus. Saving belief leads to obedience, but even when we sin, we know that god is faithful to forgive us when we confess (1:9).

John's purpose therefore appears to be two-fold:

> * Assure Christians that they have eternal life (1 Jn 5:13).
> * Counter those who denied that Jesus had come in the flesh (1 Jn 4:1-6).

SYNOPSIS:

Chapter 1

John begins his first letter like he does his gospel: With a prologue regarding the Word of Life (Jesus Christ) who dwelt in the flesh among men and made fellowship with the Father possible (1-4). Fellowship with God is maintained as we walk in the light and confess our sins that we might enjoy continual cleansing through the blood of Jesus (5-10).

> * The witness of John concerning the Word of Life.
> * The nature of the evidence for faith in Jesus.
> * The basis of our fellowship with God.

Chapter 2

We have an Advocate who is also the propitiation for our sins and to truly know Him we must keep His commandments (1-6), especially to love one another (7-11). Describing his original readers' spiritual state (12-14), John cautions against loving the world and being deceived by antichrists (15-23), by letting truth abide in them and they in Christ (24-29).

* The true test of knowing Jesus as our advocate and our propitiation.
* Things in the world we cannot not love.
* The identity of antichrists in the writings of John.

Chapter 3

John describes God's wonderful love for us, how hope as His children should motivate us to pure lives. Righteous living should be expected when we know what sin is, that Christ came to destroy it, and that one truly born of God will not persist in sin (1-9). True righteousness includes loving one another, even as Christ loved us, which in turn gives us confidence and assurance that we are abiding in Him and are of the truth (10-24).

* God's love for us, and our love for one another.
* The definition of sin, and the meaning of "does not sin" (6,9).
* The outworking of love, and the assurance it gives of our salvtion.

Chapter 4

John cautions his readers not to believe everyone who claims to be led by the Spirit, but to test them (1-6). He then exhorts them to manifest brotherly love in keeping with the character and example of God's love as demonstrated in the sacrifice of His Son (7-21).

* Distinguishing the spirit of truth from the spirit of error.
* How God's love should impact our love for one another.

Chapter 5

John writes of faith in Christ, loving God, and overcoming the world (1-5). He then reviews God's witness that gives us certainty regarding eternal life in Christ (6-13), and concludes with teaching on prayer (14-17) and the sure knowledge found in the Son of God (18-21).

* The importance of faith, love, and obedience.
* The nature of eternal life as a present possession.
* Sin, which does not lead to death versus sin, which does lead to

death.

SECOND LETTER OF JOHN

AUTHOR:

The Apostle John according to church tradition. The author is identified only as "the elder" (1:1). Many conservative scholars support the internal evidence:

> * The *three letters* attributed to John utilize much the same language and ideas.
> * All bear similarity to concepts and language to the Gospel of John.
> * The term "elder" would be a fitting description of John as the author writing in his old age.

DATE:

Estimation of the date of writing varies widely, some placing it before the destruction of Jerusalem, 70 AD. Most however, place it around 90–95 AD.

INSIGHT INTO LETTER:

The letter is addressed to "the elect lady and her children" (1:1).

There are two views of thought in regards to the elect lady. The first – **Literal.** Taken literally, the letter is written to a particular woman and her children. The second – **Figurative.** Taken figuratively, it could refer to a local church "elect lady and her children" (1) and "children of your elect sister" (13) refer to two particular congregations.

Within this short letter, the purpose is rather straightforward and twofold:

> * Encourage brotherly love, and keeping the commandments of God. (2 Jn 1:5-6)
> * Warning against supporting or encouraging false teachers. (2 Jn 1:10-11)

SYNOPSIS:

Chapter 1

The Elder greets the elect lady and her children (1-3), expressing joy over hearing her children were walking in truth, with a plea to love one another (4-6). He then warns of deceivers (antichrists) who deny Jesus as coming in the flesh, telling her not to receive into her home those

who do not bring the doctrine of Christ (7-11). Hoping to see her soon, he concludes with greetings from the children of her elect sister (12-13).

* Walking in truth and love, abiding in the doctrine of Christ.
* Identifying antichrists, refusing to support false teachers.

THIRD LETTER OF JOHN

What was the early church like? We know a lot about its early leaders, such as Apostles Paul and Peter; but what about the average Christians themselves? Were they more spiritual than Christians today? Did they experience the kind of problems seen so often in churches today? Several books of the New Testament reflect the life of the early church, and this is especially true of *The Third Letter of John*. It is a private letter, between "The Elder" and a Christian named Gaius. It provides portraits of three different men, and in so doing gives us a glimpse of the first century life in local churches. When one examines the portraits found in this letter, we learn that there is not much difference between people back then, and in the church today. Therefore, this epistle is very relevant, though we may live almost two thousand years later.

AUTHOR:

"The Elder" (3 Jn 1:1) is believed by most conservative scholars to be the Apostle John. Again, the internal evidence for the third letter is similar to that of the second:

> * The three letters of John utilize much the same language and ideas.
> * All bear similarity to concepts and language to the Gospel of John.
> * The term "elder" would be a fitting description of John as the author, writing in his old age.

DATE: Approximately 90–95 AD.

INSIGHT INTO LETTER:

The letter is addressed to "beloved Gaius." Gaius was a common Roman name, and appears five times in the New Testament (Act 19:29; 20:4; Ro 16:23; 1 Co 1:14; 3 Jn 1:1). Whether he is one of those mentioned by Luke or Paul cannot be determined. He was evidently a dear friend of the Apostle John, known for his hospitality. The letter is threefold, written to the three men mentioned by name:

> * To confirm that **Gaius** did right in supporting those teachers who came his way, encouraging him to continue this hospitality. (3 Jn 1:5-8)

* To express his condemnation of **Diotrephes** for rejecting John and others whom he   should had received. (3 Jn 1:9-10)

* To encourage Gaius to imitate what is good, commending **Demetrius** as a good example. (3 Jn 1:11-12)

SYNOPSIS:

Chapter 1

John greets Gaius, praying for his prosperity and health, rejoicing to hear that he is walking in truth (1-4). John approves his hospitality toward brethren and strangers, especially those serving the Lord (5-8). John condemns the deeds of Diotrephes (9-10), commends the testimony of Demetrius (11-12), and concludes with a hope to see Gaius soon (13-14).

* The joy of seeing one's converts growing in Christ.

* The importance of hospitality in the spread of the gospel.

* The contrast between spirituality and carnality among Christians.

THE LETTER OF JUDE

AUTHOR: Jude, as stated in the salutation (Jude 1:1). That he does not identify himself as an apostle, and appears to distinguish himself from the apostles (Jude 1:17), suggests he was not the apostle Jude (cf. Lk 6:16; Ac 1:13). His self-identification as "the brother of James" leads
many to believe the author to be Judas, brother of James and also of the Lord Jesus (cf. Mt 13:55). Like James, Jude chose not to accentuate his physical relation to Jesus, but his spiritual one ("a bondservant of Jesus Christ," cf. Jude 1:1; Jm 1:1).

DATE: Approximately 82 AD.

INSIGHT INTO LETTER: The letter is addressed "to those who are called" (Jude 1:1) without any specific designation as to who they were or where they lived. The references to Old Testament incidents and extra-biblical sources (Jude 1:5-7,9,11,14) strongly suggests that the original readers were Jewish Christians, perhaps living in Palestine. Jude's original purpose in penning this letter was to write of the common salvation he and his readers shared (Jude 1:3). But the presence of ungodly men and the danger of them leading Christians astray forced a change in purpose:

> * To encourage his readers to contend earnestly for the faith that
> had been delivered to the saints (Jude 1:3).

SYNOPSIS:

Chapter 1

Following his salutation (1-2), Jude explains the purpose for writing (3-4). He reminds his readers of God's judgments in the past (5-7), then describes the character and ultimate doom of false teachers (8-19). Exhorting them to build up their most holy faith (20-23), he concludes with praise to God (24-25).

THE BOOK OF REVELATION

AUTHOR:
John, identified as one "who bore witness to the word of God, and to the testimony of Jesus Christ" (Re 1:1-2). His authorship of this book is supported by the testimony of Justin Martyr (165 AD), Clement of Alexandria (220 AD), Hippolytus (236 AD), and Origen (254 AD).

DATE: Approximately 95–96 AD., during the reign of emperor Domitian.

INSIGHT INTO LETTER:

The early church likely did not have the problem understanding the book as we do today. They were well acquainted with the style of apocalyptic literature. They were living at a time when the symbols of the book were likely familiar to them (similar to how a picture of a donkey fighting an elephant would be understood by us as depicting conflict between the Democratic and Republican parties).

Our difficulty with this book is due to our unfamiliarity with apocalyptic literature as a method of communicating a message. We are also far removed from the historical and cultural context of the times, which would make the symbolism easier to understand. To properly interpret the book, we must try to understand the historical context in which it was written. We must also interpret it in a manner that would have been meaningful to those to whom it was first addressed. It also behooves us to pay close attention to those passages or statements which are clear and easy to understand.

KEY VERSE:
"These will make war with the Lamb, and the Lamb will overcome them, for He is Lord of lords and King of kings; and those who are with Him are called, chosen, and faithful." (Re 17:14)

SYNOPSIS:

Chapter 1

  I. **INTRODUCTION** (1-8)

  A. INTRODUCTION AND BENEDICTION (1-3)

      1. Introducing the Revelation of Jesus Christ (1-2):

      a.   Which God gave Him to show His servants.

      b.   Regarding things, which much shortly take place.

      c.   Sent and signified by His angel.

      d.   To His servant John, who bore witness ...

          (1) To the word of God,

          (2) To the testimony of Jesus Christ,

          (3) To all things that he saw.

2.   The benediction (3):

      a.   Blessed is he who reads and those who hear this prophecy.

      b.   Blessed are those who keep those things written in it, for the time is near.

B. GREETINGS TO THE SEVEN CHURCHES (4-6)

1.   From John, to the seven churches in Asia (4a),

2.   With grace and peace (4b-6):

      a.   From Him who is and who was and who is to come.

      b.   From the seven Spirits who are before His throne.

      c.   From Jesus Christ:

          (1) The faithful witness,

          (2) The firstborn from the dead,

          (3) The ruler over the kings of the earth,

          (4) Who loved us and washed us from our sins in His own blood,

          (5) Who made us kings and priests to His God and Father,

(6)   o Whom be glory and dominion
forever and ever!

C. ANNOUNCEMENT OF CHRIST'S COMING (7)

1.   He is coming with clouds.

2.   Every eye will see Him, and they also who
pierced Him.

3.   All the tribes of the earth will mourn because
of Him.

4.   Even so, Amen (so be it).

D. THE SELF-DESIGNATION (8)

1.   "I am the Alpha and the Omega, the
Beginning and the End."

2.   "Who is and who was and who is to come, the
Almighty."

II. THE VISION OF THE SON OF MAN (9-20)

A. JOHN'S CIRCUMSTANCES LEADING UP TO THE VISION (9-10a)

1.   Their brother and companion (9a):

a.   In tribulation.

b.   In the kingdom and patience of Jesus
Christ.

2.   On the island called Patmos (9b):

a.   For the word of God.

b.   For the testimony of Jesus Christ.

3.   In the Spirit on the Lord's Day (10a).

B. WHAT HE HEARD BEHIND HIM (10b-11)

1.   A loud voice, as of a trumpet (10b).

2.   Saying to him ... (11)

a.   "I am the Alpha and the Omega, the First
and the Last."

      b.   "What you see, write in a book."

      c.   "Send it to the seven churches which are in Asia ... "

C. WHAT HE SAW, AND HIS REACTION (12-17a)

    1.   Turning to see the voice, he saw ... (12-16)

      a.   Seven golden lampstands.

      b.   In the midst of the seven lampstands, One like the Son of Man:

        (1) Clothed with a garment down to the feet, girded about the chest with a golden band.

        (2) His head and hair white as wool, white as snow.

        (3) His eyes like a flame of fire.

        (4) His feet like fine brass, as if refined in a furnace.

        (5) His voice as the sound of many waters.

        (6) In His right hand, seven stars.

        (7) Out of His mouth, a sharp two-edged sword.

        (8) His countenance like the sun shining in its strength.

    2.   Seeing Him, John fell at His feet as dead (17).

D. THE LORD'S WORDS TO JOHN (17b-20)

    1.   "Do not be afraid" (17b-18),

      a.   "I am the First and the Last."

      b.   "I am He who lives, and was dead, and behold, I am alive forevermore. Amen."

      c.   "I have the keys of Hades and of Death."

2. "Write ... " (19)

    a. "The things which you have seen,"

    b. "The things which are,"

    c. "The things which will take place after this."

3. "The mystery of the seven stars ... and the seven golden lampstands." (20)

    a. "The seven stars are the angels of the seven churches."

    b. "The seven lampstands ... are the seven churches."

Chapter 2

In this chapter, John is instructed to write to four churches in Asia: **Ephesus, Smyrna, Pergamos, and Thyatira.** The Lord generally follows the same format: His self-designation, commendation, condemnation and related warning, exhortation and promise. Each letter closes with the admonition, *"He who has an ear, let him hear what the Spirit says to the churches."* This suggests the letters were not just for the personal benefit of the churches addressed.

The church at **Ephesus** is commended for its steadfastness, especially against false Apostles. But while standing for the truth, they had lost their first love. Exhorted to repent and be restored by doing the "first works," they are warned that their "lampstand" would be removed if they did not repent (1-7).

The church at **Smyrna** is commended for being "rich" despite their tribulation and poverty. Unlike most churches, there are no words of condemnation directed toward it. While they would experience a little persecution, they are exhorted to remain faithful to death (8-11). The church at **Pergamos** is also praised for its steadfastness, but faulted for allowing false teachers in their midst. The Lord threatens to come and fight with the sword of His mouth, if there is no repentance (12-17).

The church at **Thyatira** is also commended for their last works are more than their first. But they too have a false teacher and followers, which jeopardize the condition of the church. Despite giving this "Jezebel" time to repent, she has not and so the Lord intends to make

her and her followers an example before the other churches (18-29).

Chapter 3

The Lord continues His letters to the churches in Asia, with this chapter containing those written to Sardis, Philadelphia, and Laodicea. The church in **Sardis** is rebuked for having a name that they are alive, when in reality they are dead. With their works not perfected before

God, they are exhorted to be watchful and to strengthen the things which remain. They are also told to remember how they had received and heard in the past, to hold fast and repent. Otherwise, the Lord will come upon them as a thief in the night. Notice is taken, however, of a few in Sardis who had not defiled their garments and are still worthy, who are promised to walk with the Lord in white (1-6).

The church in **Philadelphia** is promised an open door that none can shut because they had kept the Lord's word and not denied His name. Their enemies, those who claim to be Jews but are not, will be made to worship before them, and the church will be kept from the trial that

was about to test those on the earth. With an announcement of His quick coming, they are exhorted to hold fast what they have that none take their crown (7-13).

The church of **Laodicea** is then described as lukewarm, for which the Lord threatens to spew them out of His mouth. While claiming to be rich, they are blind to their true condition. Therefore, the Lord counsels them to buy from Him those things they truly need. His strong

words are indicative of His love for them, and the fact that He stands ready to re-enter their hearts, if they will open to Him (14-22). As before, each letter ends with wonderful promises to those who overcome. In most cases, the manner in which the promises are to be fulfilled is illustrated in the visions to come.

Chapter 4

The visions of Revelation now begin in earnest. Upon seeing a door standing open in heaven and hearing a trumpet-like voice promising to show him of things that must take place, John is transported to **the throne**

room of God. He describes what he hears and sees with vivid and colorful imagery. The One on the throne radiates like jasper and sardius stones, surrounded by an emerald rainbow. The colors may reflect the characteristics of God, such as holiness, righteousness, justice, and mercy, or they may simply signify His splendor and majesty (1-3). John takes special note of **twenty-four elders** clothed with white robes and crowns of gold, sitting on thrones around the throne of God. Summers and Hailey suggest that they depict the twelve patriarchs of Israel and the twelve apostles, who represent the redeemed of both covenants now united in Christ. Note that in Rev 5:8-9 they do seem to speak in behalf of the redeemed (4). From the throne proceeded lightning, thunder, and voices, which may illustrate divine power and judgments coming from God. Before the throne are **seven lamps** of fire, explained as the seven Spirits of God. This likely symbolizes the Holy Spirit in His work of illumination and revelation of God's word to man (Summers). A **sea of glass** like crystal is also before the throne, perhaps symbolizing the transcendence of God that presently separates God and His people (5-6a). There are **four living creatures**, similar in some respects and yet different in others, united in their constant praise of God for His eternal holiness. Though not exactly like the cherubim seen by Ezekiel (Ezek 1, 10), they appear to serve similar functions. Hailey suggests they may be a special order of heavenly beings, perhaps the highest and closest to the throne, who serve God's majestic will (6b-8). As the four living creatures praise Him who sits on the throne, the twenty-four elders join in by falling down, casting their crowns before the throne, and praising God as the Eternal Creator (9-11).

This scene, along with that in Chapter Five, appears designed to set the stage for what follows. At the outset, we are shown the first guarantee of ultimate victory: **God is on His throne!** (Summers). The praise offered by the four living creatures and the twenty-four elders reinforce the truth that the One on the throne (and in ultimate control) is none other than the Lord God Almighty, Eternal and Holy, the Creator who holds all things together. He is therefore worthy of glory, honor and power! He is the one to revere, not some man!

Chapter 5

I. THE SCROLL AND THE LAMB (1-7)

A. **THE SCROLL IN GOD'S RIGHT HAND (1-4):**

1. Written on the inside and on the back, sealed with seven seals.

2. The proclamation by the strong angel:

    a. "Who is worthy?"

    b. "To open and the scroll and to loose its seals?"

3. The initial response:

    a. No one, in heaven, on the earth, under the earth!

    b. No one, able to open the scroll, or to look at it!

4. John's reaction: "So I wept much, because no one was found worthy ... "

B. **THE ONE WORTHY TO OPEN THE SCROLL** (5-7)

1. Comforting words of the elder to John:

    a. "Do not weep."

    b. "Behold, the Lion of the tribe of Judah, the root of David."

    c. He "has prevailed:"

        (1) "To open the scroll."

        (2) "To loose its seven seals."

2. John's description of the Lamb:

    a. Standing in the midst of the throne, the four living creatures, and the elders.

    b. A Lamb as though it had been slain:

        (1) Having seven horns,

        (2) With seven eyes, which are the seven Spirits of God sent into all the earth.

      c.   Who takes the scroll out of God's right hand.

II. <u>THE LAMB IS PRAISED</u> (8-14)

A. BY THE FOUR LIVING CREATURES AND TWENTY-FOUR ELDERS (8-10)

1. Each having:

   a. A harp,

   b. Golden bowls full of incense, which are the prayers of the saints.

2. They sang a new song ...

   a. The Lamb is worthy!

      (1) To take the scroll.

      (2) To open its seals.

   b. Because:

      (1) He was slain.

      (2) He has redeemed them to God by His blood out of every tribe, tongue, people and nation.

      (3) He has made them kings and priests to God, to reign on the Earth.

B. BY THOUSANDS UPON THOUSANDS OF ANGELS (11-12)

1. Their voices heard around the throne, along with the living creatures and the elders.

2. Saying with a loud voice:

   a. Worthy is the Lamb who was slain,

   b. To receive power, riches, wisdom, strength, honor, glory, and blessing.

C. TOGETHER WITH HIM WHO SITS ON THE THRONE (13-14)

1. John now hears those in heaven, on earth, under the earth, and in the sea saying:

   a. "Blessing and honor and glory and power ... "

   b. "Be to Him who sits on throne, and to the Lamb, forever and ever!"

2. Upon which:

   a. The four living creatures said, "Amen!"

   b. The twenty-four elders fell down and worshipped Him who lives forever and ever.

Chapter 6

I. THE FOUR HORSES AND THEIR RIDERS (1-8)

A. FIRST SEAL – RIDER ON THE WHITE HORSE (1-2)

1. The Lamb opens the first seal.

2. One of the four living creatures says "Come."

3. John sees a white horse and its rider:

   a. The man had a bow.

   b. A crown was given to him.

   c. The man went out conquering and to conquer.

B. SECOND SEAL – RIDER ON THE RED HORSE (3-4)

1. The Lamb opens the second seal.

2. The second living creature says "Come."

3. John sees a fiery red horse and its rider:

   a. The rider was granted to take peace from the earth, and for people to kill one another.

   b. A great sword was given to him.

C. THIRD SEAL – RIDER ON THE BLACK HORSE (5-6)

1. The Lamb opens the third seal.

2. The third living creature says "Come."

3. John sees a black horse and its rider:

    a. A pair of scales is in the hand of the rider.

    b. A voice in the midst of the four living creatures says, "A quart of wheat for a denarius, and three quarts of barley for a denarius; and do not harm the oil and the wine."

D. FOURTH SEAL – RIDER ON THE PALE HORSE (7-8)

1. The Lamb opens the fourth seal.

2. The fourth living creature says "Come."

3. John sees a pale horse and its rider:

    a. On the horse sits Death, and Hades followed with him.

    b. Power was given to them over a fourth of the earth.

    c. Power to kill with the sword, with death, and by beasts.

II. THE SOULS UNDER THE ALTAR (9-11)

A. THE FIFTH SEAL – SOULS UNDER THE ALTAR (9-10)

1. The Lamb opens the fifth seal.

2. John sees under the altar those who had been slain:

    a. For the word of God.

    b. For the testimony they held.

3. They cried with a loud voice:

    a. "How long, O Lord, holy and true,"

    b. "Until you judge and avenge our blood on those who dwell on the earth?"

B. **THEIR CONSOLATION** (11)

1. A white robe was given to each of them.

2. hey were told to rest a little while longer, until both their fellow servants and brethren would be killed.

III. <u>COSMIC DISRUPTIONS IN THE DAY OF THE LAMB'S WRATH</u> (12-17)

A. **THE SIXTH SEAL – COSMIC DISRUPTIONS** (12-14)

1. The Lamb opens the sixth seal.

2. Cataclysmic events occur:

    a. A great earthquake.

    b. Sun becomes black as sackcloth of hair.

    c. Moon became like blood.

    d. Stars fall to the earth, like ripe figs shaken from a tree by a mighty wind.

    e. Sky receded as a scroll when rolled up.

    f. Every mountain and island moved out of its place.

B. **THE REACTION OF MANKIND** (15-17)

1. Great and small, slave and free, hid themselves in the caves and rocks of the mountains.

2. They cry out to the mountains and rocks:

    a. "Fall on us and hide us from the face of Him who sits on the throne and from the wrath of the Lamb!"

    b. "For the great day of His wrath has come, and who is able to stand?"

<u>Chapter 7</u>

I. <u>THE 144,000 SEALED ON EARTH</u> (1-8)

A. **THE ANGELS RESTRAINED** (1-3)

1. John saw four angels at the four corners of the earth:

    a. Holding the four winds of the earth,

    b. That the winds would not blow on the earth, sea, or any tree.

2. John saw another angel ascending from the east:

    a. Crying with a loud voice to the four angels granted to harm the earth and sea.

    b. Instructing them not to harm the earth, sea, or trees until the servants of God were sealed on their foreheads.

B. THE 144,000 SEALED (4-8)

John "heard" the number of those sealed.

1. Those sealed were 12,000 each of the tribes of Israel:

    a. Judah g. Simeon

    b. Reuben h. Levi

    c. Gad i. Issachar

    d. Asher j. Zebulun

    e. Naphtali k. Joseph

    f. Manasseh l. Benjamin

II. THE GREAT MULTITUDE IN HEAVEN (9-17)

A. JOHN SEES A GREAT MULTITUDE (9-12)

1. Which none could number, from all nations, tribes, peoples and tongues.

2. Standing before the throne and before the Lamb:

    a. Clothed with white robes,

    b. With palm branches in their hands.

3. Crying with loud voices: "Salvation belongs to our God who sits on the throne, and to the Lamb!"

4. Angels, the elders, and the four living creatures also join in with praise:

    a. Falling on their faces before the throne and worshipping God.

    b. Ascribing blessing, glory, wisdom, thanksgiving, honor, power, and might to God.

B. **THE GREAT MULTITUDE IDENTIFIED** (13-17)

1. Asked by one of the elders, John puts the question back to him.

2. The elder identifies the great multitude:

    a. Those who come out of the great tribulation.

    b. Who have washed their robes and made them white in the blood of the Lamb.

  c. Who are before the throne of God and serve Him day and night in His temple.

3. The elder describes their future blessedness:

    a. The One on the throne will dwell with them.

    b. They shall not hunger nor thirst anymore; the sun nor any heat shall strike them.

    c. The Lamb will shepherd them and lead them to living fountains of water.

    d. God will wipe away every tear from their eyes.

Chapter 8

Following the "interlude" of the previous chapter, in which reassuring and comforting scenes concerning the saints were seen, **the Seventh Seal** is now opened. For about a half hour, there is silence in heaven (1).

In contrast to all that happened before, the silence must have been striking! Possibly it signifies awe in heaven for what has already been revealed, or for what is about to be revealed. When God acts, those on earth should be in awe (Hab 2:20; Zec 2:13). Should we not expect a similar reaction from His creatures in heaven (Zep 1:7)? **Seven angels** are seen standing before God to whom are given **seven trumpets**. Before they sound the trumpets, **another angel with a golden censer** comes and stands before the altar. To this angel is given much incense to offer along with the prayers of the saints upon the golden altar before the throne. The smoke of the incense and the prayers of the saints ascend before God from the angel's hand. Then, the angel takes the censer, fills it with fire from the altar, and throws it to the earth. Noises, thundering's, lightning's and an earthquake follow, and the seven angels with the seven trumpets prepare to sound (2-6). The scene appears to suggest that the sounding of the seven trumpets and the things to follow is God's response to the prayers of the saints. It is reminiscent of what Jesus taught in His parable of the persistent widow: *"And shall God not avenge His own elect who cry out day and night to Him, though He bears long with them?"* (Lk 18:7; cf. also Re 6:9-10). As the first four angels sound their trumpets in turn, the environment in particular is impacted:

> * **The first trumpet** –
> Hail and fire, mingled with blood, are thrown to earth; a third of the trees and all the green grass were burned up (**7**).
> * **The second trumpet** –
> Something like a great burning mountain is thrown into the sea, turning a third of it into   blood; a third of the sea creatures died, and a third of the ships were destroyed (**8-9**).
> * **The third trumpet** –
> A great burning star named Wormwood falls on a third of the rivers and springs of water; a third of the waters became wormwood (a bitter wood) and many men died from the bitter water (**10-11**).
> * **The fourth trumpet** –

A third of the sun, moon, and stars are struck, so that a third of them were darkened; thus, a third of the day and night did not shine (12).

The first four trumpets may signify **natural calamities** that God would use in His judgment **against apostate Israel** who oppressed His people. They are reminiscent of the Egyptian plagues (Ex 9-10), brought now against herself that is later called "Egypt" (Re 11:8). That only a third is affected, along with the symbolism of trumpets, suggests that the purpose of these judgments would be to warn, giving many opportunity to repent. Before the final three trumpets sound, an angel flies through the midst of heaven with a loud voice proclaiming a **three-fold woe** on the inhabitants of the earth (13).

While the first four trumpets were bad enough, **the worst was yet to come!**

Chapter 9

I. THE FIFTH TRUMPET: LOCUSTS FROM THE BOTTOMLESS PIT (1-12)

A. THE "STAR" FALLEN FROM HEAVEN (1-2)

1. With the sounding of the fifth trumpet ...

   a. John saw a star fallen from heaven to the earth,

   b. To whom was given the key to the bottomless pit.

2. When the bottomless pit was opened ...

   a. Smoke like that of a great furnace arose out of the pit.

   b. The sun and the air were darkened because of the smoke.

B. THE "LOCUSTS" AND THEIR POWER (3-10)

1. Out of the smoke locusts with great power came upon the earth:

   a. Power like scorpions.

     b.   Commanded not to harm the grass, any green thing, or any tree.

  2.   The extent and nature of their power:

     a.   Could harm only those who do not have the seal of God on their foreheads.

     b.   Could not kill, but only torment them for five months.

     c.   Men will seek death, but death will flee from them.

  3.   The locusts described:

     a.   Their shape like horses prepared for battle.

     b.   On their heads were crowns of something like gold.

     c.   Their faces were like those of men.

     d.   Their hair was like women's hair.

     e.   Their teeth was like lions' teeth.

     f.   With breastplates like those of iron.

     g.   The sound of their wings like chariots with many running horses.

     h.   With tails like scorpions, and stings in their tails (though

     i.   limited in power).

C. THE "KING" OVER THEM (11-12)

  1.   The angel of the bottomless pit,

  2.   Whose name in Hebrew is Abaddon, and in Greek, Apollyon.

  3.   The first of three woes is past; two more to come.

II. THE SIXTH TRUMPET: THE TWO HUNDRED MILLION ARMY (13-21)

A. THE FOUR ANGELS BOUND AT THE EUPHRATES (13-15)

1. With the sounding of the sixth trumpet ...

   a. John heard a voice from the four horns of the golden altar before God,

   b. Speaking to the sixth angel who had the trumpet,

   c. Telling him to release the four angels bound at the river Euphrates.

2. The four angels released ...

   a. Who had been prepared for the hour, day, month, and year.

   b. Who were to kill a third of mankind.

B. THE ARMY OF TWO HUNDRED MILLION HORSEMEN (16-19)

1. John heard the number of them.

2. What he saw in the vision ...

   a. Those on the horses had breastplates of fiery red, hyacinth blue, sulfur yellow.

   b. The horses had heads like those of lions.

   c. Out of their mouths came fire, smoke, and brimstone.

3. The power of this great army ...

   a. A third of mankind killed by the fire, smoke, and brimstone.

   b. The power to harm is in their mouth and tails like serpents' heads.

C. THE FAILURE OF THE SURVIVORS TO REPENT (20-21)

1. Those not killed did not repent of their idolatry.

2. Nor did they repent of their murders, sorceries, sexual immoralities, or thefts.

Chapter 10

I. THE MIGHTY ANGEL WITH THE LITTLE BOOK (1-7)

A. THE ANGEL, THE BOOK, AND THE SEVEN THUNDERS (1-4)

1. John describes another mighty angel coming down from heaven:

   a. Clothed with a cloud.

   b. A rainbow on his head.

   c. His face like the sun.

   d. His feet like pillars of fire.

   e. A little book in his hand.

   f. His right foot on the sea, his left foot on the land.

   g. Who cried out with a loud voice, as when a lion roars.

2. When the angel cried out, seven thunders uttered their voices:

   a. John prepared to write what he heard.

   b. But a voice from heaven instructs him to seal up the things uttered by the seven thunders, and not write them.

B. THE ANGEL AND HIS OATH (5-7)

1. John sees the angel lift his hand to heaven.

2. The angel swears by God that there will be delay no longer:

   a. For in the days of the sounding of the seventh angel, the mystery of God would be finished.

        b.   As God declared to His servants the prophets.

II. <u>JOHN EATS THE LITTLE BOOK</u> (8-11)

A. **JOHN IS INSTRUCTED TO EAT THE BOOK** (8-9)

    1.   The same voice from heaven instructs him to take the book from the angel's hand.

    2.   He is told to eat the book, which will be sweet as honey in his mouth, but will make his stomach bitter.

B. **JOHN EATS THE BOOK** (10-11)

    1.   Taking it from the angel's hand, he ate it.

    2.   It was sweet as honey in his mouth, but his stomach became bitter.

    3.   He is told: "You must prophesy again about many peoples, nations, tongues, and kings."

<u>Chapter 11</u>

I. <u>MEASURING THE TEMPLE OF GOD</u> (1-2)

A. **THE COMMAND TO MEASURE THE TEMPLE AND ITS OCCUPANTS** (1)

    1.   John is given a reed like a measuring rod.

    2.   Told to measure the temple of God, the altar, and those who worship there.

B. **THE COMMAND NOT TO MEASURE THE OUTER COURT** (2)

    1.   Told not to measure the court outside the temple.

    2.   For it has been given to the Gentiles, who will tread the holy city under foot for forty-two months

II. <u>THE TWO WITNESSES</u> (3-14)

A. **PROPHESYING FOR 1260 DAYS** (3-6)

1. Two witnesses given power to prophesy, clothed in sackcloth.

2. Identified as the two olive trees and two lampstands standing before God.

3. Those trying to harm them are devoured by fire from their mouths.

4. Having power:

   a. To shut heaven so no rain falls during their prophesying.

   b. To turn water to blood.

   c. To strike the earth with plagues as they desire.

B. **KILLED AND DEAD FOR THREE AND A HALF DAYS** (7-10)

1. Their testimony finished, the beast will kill them:

   a. The beast that ascends from the bottomless pit,

   b. Who will make war against them and overcome them.

2. Their dead bodies will lie in the street of the great city:

   a. Spiritually called Sodom and Egypt,

   b. Where our Lord was crucified.

3. The peoples, tribes, tongues, and nation who dwell on the earth:

   a. Will see their bodies three and a half days.

   b. Will not allow them to be put into graves.

      c.   Will rejoice over them, make merry, and exchange gifts, because the two prophets had tormented those who dwell on the earth.

C. **RAISED AND ASCENDED TO HEAVEN** (11-14)

1. After three and a half days, the breath of life from God entered them.

2. They stood, and great fear fell on those who saw them.

3. A loud voice from heaven tells them to "Come up here."

4. They ascend to heaven in a cloud as their enemies saw them.

5. In that same hour there was an earthquake:

      a.   A tenth of the city fell.

      b.   Seven thousand men were killed.

      c.   The rest were afraid and gave glory to the God of heaven.

6. The second woe is past; the third woe is coming quickly.

III. <u>THE SEVENTH TRUMPET: THE KINGDOM PROCLAIMED</u> (15-19)

A. **VICTORY PROCLAIMED** (15)

1. The seventh angel sounded his trumpet and there were loud voices in heaven,

2. Saying, "The kingdoms of this world have become the kingdoms of our Lord and of His Christ, and He shall reign forever and ever!"

B. **THE TWENTY-FOUR ELDERS WORSHIP GOD** (16-18)

1. The elders fell on their faces and worshiped God.

2. Giving thanks to the Lord God Almighty, the One who is and who was and who is to come.

3. Because He has taken His great power and reigned.

4. The nations were angry, and His wrath has come.

5. he time has come:

    a.   That the dead should be judged.

    b.   That His servants the prophets, the saints, and those who fear His name, should be rewarded.

    c.   That He should destroy those who destroy the earth.

C. THE TEMPLE OF GOD OPENED IN HEAVEN (19)

1. The temple of God was opened in heaven, and the ark of His covenant was seen in His temple.

2. There were lightning's, noises, thundering's, an earthquake, and great hail.

Chapter 12

I. THE WOMAN, THE CHILD, AND THE DRAGON (1-6)

A. THE WOMAN WITH CHILD (1-2)

1. A great sign appeared in heaven, in which woman is clothed:

    a.   With the sun.

    b.   With the moon under her feet.

    c.   A garland of twelve stars on her head.

2. Being with child, she cried out in labor and pain to give birth.

B. THE DRAGON READY TO DEVOUR THE CHILD (3-4)

1. Another great sign appeared in heaven: A great, fiery red dragon:

    a.   With seven heads, ten horns, seven diadems on the heads.

    b.   With a tail, which threw a third of the stars of heaven to the earth.

2. Standing before the woman, ready to devour the child as soon as it is born.

C. THE OUTCOME OF THE CHILD AND THE WOMAN (5-6)

1. The male child is born:

        a.   Who was to rule all nations with a rod of iron.

        b.   Who was caught up to God and His throne.

  2.   The woman fled into the wilderness:

        a.   Where she has a place prepared by God.

        b.   Where she is fed for 1,260 days.

II. <u>SATAN THROWN OUT OF HEAVEN</u> (7-12)

A. **A WAR IN HEAVEN** (7-9)

  1.   Between Michael and his angels, and the dragon and his angels.

  2.   The dragon and his angels did not prevail:

        a.   No place was found for them in heaven any longer.

        b.   The dragon and his angels were cast to the earth.

        c.   The dragon identified:

            (1) That serpent of old, called the Devil and Satan,

            (2) Who deceives the whole world.

B. **A LOUD VOICE IN HEAVEN** (10-12)

  1.   Proclaiming victory for Christ and His brethren:

        a.   Salvation, strength, the kingdom of God, and the power of Christ have come:

            (1) For the accuser of the brethren has been cast down,

            (2) Who had accused them before God day and night.

        b.   How the brethren overcame the accuser:

            (1) By the blood of the Lamb.

(2) By the word of their testimony.

(3) They did not love their lives to the death.

2. A call to rejoice, along with a warning:

    a. For those in heaven, rejoice!

    b. For the inhabitants of the earth and sea, woe!

      (1) For the devil has come down to them having great wrath,

      (2) Knowing that he has only a short time.

III. <u>THE FAILED ATTEMPT TO PERSECUTE THE WOMAN</u> (13-17)

A. THE DRAGON'S ATTEMPT TO PERSECUTE THE WOMAN (13-16)

1. Cast to the earth, he persecuted the woman who gave birth to the male child.

2. But the woman was given two wings of a great eagle:

    a. That she might fly into the wilderness to her place,

    b. Where she is nourished for a time, times, and half a time,

    c. Safe from the presence of the serpent.

3. The serpent spewed water out of his mouth like a flood after the woman:

    a. Hoping to cause her to be carried away.

    b. But the earth helped the woman by opening its mouth and

    c. swallowing up the flood.

B. THE DRAGON'S INTENT TO PERSECUTE HER OFFSPRING (17)

1. Enraged with the woman he cannot reach, the dragon goes to make war with the rest of her offspring

2. The rest of her offspring identified:

    a. Those who keep the commandments of God.

    b. hose who have the testimony of Jesus Christ.

Chapter 13

I. THE BEAST FROM THE SEA (1-10)

A. THE BEAST DESCRIBED (1-3a)

1. Seen by John as rising up out of the sea.

2. Having seven heads, ten horns, with ten crowns on his horns, and on his heads a blasphemous name.

3. Like a leopard with feet like those of a bear and a mouth like that of a lion.

4. His power, throne, and great authority given to him by the dragon.

5. One of his heads was mortally wounded, but healed.

B. THE ACTIVITY INVOLVING THE BEAST (3b-8)

1. All the world marveled and followed the beast:

    a. Worshipping the dragon who gave authority to the beast.

    b. Worshipping the beast because of his apparent invincibility.

2. What the beast was given:

    a. A mouth speaking great things and blasphemies.

    b. Authority to continue (make war) for forty-two months.

3. With this authority:

      a.   He blasphemed God, His name, His tabernacle, and those dwelling in heaven.

      b.   He was granted to make war with the saints and overcome them.

      c.   He was given authority over every tribe, tongue, and nation.

      d.   All who dwell on earth would worship him, unless their names are in the Book of Life of the Lamb.

C. A NOTE OF CAUTION (9-10)

1. If anyone has an ear, let him hear.

2. He who leads into captivity shall go into captivity; he who kills with the sword must be killed with the sword.

3. Here is the patience and the faith of the saints.

II. <u>THE BEAST FROM THE LAND</u> (11-18)

A. THIS BEAST DESCRIBED (11)

1. Seen by John as coming up out of the earth.

2. With two horns like a lamb, but speaking like a dragon.

B. **THE ACTIVITY OF THIS BEAST** (12-17)

1. He exercises all the authority of the first beast in his presence.

2. He causes the earth and those who dwell in it to worship the first beast:

      a.   Performing great signs, making even fire come down from heaven.

      b.   Deceiving the world by the signs.

3. He tells the world to make an image to the first beast:

      a.   To which he is granted power to give breath.

      b.   So the image could both speak and cause those who do not worship it to be killed.

   4.   He causes all to receive a mark on the right hand or on their foreheads:

      a.   Without which none can buy or sell.

      b.   Which is the name of the beast, or the number of his name.

C. A NOTE OF WISDOM (18)

   1.   Let those with understanding calculate the number of the beast.

   2.   For it is the number of a man: His number is 666.

Chapter 14

I. THE 144,000 ON MOUNT ZION (1-5)

A. STANDING WITH THE LAMB (1)

   1.   144,000 together with the Lamb on Mount Zion.

   2.   With the Father's name written on their foreheads.

B. SINGING A NEW SONG (2-3)

   1.   John heard a voice from heaven:

      a.   Like the voice of many waters.

      b.   Like the voice of loud thunder.

   2.   John heard the sound of harpists playing their harps.

   3.   The 144,000 sang a new song:

      a.   Before the throne, the four living creatures and the elders,

> b.   Which none could learn except the
>   144,000 redeemed from the earth.

C. **DESCRIBED MORE FULLY** (4-5)

1.   They are virgins, who had not defiled them-
      selves with women.

2.   They follow the Lamb wherever He goes.

3.   They were redeemed from among men, the
      first fruits to God and to the Lamb.

4.   They are without fault before the throne of
      God, with no guile in their mouths.

II. <u>THREE ANGELIC PROCLAMATIONS</u> (6-13)

A. **THE FIRST PROCLAMATION** (6-7)

1.   By an angel flying in the midst of heaven,
      having the everlasting gospel:

> a.   To preach to those who dwell on the
>   earth.

> b.   To every nation, tribe, tongue, and
>   people.

2.   Saying with a loud voice ...

> a.   "Fear God and give glory to Him, for the
>   hour of His judgment has come."

> b.   "Worship Him who made heaven and
>   earth, the sea and springs of water."

B. **THE SECOND PROCLAMATION** (8)

1.   By another angel, which followed the first.

2.   Saying ... "Babylon is fallen, is fallen, that
      great city."

> a.   "Because she has made all nations
>   drink of the wine of the wrath of her
>   fornication."

C. **THE THIRD PROCLAMATION** (9-11)

1. By a third angel, which followed the first two.

2. Saying with a loud voice ...

   a. "If anyone worships the beast and his image, and receives his mark on his forehead or on his hand ... "

   b. "He himself shall also drink of the of wine of the wrath of God, which is poured out full strength into the cup of His indignation."

   c. "He shall be tormented with fire and brimstone ... "

      (1) "In the presence of the holy angels and in the presence of the Lamb."

      (2) "The smoke of their torment ascends forever and ever."

      (3) "They have no rest day or night."

      (4) "Who worship the beast and his image, and whoever receives the mark of his name."

D. **A WORD OF WISDOM AND A BEATITUDE** (12-13)

1. Here is the patience of the saints: Those who keep ...

   a. The commandments of God.

   b. The faith of Jesus.

2. A voice from heaven saying ...

   a. "Write: 'Blessed are the dead who die in the Lord from now on.'"

   b. "Yes," says the Spirit, "that they may rest from their labors, and their works follow them."

III. <u>THE TWO HARVESTS</u> (14-20)

A. REAPING THE EARTH'S HARVEST (14-16)

1. The Son of Man sitting on a white cloud:

   a. With a golden crown on His head.

   b. With a sharp sickle in His hand.

2. An angel came out of the temple, crying with a loud voice ...

   a. "Thrust in Your sickle and reap."

   b. "For the time has come for You to reap, for the harvest of the earth is ripe."

3. He who sat on a cloud thrust in His sickle on the earth, and it was reaped.

B. REAPING THE GRAPES OF WRATH (17-20)

1. An angel came out of the temple in heaven, also having a sharp sickle.

2. Another angel, having power over fire, cried with a loud voice   to the angel with the sickle ...

   a. "Thrust in your sharp sickle and gather the clusters of the vine of the earth."

   b. "For her grapes are fully ripe."

3. So the angel ...

   a. Thrust his sickle into the earth,

   b. Gathered the vine of the earth,

   c. Threw it into the great winepress of the wrath of God.

4. The winepress was trampled outside the city:

   a. Blood came out of the winepress.

   b. Up to the horses' bridles, for 1,600 furlongs.

Chapter 15

I. <u>PRELUDE TO THE SEVEN BOWLS OF WRATH</u> (1-4)

A. A GREAT AND MARVELOUS SIGN IN HEAVEN (1-2)

1. John sees seven angels:

   a. Having the seven last plagues,

   b. In which the wrath of God is complete.

2. John sees a sea of glass mingled with fire, and a great multitude.

   a. It is those who have the victory over the beast, his image,

   b. his mark, and the number of his name.

   c. They are standing on the sea of glass, with harps of God.

B. SINGING THE SONG OF MOSES AND OF THE LAMB (3-4)

1. The multitude is singing the song of Moses, and the song of the Lamb.

2. A song, which praises the Lord God Almighty, King of the saints:

   a. For His great and marvelous works.

   b. For the truth and justice of His ways.

   c. For He is worthy of reverence and glory.

   d. And all nations shall come and worship before Him, for the manifestations of His judgments.

II. <u>SEVEN ANGELS AND SEVEN BOWLS OF WRATH</u> (5-8)

A. THE SEVEN ANGELS (5-6)

1. The temple of the tabernacle of the testimony in heaven is opened.

2. Out come the seven angels having the seven plagues:

a. Clothed in pure bright linen,

b. Having their chests girded with golden bands.

B. THE SEVEN GOLDEN BOWLS (7-8)

1. One of the four living creatures gave to the seven angels:

   a. Seven golden bowls,

   b. Full of the wrath of God who lives forever.

2. The temple was filled with smoke:

   a. From the glory of God and from His power.

   b. No one was able to enter the temple until the seven plagues were completed.

Chapter 16

I. THE PRONOUNCEMENT (1)

A. BY A LOUD VOICE FROM THE TEMPLE (1a)

B. TO THE SEVEN ANGELS TO POUR OUT THE BOWLS OF WRATH (1b)

II. THE SEVEN BOWLS OF WRATH (2-21)

A. FIRST BOWL: TERRIBLE SORES (2)

1. The bowl is poured out upon the earth.

2. Loathsome and foul sores came upon those who had the mark of the beast and who worshipped his image.

B. SECOND BOWL: SEA OF BLOOD (3)

1. The bowl is poured out on the sea, turning it to the blood of a dead man.

2. Every living creature in the sea died.

C. THIRD BOWL: RIVERS AND SPRINGS OF BLOOD (4-7)

1. The bowl is poured out on the rivers and springs, turning them to blood.

    2.   The angel of the waters declares God's justice:

        a.   His judgments are righteous.

        b.   For it is just due upon those who shed the blood of saints and prophets.

    3.   Another voice from the altar also proclaims God's judgments as true and righteous.

D. **FOURTH BOWL: MEN SCORCHED** (8-9)

    1.   The bowl is poured out on the sun, giving the fourth angel power to scorch men with fire.

    2.   Men were scorched with great heat:

        a.   They blasphemed the name of God who had power over these plagues.

        b.   They did not repent or give glory to Him.

E. FIFTH BOWL: PAIN AND DARKNESS (10-11)

    1.   The bowl is poured out on the throne of the beast, his kingdom became full of darkness.

    2.   Men gnawed their tongues because of the pain:

        a.   They blasphemed God.

        b.   They did not repent.

F. **SIXTH BOWL: KINGDOMS GATHERED AT ARMAGEDDON** (12-16)

    1.   The bowl is poured out on the great river Euphrates:

        a.   Its water was dried up.

        b.   Preparing the way for the kings of the east.

    2.   Three unclean spirits like frogs appear:

        a.   Out of the mouths of the dragon, the beast, and the false prophet,

   b. Which are spirits of demons, performing signs,

   c. Who gather the kings of the earth to the battle of that great day of God Almighty.

  3. Jesus offers both a warning and a blessing:

   a. He is coming as a thief.

   b. Blessed is he who watches and keeps his garments, lest he walks naked and others see his shame.

  4. The unclean spirits gather the kings of the earth to the place called Armageddon.

G. SEVENTH BOWL: GREAT EARTHQUAKE; THE GREAT CITY DIVIDED AND BABYLON REMEMBERED; CATACLYSMIC EVENTS (17-21)

  1. The bowl is poured out on the air:

   a. Followed by a loud voice out of the temple of heaven, from the throne, declaring, "It is done!"

   b. There were noises, thundering's, lightning's, and a mighty earthquake unlike any before.

  2. The great city was divided into three parts, and the cities of the nations fell.

  3. Great Babylon was remembered, to receive the cup of the wine of the fierceness of God's wrath.

  4. Great cataclysmic events occur:

   a. Every island fled away and the mountains were not found.

   b. Great hail fell upon men, and they blasphemed God because of the hail.

Chapter 17

  I. <u>THE SCARLET WOMAN AND THE SCARLET BEAST</u> (1-6)

    A. JOHN IS APPROACHED BY AN ANGEL (1-2)

      1.   One of the seven angels who had the seven bowls.

      2.   Who offers to show him the judgment of the great harlot:

        a.   Which sits on many waters.

        b.   With whom kings of the earth have committed fornication.

        c.   With whom inhabitants of the earth were made drunk with the wine of her fornication.

    B. JOHN IS SHOWN THE SCARLET WOMAN ON THE SCARLET BEAST (3-6)

      1.   He is carried away by the angel in the Spirit into the wilderness.

      2.   There he sees a woman sitting on a scarlet beast:

        a.   The scarlet beast:

          (1) Full of names of blasphemy.

          (2) Having seven heads and ten horns.

        b.   The woman:

          (1) Arrayed in purple and scarlet.

          (2) Adorned with gold, precious stones, and pearls.

          (3) In her hand a golden cup full of abominations and the filthiness of her fornication.

          (4) On her forehead the name written:

            a.   MYSTERY

   b. BABYLON THE GREAT

   c. THE MOTHER OF HARLOTS AND OF THE ABOMINATIONS OF THE EARTH

  (5) Drunk with:

   a. The blood of the saints.

   b. The blood of the martyrs of Jesus.

 3. He marveled with great amazement when he saw her.

II. THE MYSTERY OF THE WOMAN AND BEAST EXPLAINED (7-18)

A. THE ANGEL OFFERS TO EXPLAIN THE MYSTERY (7)

 1. Asking John why he marveled.

 2. Saying that he will tell him the mystery:

  a. Of the woman.

  b. Of the beast with seven heads and ten horns that carries her.

B. THE BEAST EXPLAINED (8-14)

 1. The beast that John saw:

  a. Was, is not, and will ascend out of the bottomless pit and go to perdition.

  b. Will be marveled by those whose names are not written in the Book of Life from the foundation of the world when they see it.

 2. The mind, which has wisdom:

  a. The seven heads are seven mountains upon which the woman sits.

  b. There are also seven kings:

    (1) Five have fallen, one is, the other has yet to come.

    (2) When the seventh comes, he must continue a short time.

  c. The beast that was, and is not, is himself the eighth:

    (1) He is of the seven.

    (2) 2) He is going to perdition (destruction).

  d. The ten horns are ten kings:

    (1) Who have received no kingdom as yet.

    (2) But receive authority for one hour with the beast.

    (3) Who are of one mind, and give their power and authority to the beast.

  e. These will make war with the Lamb, and the Lamb will overcome them:

    (1) For He is Lord of lords and King of kings.

    (2) Those with Him are called, chosen, and faithful.

C. THE WOMAN EXPLAINED (15-18)

1. The waters upon which she sits are peoples, multitudes, nations and tongues.

2. The ten horns (ten kings) on the beast:

  a. Will hate the harlot:

    (1) Make her desolate.

    (2) Eat her flesh and burn her with fire.

  b. For God has put it into their hearts to fulfill His purpose:

        (1) For them to be of one mind.

        (2) To give their kingdom to the beast.

        (3) Until the words of God are fulfilled.

3.   The woman John saw is that great city which reigns over the kings of the earth.

Chapter 18

I. THE FALL OF BABYLON PROCLAIMED (1-8)

A. BY AN ANGEL FROM HEAVEN (1-3)

1.   John sees an angel coming down from heaven:

    a.   Having great authority.

    b.   Illuminating the earth with his glory.

2.   The angel cries mightily with a loud voice:

    a.   "Babylon the great is fallen, is fallen."

    b.   "She has become ...

        (1) A dwelling place of demons,

        (2) A prison for every foul spirit,

        (3) A cage for every unclean and hated bird."

    c.   "With her ...

        (1) The nations have drunk of the wine of her fornication.

        (2) The kings of the earth have committed fornication.

        (3) The merchants of the earth have become rich."

B. BY A VOICE FROM HEAVEN (4-8)

1.   Calling God's people to come out of her:

    a.   Lest they share in her sins and her plagues.

       b.   For her sins have reached to heaven and God has remembered her iniquities.

   2.   Calling for judgment to be rendered:

       a.   Render her just as she rendered them.

       b.   Repay her double according to her works.

       c.   In the cup she has mixed, mix double for her.

       d.   To the degree she glorified herself and lived luxuriously ...

          (1) Give her torment and sorrow.

          (2) For she says in heart that she is a queen and will not see sorrow as a widow.

       e.   Her plagues will come in one day ...

          (1) Death, mourning, and famine.

          (2) Utterly burned with fire.

          (3) For great is the Lord God who judges her.

II. THE FALL OF BABYLON MOURNED (9-20)

A. BY THE KINGS OF THE EARTH (9-10)

   1.   Those who committed fornication and lived luxuriously with her.

   2.   They shall weep and lament when they see the smoke of her burning.

   3.   They shall stand afar off for fear of her torment, saying ...

       a.   "Alas, alas, that great city Babylon, that mighty city!"

       b.   "For in one hour your judgment has come."

B. BY THE MERCHANTS OF THE EARTH (11-17a)

1. They shall weep and mourn over her.

2. For no one buys their merchandise anymore.

3. All that they longed for, both rich and splendid, they shall find no more.

4. The merchants shall stand at a distance for fear of her torment, weeping and wailing ...

    a. "Alas, alas, that great city that was clothed in fine linen, purple, and scarlet, and adorned with gold and precious tones and pearls!"

    b. "For in one hour such great riches came to nothing."

C. BY THE TRADERS AND TRAVELERS ON THE SEA (17b-19)

1. They stood at a distance, crying when they saw the smoke of her burning, "What is like this great city?"

2. Throwing dust on their heads, they cried out, weeping and wailing ...

    a. "Alas, alas, that great city, in which all who had ships on the sea became rich by her wealth!"

    b. "For in one hour she is made desolate."

D. BUT NOT BY THE HOLY APOSTLES AND PROPHETS (20)

1. They are to rejoice over her.

2. For God has avenged them on her.

III. THE FALL OF BABYLON JUSTIFIED (21-24)

A. THE EXTENT OF HER FALL ILLUSTRATED (21-23a)

1. By a mighty angel ...

    a. Who took a stone like a great millstone and cast it into the sea.

       b. Who then proclaims, "Thus, with violence the great city Babylon shall be thrown down, and shall not be found anymore."

   2. Neither shall be heard or seen in her ...

       a. The sound of harpists, musicians, flutists, and trumpeters.

       b. A craftsman of any craft.

       c. The sound of a millstone.

       d. The light of a lamp.

       e. The voice of bridegroom and bride.

B. THE EXTENT OF HER FALL JUSTIFIED (23b-24)

   1. For her merchants were the great men of the earth.

   2. For by her sorcery all the nations were deceived.

   3. For in her was found the blood of prophets and saints, and of

   4. all who slain on the earth.

Chapter 19

I. <u>HEAVEN REJOICES OVER THE FALL OF BABYLON</u> (1-5)

A. A GREAT MULTITUDE IN HEAVEN (1-3)

   1. Praising God, attributing salvation, glory, honor, and power to Him.

   2. Declaring His judgments on the great harlot as true and righteous:

       a. For she corrupted the earth with her fornication.

       b. He has avenged the blood of His servants, which she shed.

   3. Praising God, for her smoke rises up forever and ever.

B. **THE TWENTY-FOUR ELDERS AND FOUR LIVING CREATURES** (4)

    1.   Falling down and worshipping God who sits on the throne. saying, "Amen, Alleluia!"

C. **A VOICE FROM THE THRONE** (5)

    1.   Calling upon all God's servants and those who fear Him.

    2.   Calling upon both small and great to praise God.

II. <u>**PREPARATION FOR THE MARRIAGE OF THE LAMB**</u> (6-10)

A. **A GREAT MULTITUDE IN HEAVEN** (6-8)

    1.   Sounding like many waters and mighty thundering's:

        a.   Praising the Lord God Omnipotent for His reign.

        b.   Calling to be glad and rejoice and give God glory.

    2.   For the marriage of the Lamb has come:

        a.   His wife has made herself ready.

        b.   She was arrayed in fine linen, which is the righteous acts of the saints.

B. **A FELLOW SERVANT** (9-10)

    1.   Telling John to write: "Blessed are those who are called to the marriage supper of the Lamb!"

    2.   Proclaiming: "These are the true sayings of God."

    3.   When John fell at his feet to worship him, he is rebuked:

        a.   "See that you do not do that!"

    b. "I am your fellow servant, and of your brethren who have the testimony of Jesus."

    c. "Worship God! For the testimony of Jesus is the spirit of prophecy."

III. <u>CHRIST THE WARRIOR KING ON A WHITE HORSE</u> (11-16)

A. HIS AWESOME DESCRIPTION (11-13)

1. As heaven opened, John sees Him sitting on a white horse:

    a. He is called Faithful and True.

    b. In righteousness He judges and makes war.

1. As seen by John:

    a. His eyes were like a flame of fire.

    b. On His head were many crowns.

    c. He had a name written that no one knew but Himself.

    d. Clothed with a robe dipped in blood.

    e. His name is called The Word of God.

B. HIS GREAT RULE AND REIGN (14-16)

1. Followed by the armies of heaven:

    a. Clothed in fine linen, white and clean,

    b. Sitting on white horses.

2. From His mouth, a sharp sword to strike the nations.

    a. He Himself will rule the nations with a rod of iron.

    b. He Himself treads the winepress of Almighty God's fierceness and wrath.

3. On His robe and thigh a name written: "King of kings, and Lord of lords."

IV. THE FALL OF THE BEAST, THE FALSE PROPHET, AND THEIR FORCES (17-21)

A. THE DECLARATION OF AN ANGEL (17-18)

1. John sees an angel standing in the sun, crying with a loud voice,

2. Speaking to all the birds that fly in the midst of heaven:

   a. "Come and gather together for the supper of the great God."

   b. " ... eat the flesh of kings ... captains ... mighty men ... horses ... all people, free and slave, both small and great."

B. THE END OF THE BEAST AND FALSE PROPHET (19-21)

1. John saw the beast, the kings of the earth and their armies, gathered to make war against Him who sat on the horse and His army.

2. John saw the beast and false prophet captured.

   a. The false prophet who worked signs in the presence of the beast,

   b. By which he deceived those who received the mark of thebeast and worshiped his image.

   c. Both were cast alive into the lake of fire burning with brimstone.

3. The rest of their forces were killed

   a. With the sword which proceeded from the mouth of Him who sat on the horse

   b. All the birds were filled with their flesh

Chapter 20

I. THE THOUSAND YEAR REIGN (1-6)

A. **SATAN BOUND FOR 1,000 YEARS** (1-3)

1. John sees an angel come down from heaven:

   a. Having the key to the bottomless pit,

   b. With a great chain in his hand.

2. The angel binds Satan for a thousand years:

   a. Casting him into the bottomless pit, shutting him up and setting a seal on him.

   b. So that he should deceive the nations no more for a thousand years.

   c. But afterward he will be released for a little while.

B. **SAINTS REIGN WITH CHRIST FOR 1,000 YEARS** (4-6)

1. John sees souls upon thrones, to whom judgment was committed:

   a. Who had been beheaded for their witness to Jesus and the word of God,

   b. Who had not worshiped the beast or his image,

   c. Who had not received his mark on their foreheads or on their hands.

1. These souls lived and reigned with Christ a thousand years.

   a. The rest of the dead not live again until the thousand yearswere finished.

   b. This is the first resurrection:

      (1) Blessed and holy are those who have a part in the first resurrection.

      (2) Over such the second death has no power.

      (3) They shall be priests of God and of Christ.

(4) They shall reign with Christ a thousand years.

II. SATAN'S FINAL ATTEMPT AND DEFEAT (7-10)

A. HIS RELEASE FROM PRISON (7-8)

1. After the thousand years were completed,

2. He will go out to deceive the nations:

   a. Those in the four corners of the earth, Gog and Magog,

   b. To gather them to battle.

B. HIS FINAL ATTEMPT AND DEFEAT (9)

1. To have the nations surround the camp of the saints and the beloved city.

2. But fire from God out of heaven devoured those Satan had deceived.

C. HIS ETERNAL TORMENT (10)

1. The devil who deceived the nations was cast into the lake of fire and brimstone.

2. The same place where the beast and the false prophet are.

3. They will be tormented day and night forever and ever.

III. THE FINAL JUDGMENT (11-15)

A. THE ONE ON THE GREAT WHITE THRONE (11)

1. John sees a great white throne and Him who sat on it.

2. Before Whose face the earth and heaven fled away so no place was found for them.

B. THE JUDGMENT OF THE DEAD (12-13)

1. John sees the dead, small and great, standing before God.

2. Books were opened, including the Book of Life:

    a. The dead were judged according to their works.

    b. The dead were judged by the things written in the books.

3. All the dead were judged, each according to his works:

    a. For the sea gave the dead who were in it.

    b. For Dead and Hades delivered up the dead who were in them.

C. THE LAKE OF FIRE (14-15)

1. Death and Hades were cast into the lake of fire (which is the second death).

2. Anyone not found written in the Book of Life were cast into the lake of fire.

Chapter 21

I. ALL THINGS MADE NEW (1-8)

A. THE NEW HEAVEN AND NEW EARTH (1)

1. John sees a new heaven and a new earth.

2. The first heaven and earth had passed away, and there was no sea.

B. THE NEW JERUSALEM (2)

1. John saw the holy city coming down out of heaven.

2. It was prepared as a bride adorned for her husband.

C. THE PROCLAMATION FROM HEAVEN (3-4)

1. "The tabernacle of God is with men:"

    a. "He will dwell with them, and they shall be His people."

b. "God Himself will be with them and be their God."

2. "God will wipe away every tear from their eyes:"

    a. "There shall be no more death, nor sorrow, nor crying."

    b. "There shall be no more pain, for the former things have passed away."

D. THE PROCLAMATION FROM THE ONE WHO SAT ON THE THRONE_(5-8)

1. "Behold, I make all things new:"

    a. "Write, for these words are true and faithful."

    b. "It is done!"

2. "I am the Alpha and the Omega, the Beginning and the End:"

    a. "I will give of the fountain of the water of life freely to him who thirsts."

    b. "He who overcomes shall inherit all things:"

        (1) "I will be his God."

        (2) "He shall be My son."

3. "But the cowardly, unbelieving, abominable, murderers, sexually immoral, sorcerers, idolaters, and all liars ... "

    a. "Shall have their part in the lake, which burns with fire and brimstone,"

    b. "Which is the second death."

II. THE NEW JERUSALEM (9-21)

    A. JOHN IS SHOWN THE HOLY CITY (9-11)

1. By one of the seven angels who had the seven bowls filled with the last plagues:

    a. Who offered to show John, "the bride, the Lamb's wife."

    b. Who carried him away in the Spirit to a great and high mountain.

2. He sees the great city, the holy Jerusalem:

    a. Descending out of heaven from God,

    b. Having the glory of God,

    c. With light like a jasper stone, clear as crystal.

B. THE CONSTRUCTION OF THE CITY AND ITS WALL (12-21)

1. It had a great and high wall with twelve gates:

    a. With twelve angels at the gates.

    b. With the names of the twelve tribes of Israel.

    c. With three gates each on the east, north, south, and west.

    d. With twelve foundations, on which were the names of the

    e. twelve apostles of the Lamb.

2. The measurement of the city, the gates, and the wall:

    a. The angel had a golden reed to measure them.

    b. The city is laid out as a cube, its length, breadth, and height are each 12,000 furlongs (1,500 miles).

    c. The wall is one hundred and forty-four cubits (216 feet).

3. The construction of the city, the wall, its foundations, and the gates:

    a. The wall was of jasper; the city was pure gold, like clear glass.

    b. The twelve foundations of the wall were adorned with precious stones:

        1) Jasper 2) Sapphire 3) Chalcedony 4) Emerald 5) Sardonyx 6) Sardius 7) Chrysolite 8) Beryl 9) Topaz 10) Chrysoprase 11) Jacinth 12) Amethyst

    c. The twelve gates were twelve pearls, each gate one pearl.

    d. The street of the city was pure gold, like transparent glass.

III. <u>THE GLORY OF THE HOLY CITY</u> (22-27)

A. ILLUMINATED BY THE PRESENCE OF GOD AND THE LAMB (22-23)

1. Its temple are the Lord God Almighty and the Lamb.

2. It is illuminated by the glory of God and the Lamb.

B. ENHANCED BY THOSE WHO ENTER IT (24-27)

1. The nations of the saved shall walk in its light.

2. The kings of the earth bring their glory and honor into it.

3. Its gates shall not be shut at all by day, and there is no night there.

4. The nations shall bring their glory and honor into it:

    a. Nothing that defiles, causes an abomination or a lie, shall enter it.

       b.   Only those written in the Lamb's Book of Life enter it.

Chapter 22

I. <u>THE RIVER, THE TREE, AND THE THRONE</u> (1-5)

A. **THE RIVER OF LIFE** (1)

    1.   John sees a pure river of water of life, clear as crystal.

    2.   It proceeds from the throne of God and of the Lamb.

B. **THE TREE OF LIFE** (2)

    1.   On either side of the river was a tree of life.

    2.   The tree(s) bore twelve fruits, yielding fruit every month.

    3.   The leaves were for the healing of the nations.

C. **THE THRONE OF GOD AND OF THE LAMB** (3-5)

    1.   There shall be no more curse, but the throne of God and the Lamb shall be in it.

    2.   His servants shall serve Him:

        a.   They shall see His face.

        b.   His name shall be on their foreheads.

    3.   There shall be no night there:

        a.   They need no lamp nor light of the sun.

        b.   For the Lord God gives them light.

    4.   They shall reign forever and ever.

II. <u>THE GRAND CONCLUSION</u> (6-21)

A. **THE TIME IS NEAR, DO NOT SEAL THE BOOK** (6-11)

    1.   John is told by the angel that these words are faithful and true:

a. The Lord God has sent His angel to show His servants the things that must shortly take place.

b. The Lamb proclaims: "Behold, I am coming quickly! Blessed is he who keeps the words of the prophecy of this book."

2. John attempts to worship the angel:

a. He falls down at the feet of the angel who showed him these things.

b. The angel forbids him:

(1) The angel is his fellow servant, and of his brethren the prophets and of those who keep the words of this book.

(2) John is to worship God.

1. John is told not to seal the words of the prophecy of this book:

a. For the time is at hand.

b. Let he who is unjust be unjust still, the filthy be filthy still.

c. Let he who is righteous be righteous still, the holy be holy still.

B. THE TESTIMONY OF JESUS (12-17)

1. His first declaration:

a. "Behold, I am coming quickly."

b. "My reward is with Me, to give to everyone according to his work."

c. "I am the Alpha and the Omega."

d. "The Beginning and the End, the First and the Last."

2. The promise:

     a.   Blessed are those who do His command-ments (or wash their robes):

       (1) That they may have the right to the tree of life.

       (2) That they may enter through the gates into the city.

     b.   Those outside the city:

       (1) Are dogs, sorcerers, sexually immoral, murderers, and idolaters.

       (2) Whoever loves and practices a lie.

3.   His second declaration:

     a.   "I, Jesus, have sent My angel to testify to you these things in the churches."

     b.   "I am the Root and the Offspring of David, the Bright and Morning Star."

4.   The invitation:

     a.   The Spirit and the bride say, "Come!"

     b.   Let him who hears say, "Come!"

     c.   Whoever desires, let him take the water of life freely.

C. A WORD OF WARNING (18-19)

1.   Do not add to the words of this book, or God will add to him the plagues written in it.

2.   Do not take away from the words of this book, or God will take away his part from:

     a.   The Book (or Tree) of Life.

     b.   The holy city.

     c.   The things written in this book.

D. CLOSING PROMISE, FINAL PRAYERS (20-21)

1. The promise of Him who testifies to these things: "Surely I amncoming quickly."

2. John's two prayers:

   a. Concerning his Lord: "Amen. Even so, come, Lord Jesus!"

   b. Concerning his brethren: "The grace of our Lord Jesus Christ be with you all. Amen."

REFERENCE NOTES

Genesis through Revelation. King James, New International, and the Geneva Bible translations were used for scripture references, with insight gained from the following writers:

Charles H. Spurgeon – Spurgeon's Sermons (1958)

Aiden W. Tozer – Attributes of God/Volume 1 (2007)

Dr. David Jeremiah – Escape the Coming Night (2018)

Warren O. Langworthy – The Bible, Master Thesis (1952)

Matthew Henry's Bible Commentary, 6 volume set, (1991)

Dr. Billy Graham – The Four Horsemen of the Apocalypse (1984). The Coming Storm (1995)

Parallel Commentary of New Testament, (Charles Spurgeon, John Wesley, & Matthew Henry) (2003)

Ray C. Stedman – Gods final Word

Billy Sunday – Topics in Chronicling America (1928)

Dr. Warren W. Wiersbe – New Testament Commentary (1975)

The Great Book of Sermons – (1963)

Drs. Charles R. Swindoll, John F. Walvoord, & J. Dwight Pentecost – The Road to Armageddon (2004)

Dr. J. Vernon McGee – Book of Daniel, Walk through the Bible Series (1968)

Alfred Edersheim - Bible History Old Testament (1995)

The Natural History of the Bible, Environmental Exploration of the Hebrew Scriptures, Daniel Hillel (2005)

John MacArthur New Testament Commentary (1985)